AFTER DIFFERENCE

Wyse Series in Social Anthropology

Editors:

James Laidlaw, William Wyse Professor of Social Anthropology, University of Cambridge, and Fellow of King's College, Cambridge

Maryon McDonald, Fellow in Social Anthropology, Robinson College, University of Cambridge

Joel Robbins, Sigrid Rausing Professor of Social Anthropology, University of Cambridge, and Fellow of Trinity College, Cambridge

Social Anthropology is a vibrant discipline of relevance to many areas – economics, politics, business, humanities, health and public policy. This series, published in association with the Cambridge William Wyse Chair in Social Anthropology, focuses on key interventions in Social Anthropology, based on innovative theory and research of relevance to contemporary social issues and debates. Former holders of the William Wyse Chair have included Meyer Fortes, Jack Goody, Ernest Gellner and Marilyn Strathern, all of whom have advanced the frontiers of the discipline. This series intends to develop and foster that tradition.

AFTER DIFFERENCE

Queer Activism in Italy and Anthropological Theory

Paolo Heywood

berghahn
NEW YORK • OXFORD
www.berghahnbooks.com

First published in 2018 by
Berghahn Books
www.berghahnbooks.com

© 2018, 2022 Paolo Heywood
First paperback edition published in 2022

Library of Congress Cataloging-in-Publication Data

A C.I.P. cataloging record is available from the Library of Congress

British Library Cataloguing in Publication Data

A catalogue record for this book is available from the British Library

ISBN 978-1-78533-786-4 hardback
ISBN 978-1-80073-452-4 paperback
ISBN 978-1-78533-787-1 ebook

https://doi.org/10.3167/9781785337864

Resemblance has no reality in itself; it is only a particular instance of difference, that in which difference tends towards zero.
—Lévi-Strauss, *The Naked Man*

Everything hinges on the verb 'to tend'.
—Viveiros de Castro, *Cannibal Metaphysics*

Contents

Illustrations

Acknowledgements

In Italy: to my mother and my family, for putting me up when I first arrived, and putting up with me when I needed help; to my friends, especially Irene, Giulia, Gianluca, Clara, Gaia and Giada, for making my year in Bologna not just interesting but enjoyable; to Antonio and his delightful shop for keeping me fed; and to all those, activists and otherwise, who had the kindness and patience to answer my endless questions.

In Cambridge: at the Division of Social Anthropology at Cambridge over the years I have had inestimable teachers, colleagues, readers and friends in Susan Bayly, Naor Ben-Yehoyada, Barbara Bodenhorn, Harri Englund, Taras Fedirko, Tim Jenkins, Nick Long, Patrick McKearney, Maryon McDonald, Tom Neumark, Anthony Pickles, Anastasia Piliavsky, Branwyn Poleykett, Joel Robbins, Marlene Schäfers, Nikolai Ssorin-Chaikov, Rupert Stasch, Felix Stein and Fiona Wright.

In addition, in Marilyn Strathern and Sarah Green I have had intellectual inspirations since I first began studying anthropology, and I could not have hoped for more thoughtful, attentive and encouraging examiners for the doctoral thesis upon which much of this book is based. I am extremely grateful for their close reading of the dissertation, and their continuing support as I developed its arguments for this manuscript. Joel Robbins and Maryon McDonald have been similarly supportive series editors.

I have also been fortunate in being able to benefit from discussion with a number of other anthropologists whose work has inspired parts of this book. Giovanni da Col, James Faubion, Michael Lambek, Tanya Luhrmann and Adam Reed have been enlightening and supportive conversational partners, both in person and through their work. I am very much indebted to Michael Herzfeld for his invaluable guidance and encouragement, and for his regular and insightful reading of this manuscript and its various parts. I have also been fortunate in having had on occasion the opportunity to discuss some of the ideas behind the book with Martin Holbraad, Morten Pedersen and Eduardo Viveiros de Castro, though all resulting errors and equivocations are very much my own. Their work has been a perpetual delight and challenge to read from the moment I first encountered it as an undergraduate, and I hope that is clear throughout the book.

In Nicholas Evans, Caroline Humphrey, Jonathan Mair and Soumhya Venkatesan I have had kind friends, delightful dinner companions and the best of fellow travellers in ethics over the years.

In Matei Candea I have had a teacher, colleague and friend to whom I am thoroughly indebted for his support, encouragement and unfailing acumen as a reader. If there is merit to the arguments of this book then that is undoubtedly due in significant part to my having been able to hash them out with him over coffee, alcohol and a variety of wonderful dinners (none of which I cooked). I cannot thank him enough. And in James Laidlaw I have had all that I could have hoped for and more in a supervisor, mentor and friend. His influence on this book and on me is immeasurable, and for it I will always remain more grateful than I can say.

Finally, in Peter Heywood, Paola Gardini and Jennifer Midura I have had the love and support of a family; and in Joanna Cook, I have had the best of all things.

Introduction

On a bright Sunday at the beginning of March 2012, a month after I arrived in the city, Bologna's most famous son gave his final performance in Piazza Maggiore, on what would have been his sixty-ninth birthday. Three days previously, on tour in Switzerland, Lucio Dalla, Italy's most well-known folk singer, whose career spanned four decades, died following a heart attack. His body was brought back to his home town, where it laid in state in the square he made famous with a song about a vagrant who lives under the piazza's medieval arcades. An estimated 50,000 people from across the country flooded into the city to pay their respects, and for days the piazza was the site of an endless, snaking queue of fans, young and old, who waited for hours to file past the coffin. The street on which he lived, itself a few metres from the square, was awash in a sea of flowers and other offerings, and for months afterwards restaurants, bars, and other public places in the city decorated their windows with banners declaring 'Ciao Lucio' and set out books of condolence for patrons to sign.

The funeral itself took place in the Basilica of Saint Petronius, the enormous and imposing church that dominates the southern side of the square. The mayor had declared an official day of mourning, and the flag above the seat of the city's government flew at half-mast. A long list of dignitaries, including celebrities and politicians, attended the funeral at the Basilica, which was broadcast live on national television, whilst thousands continued to gather outside. A homily was delivered by a Dominican friar who had been Dalla's confessor, who wished his friend a posthumous happy birthday, and declared that he had had 'an incredible relationship with God'. Acclaimed as the most touching and beautiful part of the service, however, was a tribute delivered by a thirty-two-year-old man from Puglia, Marco Alemanno, who had collaborated with Dalla on some of his compositions. In a voice quavering with emotion and evidently struggling not to weep, he recalled the first time he and Dalla had met, and expressed his incredulity and gratitude at having had the 'honour and the privilege to grow by his side', before finally bursting into tears.

Why did this young man's speech create such a stirring impression and strike such a chord? Because Marco Alemanno was not simply, as he was

described in the service, Dalla's collaborator, he was also his long-term romantic partner, and everybody knew it.

The funeral occasioned a degree of soul-searching, both locally and nation-
ally, about the status of homosexuality in Italy. A few Catholics I knew queried
the appropriateness of providing such a lavish religious ceremony to honour a
man who was not only gay but also famously left-wing. No one that I met
countenanced such a position in Bologna however, where Dalla was mourned
as a local hero; even my landlady, whose political views were far to the right of
anybody else I ever met in a city famous as a bastion of socialism, lauded the
decision to hold the funeral at the Basilica, declaring to me that Dalla was 'a
good man whose private life is nobody's business'.

Such an assertion was possible because despite the fact that Dalla's sexuality was an open secret, a secret it remained: he never came out publicly. This,
indeed, was the official justification for the funeral in the Basilica by the
Church, a stance comparable to the US military's former policy of 'don't ask,
don't tell'. Like the latter, this position was the target of much criticism. Many
in the city's LGBTQ community were apathetic about the funeral, seeing it as
yet another instance of hypocritical attitudes towards homosexuality in Italy,
both on Dalla's part, for not coming out publicly, and on the part of the
Church, for celebrating the life of a prominent and popular homosexual whilst
simultaneously condemning homosexuality from the pulpits of churches
across the country on a weekly basis.

A Dominican friar describes a gay man as having had 'an incredible relationship with God', whilst representing a Catholic Church whose opposition to
the progress of LGBTQ rights in Italy is vocal and vituperative; that same gay
man, despite his sexuality and his political views, is a famously devoted
Catholic; his romantic partner speaks at his funeral but only as his 'collaborator'; and people such as my landlady, the majority of whose pronouncements
on homosexuality were similar in tone and content to those of the Church, are
spontaneously able to set aside their homophobia when it comes to a man
whose music tugs at their heartstrings. These exemplify a curious and somewhat paradoxical way of relating to something, whether it be to a faith, an
ideology, a person, or a moral code, that is one of partial fidelity rather than
wholehearted subscription, one in which what is most remarkable is the distance or difference maintained between oneself and the object with which one
is supposed to identify. Relationships of this form – relationships that sustain,
rather than cancel out, the differences between their terms – are the central
concern of this book.

Difference from What?

Relations, we are often wont to think, are about identification. As Rupert
Stasch has recently argued (2009), the ideal of *Gemeinschaft*, first set out by

Ferdinand Tönnies in the nineteenth century, has long dominated social science studies of community as 'a perfect unity of wills' (1887: 37), and Marilyn Strathern has highlighted the etymological connections between relation and the idea of connection itself, noting that anthropologists usually speak of relations as the means 'through which people connect themselves to one another' (1995: 11). But as both these authors – and a growing number of others – argue, there is another side to relations: the 'perfect unity' Tönnies writes of always risks collapsing a relation of two or more terms into a singularity; without difference, as well as identity, a relation is no longer a relation. The ethnographic relations this book is concerned with are cases in which that difference is made highly visible; and one of the tasks of this book is to make highly visible the difference in a more theoretical relationship, namely that between ethnography and theory itself.

This book situates itself in a vein of literature on relating through difference by describing a set of empirical relations surrounding LGBTQ activism in Italy in which the difference between the terms being related is more important than the identities between them. My claim is not that this form of relationship is unique to the context I describe. Some of the relations I discuss will be recognizable to many as themselves related to other forms of political and ethical life, and partly for this reason I will draw from them more general theoretical arguments about the ways in which it is possible to relate – through difference – to political ideologies, or to moral codes, for example. What I will also suggest though is that the context of LGBTQ activism has something particular to teach us about the relationship between difference and identity, and that anthropologists, in particular, have something to learn from it. It forms a special and unusual example of a broader problem, namely that of how identities are constituted: particular and unusual because what constitutes identity in the context of Italian LGBTQ activism is in fact a radical rejection of identity politics in favour of a belief in the necessity and virtue of making or producing difference.

The problem of identity, or solidarity, is a problem for a particular reason. As Stasch eloquently describes, Tönnies' arguments about *Gemeinschaft* had a critical edge: his 'unity of wills' was an 'idyllic alternative possibility' to the reality of urban strangeness and difference that he called *Gesellschaft* and that he understood to be characteristic of modern life (Stasch 2009: 7). Far from being something the existence and persistence of which could be assumed, bonds of identification were, at least implicitly, an ideal to be worked towards. Bringing people together has never been an easy task, though, as Stasch goes on to note, anthropologists have continued to find examples of the *Gemeinschaft* ideal in non-Western societies (2009: 8).

The context I describe is a modern, urban one, the city of Bologna in Italy, and thus one in which bringing people together should be as difficult, if not more so, as in that of Tönnies. Moreover, the particular community with which this book is concerned is one of political activists, and thus, popular wisdom would have it, liable to suffer from the problem of what Freud – following anthropologist Ernest Crawley – called 'the narcissism of minor differences' (1957 [1917]: 119). Another Italianist, Anton Blok, begins a survey of anthropological and sociological literature on the 'minor differences' question with a Sicilian proverb: 'in the same face, the right eye hates the left', and as he goes on to note, the phenomenon of *campanilismo* (or the idea that one's own village is infinitely better in every possible way than the one just down the road) is a quintessential version of this problem, even if it is as liable to be found in Cambridge colleges as in Italian villages (Blok 1998: 33).

So one would imagine that the people this book is concerned with do not easily form a community, let alone a 'unity of wills'. Indeed, this is true to a large extent, and much of this book will describe the internal heterogeneity of an extremely diverse movement, and the ways in which this heterogeneity reveals itself through a variety of media, and often through intensely passionate debate and disagreement.

There is one respect, however, in which the question of identity and identification for LGBTQ activists in Bologna takes on a peculiar and perhaps somewhat unique colour, and that is the fact that if there is one thing with which most activists can identify, if there is one aspect of their activism that does indeed bring them together, it is their rejection of identity, and their valuation instead of difference. So the central ethnographic argument of this book will be that they are in the interesting position of being brought together by precisely what sets them apart, and set apart by what brings them together.

What I mean by that is that a dominant and even constitutively essential aspect of being an LGBTQ activist is performing and producing difference from the world around one. Activism, in a generic sense, is premised on a certain relationship of difference: that between what is and what ought to be (Dave 2012; see also Ferrara 2008; Robbins forthcoming). It is a deeply worldly activity, in the Weberian sense (2001 [1930]) but its relationship with the world is based around the fact that there is something wrong with it, something lacking or otherwise deficient, something to be changed (Dave 2012; Marx 1845): that it should be different from the way it is. It is about, as the cliché goes, 'making a difference'.

But difference is important in a distinctive and unique sense for LGBTQ activism. As in much of the writing which inspires such activism (e.g. Butler 1990; De Lauretis 1991; Sedgwick 1990), many of the LGBTQ activists I worked with seek to embody a radical difference from the rules, norms and identities they see as undergirding Italian society, whether as 'ethical sluts', polyamorists, drag queens or kings, or just by living a life that runs against the grain of what they understand to be Catholic and conservative orthodoxy. Thus, as with activism in the more generic sense, what they do and what they believe is saturated with a concern for what they do not do and do not believe, for what they must differ from: transgression requires something to transgress (Bourg 2007).

For some activists this relationship is further complicated by their desire to erase this difference: those who seek equal treatment under the law from a state that currently excludes them from a range of institutional spheres aim to 'make a difference' by making certain differences disappear. But for many of those with whom this book is primarily concerned, their difference from others is something to be valued and celebrated. It is something to be produced and reproduced on a regular basis.

This leads to a conundrum of a sorts that is the central ethnographic focus of this book: producing difference from fixed identities like gay, lesbian or straight is a defining project of much queer activism in Bologna. But precisely as such, it is always on the verge of undoing itself, as it risks becoming its own kind of identity, as fixed, clear and easily recognizable as those to which it is opposed.

So if that is the primary ethnographic concern of this book, what of its theoretical focus? Raising this as a question may appear curious to some readers. For many it will seem obvious that the theoretical focus of a work of anthropology is simply an extension of its ethnography – an explication or description of whatever facts about the world it purports to represent. That is both true, and not true, of my argument here, as I hope will become clear. For my theoretical interest is in the nature of anthropological theory itself, and its relation to ethnography. To take this as a question cannot mean assuming an answer in advance. So I do not presume that the nature of that relationship will automatically be one of resemblance and proximity. Instead I aim to develop an argument through demonstrating the consequences of occupying certain positions in regard to this relationship.

That is also a partial answer to the obvious question of why a book about queer activism should also interest itself in the nature of anthropological theory. A more straightforward answer is that the issue of how one's theoretical concepts relate to one's empirical material is a question that preoccupies any anthropologist to some extent, and indeed has stimulated some of the most important pieces of methodological reflection in the discipline's history (e.g. Clifford and Marcus 1986; Geertz 1973; Herzfeld 1987; Leach 1961; Strathern 1988). But concerns about the nature of the relationship between analysis and ethnography seem far removed from the empirical context of the LGBTQ activist movement in Bologna; the two issues appear disparate and unconnected.

Yet, as I hope to show, the more complex answer to the question of why a book about LGBTQ activism should concern itself with the nature of anthropological theory is that the two both are and are not connected, and indeed, precisely in being so they may aid us in coming to some conclusions about whether connection is always the most apposite form of relation between ethnography and theory.

The extent to which the two issues – one ethnographic and one theoretical – appear different from one another is obvious. At no point in this book will I shy away from that fact. In fact, I will often emphasize it, for that difference will form a central plank of the overall thrust of the argument.

Yet I will also argue that they are more similar than they might first appear. This is evident if we examine some recent literature in anthropology that endeavours to take relationships of difference as its starting point.

Some readers will already have noted some similarities between the way in which I have described this kind of relationship, in which it is difference, rather than identity, that is important, and other anthropological reflections on difference, particularly perhaps those of Viveiros de Castro on equivocation (2004a; see also Stasch 2009). He describes affinity as the paradigmatic form of such a relationship, arguing that unlike consanguinity, which is based on a common referent ontologically prior to the terms being related, affinity is premised on an equivocation: instead of the parent uniting two brothers, we have the wife/sister uniting two brothers-in-law, 'a mediating term, which is seen in diametrically opposite ways by the two poles of the relation' (2004a: 16).

Viveiros de Castro's discussions of equivocation are part of a now extensive theoretical literature in anthropology often described as an ontological or recursive 'turn' in the discipline. Though a diverse and varied movement whose subjects range from lab technicians and scientists to jaguars and shamans (e.g. Mol 2002; Pedersen 2011), the spirit of the turn, whose progenitors include Viveiros de Castro, Marilyn Strathern, Roy Wagner and Bruno Latour, concerns precisely the question of difference.

The fundamental theoretical premise of recursivity in anthropology is the idea that ethnographic data should have a transformative effect on anthropological concepts. A corollary of this premise is that there is not thus a substantive difference between those ethnographic data and those concepts, hence also the turn's 'ontological' nature: it famously aims to collapse the distinction between concepts and things (Henare et al. 2006). When I use the word in this book I will primarily be referring to those claims.

They are a gloss of what are in fact a range of extremely complex arguments, which have generated a rich range of further ethnographic insights. My interest here, however, is with difference as an ethnographic object, and as a relationship between ethnographic objects and analytical categories. Hence, I raise the issue of recursivity here for several reasons.

Firstly, and most obviously, because the ideas about difference and equivocal relationships that the 'turn' encapsulates are the latest set of interventions in that grand tradition of anthropological reflection on the status of anthropological knowledge itself that I have already mentioned. Indeed, it draws heavily on earlier work on precisely those issues, such as that of Roy Wagner and Marilyn Strathern.

Secondly, because the 'recursive turn' provides perhaps the clearest and most coherent example of an answer to the theoretical question of this book, namely how theory and ethnography relate to one another. It is, I will suggest in Part Three, the most paradigmatic and logically elegant instance of a broader trend in anthropology towards seeing 'good' theory as closely and directly tied to ethnography. This is a perspective that I will go on to suggest is at least implicitly common to much contemporary anthropological writing, and which Matei Candea and I elsewhere call 'ethnographic foundationalism' (Heywood forthcoming). What I mean by this is that according to this perspective, it is ethnography that is alleged to justify whatever analysis is presented, whether via a commitment to empiricism, politicized intersubjectivity or conceptual novelty, and unlike in earlier reflections on anthropological method (e.g. Leach 1961; Nadel 1951).

Finally, and as I have already suggested, I raise it because the kinds of relationships of otherness upon which authors such as Viveiros de Castro focus resemble those that my own ethnography treats.

This returns us to the question of the resemblance, or difference, between the ethnographic and theoretical foci of this book. I have noted that the two obviously differ in some ways. But they are also related, to the extent that the idea of a relationship of partial fidelity, a relationship through difference, very much resembles that of equivocation: in such a relationship one is connected differently to an object depending upon the position or context involved. As Viveiros de Castro puts it with a phrase that could equally well apply to LGBTQ activists, in such a relationship one finds oneself 'united by that which divides ... linked by that which separates' (2004: 17). Thus, with this comparison in mind, the arguments this book will make regarding the connection between theory and ethnography will be connected (recursively) to the relationships of difference I describe amongst LGBTQ activists in Bologna.

But for similar reasons, that cannot be the end of the answer: for the analogy undoes itself, just, as I will argue later, as do those internal to it. Connecting ethnographic relations in which disconnection, not connection, is key, to theoretical questions cannot mean entirely assimilating the two, for to do so would be to obscure how they connect in the first place: over difference. It would not 'make a difference', in the manner of my LGBTQ activist interlocutors.

Thus, doing what anthropologists usually do – connecting a theoretical issue to an ethnographic one – will not suffice on its own when the ethnographic issue in question is that of connections through difference. Instead, like the empirical differences this book describes, the book itself differs from them by connecting them to precisely these theoretical questions about theory and ethnography. In other words, the argument I will go on to make about the value of disconnecting theory from ethnography is partly an instance of itself. So this equivocal relationship, of both connection and disconnection, between queer activism and anthropological theory, mirrors – but also of course differs from – the equally equivocal relationships the ethnographic sections of this book will describe. What this further involves is a similarly partial relationship with recursivity, as in this case being recursive means being paradoxically non-recursive as well. A part of the effect of the arguments of the book will thus be to widen, not just to narrow, the gap between analysis and ethnography.

Hence, 'making difference' is both what LGBTQ activists in Bologna seek to do in a range of different ways, and what the book itself will seek to do by connecting (through their differences) the activities of LGBTQ activists to issues surrounding the relationship between theory and ethnography in anthropology. In line with this argument, what I will suggest in the concluding chapters of this book is that a possible direction for a 'post-recursive' anthropology (Pedersen 2012) to take is to abandon our quest for recursivity itself.

Difference from Whom?

My fieldwork was conducted over the course of the calendar year of 2012, during which I encountered a wide range of activist groups in Bologna. As I will describe in detail in Chapter 1, the city has long been a centre for radical left-wing politics in Italy. It witnessed the rise and fall of Europe's largest and most successful communist party at first hand, having been governed by the Italian Communist Party from the end of World War II until the party's dissolution in 1991, following a crisis meeting in Bologna itself. It was the site of worker protests during the 'Hot Autumn' of 1969, saw even larger student protests that ended in the death of a demonstrator in 1977, and was left scarred by the 'Years of Lead' – a period of left- and right-wing terrorism – after a bomb exploded at its train station in 1980, the worst atrocity of its kind at the time and the deadliest act of terror to take place on European soil before the Madrid train bombings of 2004.

At the time of my fieldwork it was home to several major centres of left-wing activism, and dozens of smaller ones. Amongst the former (housed in spaces known as *centri sociali*, often illegally occupied buildings) prominent examples were Ex Mercato 24 (XM24), a collective that emerged in the wake of the No Global movement of the late 1990s and by 2012 occupied itself with a variety of initiatives ranging from a language school for immigrants to the promotion of recycling; Teatro Polyvalente Occupato (TPO), originally a cultural collective founded by university students but which went on to concern itself with immigration and globalization; Laboratorio Crash!, another anti-globalization collective; and Vag61, a cultural centre that focused on immigration and local politics, amongst other issues.

These descriptions are brief, for though I spent time at each of these places and interviewed some of their members, they were not the focus of my fieldwork, which was instead spent largely examining groups that occupied themselves specifically with issues surrounding sexuality, which I describe below. I should also say that although my descriptions have made them sound relatively homogenous, they are in fact distinct in a number of ways. Some differences are broad and familiar even to casual observers of the activist scene: TPO, for example, partly because some of its funding comes from local government and because it considers itself to be more of a cultural than a political group, is viewed as a very different kind of entity from, say, Crash!, which is much more oriented towards anarchism and direct political action. Members of either organization make these distinctions themselves, often in a manner critical of the other. Other differences are less clear, and newcomers to the scene often spend time in a number of centres before finding one that they are most comfortable with.

Lines of conflict within LGBTQ activism are also focused on questions of institutionalization. Bologna is home to the largest and oldest local base of Italy's most prominent LGBTQ rights organization, Arcigay. In contrast to the majority of the *centri sociali*, Arcigay is housed in a large and elegant space given over to it by the city's government, known as Cassero. Cassero, as the Bologna chapter of Arcigay is often thus called, is home to a sophisticated and complex organization that includes an extensive library, a youth and schools outreach programme, a counselling and health service, and a large disco. Again, unlike the *centri sociali*, which almost universally emphasize self-government and decision by consensus, it is formally structured, with a President and Vice-President responsible for its operations. As I will describe in detail in the second part of this book, these features, coupled with its focus on lobbying for familial and reproductive rights, mean it is perceived by many LGBTQ activists as being too close to mainstream politics in Italy, both literally through its asso-ciation with the city's government, and conceptually in the sense that the prin-cipal objects of its activism (the legalization of gay marriage[1] and adoption and fertility rights for gay couples) are about normalizing LGBTQ life in Italy. Associated with Cassero – particularly with its lobbying aims – but organiza-tionally distinct are two smaller groups that focus exclusively on issues regard-ing the family: Famiglie Arcobaleno and Agedo both dedicate themselves to helping LGBTQ couples adopt or receive fertility treatment abroad, and on providing counselling for those in problematical domestic situations.

On the other side of the divide in LGBTQ political activism are a range of smaller groups that are structured along lines similar to *centri sociali* and much more radical in their politics than Cassero. During the course of my fieldwork, a number of these groups were united by a generalized opposition to Cassero's plans for the 2012 national Pride which took place in Bologna (see Part Two), and by an informal network, and it was with members of this network – of varying degrees of dedication to it – that a large part of my fieldwork time was spent. This network – known as the PutaLesboTransFemministaQueer Network, which I shorten to 'Puta Network' – was loosely based around an occupied building in the south of the city, close to where I lived.

The network originated in two ways: firstly with the Pride celebrations of 2010, in which various LGBTQ activist groups banded together to hold a fes-tival at a local LGBTQ-friendly bar, in order to raise money for activists to travel to Naples for the national gathering (though this itself was an 'alterna-tive' Pride, in opposition to the official one in Rome that year); and secondly with the massive demonstrations of 15 October 2011, against European and global financial institutions and the government of Silvio Berlusconi, for which these same groups collaborated.

Resisting institutionalization was of great importance for the Puta Network, and so pinning down its precise constituent parts is no easy task. The most visible elements of it were as follows: Antagonismogay/Laboratorio Smaschieramenti were two groups composed largely of the same individuals. The first was one of the earliest occupiers of Atlantide, a queer collective composed of gay, lesbian and transgender activists who seek to relate LGBTQ activism to the struggles of migrants, women, ethnic minorities and the unemployed, and to make the politics of LGBTQ activism into something more than a struggle for normalization. The second was formed by members of Antagonismogay in 2008 with the specific goal of investigating alternative forms of masculinity to be found amongst the LGBTQ and activist community of the city. FrangettEstreme emerged from XM24 in 2008 with the aim of pushing back against what they saw as an increasing commercialization of the LGBTQ movement, particularly with regard to Pride. Let's Queer were a largely cultural group of post-feminists who emphasize the ludic aspects of activism, and stage events, workshops and concerts in the city. Made in Woman were a similarly cultural group that produces and promotes goods and events made and organized by its members. Movimento Identità Transessuale (MIT) is the oldest and most well-established transgender organization in Italy, and is based in Bologna. Its position in the network was somewhat ambiguous, as it was simultaneously collaborating with Cassero on the organization of the official Bologna 2012 Pride. Finally, the group with whose members I spent the most time was known as SexyShock/Betty&Books; SexyShock emerged in 2001 as a group within TPO dedicated to exploring female desires, but split from it in 2004, believing it to be too rigid in both its structure and its political ideology. Betty&Books is the cultural/commercial arm of SexyShock, selling sex toys and related products, at one point through a shop in the Castiglione section of the city, but later through its website, or through temporary stalls.

Apart from MIT, these groups were made up of small numbers of dedicated individuals who met relatively regularly either in Atlantide or similar locations. Meetings would usually revolve around planning activities and events for the forthcoming period, but might also involve workshops on sexuality, book readings and film projections. The people involved also tended to frequent the same bars, clubs and cafes and so formed a close-knit community. This was true also because they tended to be similar in other respects, ranging in age from late twenties through to mid-forties but rarely beyond these limits, and were for the most part either unemployed, employed in part-time precarious labour, or students. Despite these similarities however, there were also differences between them – not least because the performance of difference was an essential aspect of their activism, and Part Two of the book will describe these tensions over identity and difference in detail.

A number of key names will recur throughout this book, and though I will describe these individuals as they appear, I introduce a few of the most important ones here briefly as well, because they broadly characterize some of the different types of activist I encountered in Bologna.

Marina and Massimo were key figures in the Puta Network, its *de facto* leaders in many respects, as I describe in Chapter 4. Marina was a recent graduate from Bologna University in her late twenties, working part time alongside her activism. Quiet, serious and earnest, her personality contrasted with that of Massimo, a flamboyant and charismatic man in his early forties who tended to dominate many of the meetings I attended, and was a driving force in the debates around the 2012 Pride described in Chapter 4. He was one of the few activists I met with a permanent job with the local city council. Both Marina and Massimo were unswerving in their convictions about the merits of the Puta Network over Cassero, and queer politics more broadly over what they saw as the conservative identity politics of the institutionalized movement.

On the more institutionalized side of the movement, Gaia was an imposing woman in her sixties, a matriarchal figure who commanded a great deal of respect even from those who disagreed with her. Not herself gay, she had come to LGBTQ activism through her son's difficulties in coming out, and was a prominent member of groups associated with and lobbying for LGBTQ families. Despite her strong opinions and forceful personality, she was a firm advocate of compromise and unity amongst the various factions within the LGBTQ movement, and in our discussions would often do her best to see the positive side of any position. She saw no harm in working with rather than simply against local government, and though her instincts could often be as antinomian as those of Marina and Massimo, she was convinced – like many in Cassero – that the movement's most important contemporary task was the achievement of equal rights.

Finally, Laura, an activist with Betty&Books/SexyShock, was a woman in her early thirties, a graduate in semiotics, employed part-time writing grant proposals for a local healthcare institution, and otherwise supported by her parents. In these respects and others she was in many ways typical of the female queer activists I encountered in my fieldwork. She was not as rigid in her beliefs as Marina and Massimo could sometimes seem, but she was deeply unsympathetic to Cassero and to institutions like it. Like many other queer activists in Bologna, she had begun her activism with Cassero, but become disillusioned with its focus on marriage to the exclusion of other political issues, and so had gravitated towards more radical LGBTQ activist groups such as those in the Puta Network. Yet she was far from being in complete agreement with Massimo and Marina, and argued with them on a number of occasions. As Chapter 4 will describe, she was suspicious of any attempt to reduce the pluralism of the radical LGBTQ movement to a singular perspective. This led her – as it did others – to drift in and out of initiatives, whilst retaining an absolute conviction in the value of activism *per se*. She was usually to be found dressed casually but elegantly in jeans and a t-shirt, often with a dash of lipstick on, and could be relied upon to be present at a range of the regular gatherings or meetings that took place in the city. Kind, open and extremely confident, she became both a close friend and an invaluable interlocutor.

Needless to say, these brief descriptions are intended only to give an introductory sense for the kinds of activist characters I encountered in my fieldwork. Most, like Laura, fell somewhere in between Gaia and Marina in many respects: university graduates in their thirties, without – like many Italians of that generation – fixed employment, unhappy with the leadership and aims of Cassero but not fully convinced by alternative organizations like the Puta Network either.

A final point worth emphasizing is that this book is not intended to be, or even to resemble, a comprehensive ethnographic account of queer activism in Bologna. It is a partial description of a specific set of practices and problems involved in such activism, ones which throw into relief an equally specific set of anthropological problems. That is not an unusual strategy in anthropological writing, though some may prefer that it were. I make no attempt to defend such strategies, because it is precisely the question of how ethnographic material and anthropological problems relate that I aim to address. I have chosen to do so by demonstrating the consequences of self-consciously adopting the conceits of some forms of anthropological writing. My reasons for doing so will, I hope, be clear by the book's conclusion.

In *Anthropology Through the Looking Glass* (1987), a foundational text for Europeanist anthropologists, Michael Herzfeld makes an argument about Greece and about anthropology as a discipline. Highlighting the ways in which Greeks, at the margins of Europe and the Orient, have been subjected to a discourse that on the one hand sanctions those aspects of its culture considered appropriately 'European' and on the other condemns 'exotic' yet traditional Greek practices, Herzfeld contends that anthropology has long been engaged in the same process of distillation, in which its European origins are subtly elevated to the pinnacle of civilization through an obsessive focus on the 'exotic' other. To rectify this, he calls for an increased attention to the anthropology of Europe, in an effort to force the discipline to come to terms with its own historical and cultural context.

The argument Herzfeld makes about Greece could be made in much the same form with regard to Italy: the cultural, racial and even criminological 'peculiarities' of the *mezzogiorno* had been preoccupying native scholars for the best part of a century prior to the publication of Edward Banfield's *Moral Basis of a Backward Society* (1958; Gibson 1998), and as Bonaccorso notes (2009: 8), anthropology has often reproduced this tendency to concern itself with 'predominantly small peasant communities in the south of the country, in impoverished and economically underdeveloped areas'. Since Banfield, ethnographers, both native and otherwise, have continued to focus largely on areas south of the capital (e.g. Belmonte 1979; Blok 1975; Brogger 1971; Douglass 1975; Galt 1980; Gambetta 1993; Giovannini 1981; Schneider and Schneider 1976, 1996, 2003; Schneider 1998; Silverman 1968; Tarrow 1967) and to emphasize the 'Mediterranean' theme of honour and shame.[2]

Herzfeld's argument in *Anthropology Through the Looking Glass* has rightly shaped the way in which subsequent ethnographers have approached the study of Europe, including this one. The principal arguments I will make in this book are deeply influenced by Herzfeld's concern for the relationship between theory and ethnography, yet I aim to experiment with an alternative manner of approaching that relationship. *Anthropology Through the Looking Glass* is premised on a symmetry between 'modern anthropological theory and the ethnographic study of modern Greece'; Herzfeld argues that 'boundary creation … should be seen as a problem in the ethnography of anthropological theory' (1987: 15). Instead of being bounded off from one another, he suggests, 'in the Mediterranean context … [anthropological categories] reproduce the ambiguities of identity … that the local populations directly experience for themselves. In this way anthropological theory and indigenous experience come together in an accessible framework of comparison' (1987: 16).

As I noted at the beginning of this section, a very similar argument might be made with regard to Italy: for decades (at least prior to Herzfeld's writing) Italianist ethnography was overwhelmingly focused upon the rural south, or upon the 'honour and shame complex'. Yet a range of recent work has challenged this predominance through studies of immigration, urban life and political economy (e.g. Dines 2012; Goddard 1996; Herzfeld 2009; Kertzer 1980; Krause 2009; Mahmud 2014; Però 2007; Molé 2012a; Muehlebach 2012; Yanagisako 2002). Thanks at least in part to its own persuasiveness, in this respect Herzfeld's argument no longer rings completely true. This is not, however, the only sense in which the kind of comparison Herzfeld had in mind might apply to my own argument. I will describe the political thought of the activists with whom I worked in detail in Chapters 3 and 4, but even the rudimentary outlines I have provided here should make it clear that they are far from being worlds apart from some aspects of anthropological theory. My interlocutors talked about Foucault, and they talked about Judith Butler; they talked about constructivism, and about performativity; and as I have mentioned already, their interest in difference unites them both intellectually and in many senses politically with the anthropological enterprise.

But it is precisely this interest in difference – and the broader focus of this book on relations of difference, rather than similarity – that makes a straightforward comparison with anthropology inappropriate. To be 'symmetrical' as an account of such relations of difference cannot mean erasing the difference between that account and those relations.

This is more than just a question of analytical strategy. Assuming a straightforward equation between the categories of anthropological analysis and those of Euro-American thought is no longer unproblematic. The developments in

anthropological theory which make some of the arguments of this book possible are derived from ethnographic material from places as diverse as
Amazonia, Cuba and Mongolia; and even if we dispute the claims to recursivity that these authors make, we must at least acknowledge the difference
between the theoretical models they employ and those that Herzfeld identifies
as being based on ethnocentric assumptions.

Does this imply, then, that contemporary anthropological concepts have
now advanced radically beyond those with which we were accustomed to
think when the discipline was still blinkered by its 'Western' origins? The
claim I wish to make here is less ambitious than that. What I want to argue is
that though the contents of the arguments of Herzfeld and of recent thinkers
on recursivity are very different, they in fact share both a question and the
form of a certain kind of response: both are concerned with the way in which
ethnography ought to relate to theory, and both look to ethnography for an
answer to this question.

What I will argue here instead is that the question is by its nature an intrinsically anthropological one. In asking it, we presuppose a distinction – or at
least an equivocal relationship – between the ethnographic data we observe in
the field and the analysis of it we provide subsequently, one that cannot exist
for those who do not do both. Note that there is absolutely no consequential
claim that this makes us in any sense whatsoever 'superior' to those we study.
The claim instead is no more than the bland truism that our task is not the
same as theirs.

So rather than proposing an alternative to Herzfeld's formulation of 'comparison' because thinkers such as Viveiros de Castro have provided us with
categories that are not 'Euro-American', I am suggesting that 'comparison' may
not be an appropriate formulation because in so far as we are concerned with
this relationship, our categories are not – and perhaps were never – identical
with those of any particular ethnographic location, an argument I develop
further in my conclusion. Viveiros de Castro and others have shown us that
'culture' is not the relative answer to universal questions but that questions
themselves differ across contexts. To which I add merely that anthropology
may have its own distinct set of questions too, of which perhaps the most
crucial is that which both Viveiros de Castro and Herzfeld pose: how do our
questions relate to those of our interlocutors? But that is itself our question,
not theirs.

Given this, the experiment I will conduct with this book is to try to respond
to this question not with 'comparison' or recursivity, but with equivocation
and partial fidelity. What will it look like to try to 'take seriously' a Euro-
American ethnographic context with theories influenced by the thought of
Amerindian shamans? What kind of account can we produce when we seek
not a confluence of concepts and materials, but a separation, not only from
those materials but from the aim of confluence itself? How can we be recursive
when 'making a difference' is both object and method of analysis?

As many readers will already be thinking, this kind of project has obvious ethical implications, particularly given that it is concerned with people struggling for various forms of recognition. The following section will seek to address some of these implications.

Why Make Difference?

In their landmark introduction to a symposium dedicated to anthropology and human rights (2005), Jean-Klein and Riles make a startling suggestion: instead, they argue, of asking what anthropology can do to be relevant to the human rights sector, they pose the question of 'what anthropological encounters with human rights contribute to the development of our discipline' (2005: 174). Flying in the face, they note, of a widespread preoccupation with 'anti-disciplinarity' as a cure for all the political and analytical ills of the academy, and of an equally widespread sense that to care about discipline – our discipline – 'constitutes a form of perversion – a kind of lapse of professional ethics' (2005: 174), they follow Pels (2002) in arguing that 'self-disciplined ethnographic engagement is a form of professional commitment to humanitarian ethics ... [and] also necessarily a form of care for the discipline itself' (2005: 175). In a statement phrased much more eloquently than the way in which I have tentatively echoed it above, they argue that '[e]thnography, and the commitments it demands, is in fact the only form of engagement that our profession is uniquely qualified to administer' (2005: 175).

The reason their discussion of the relationship between anthropology and human rights is pertinent to my own argument is not only because of their stirring defence of a concern for anthropology's own interests, but also because of the curious parallels between the kind of human rights literature to which they object and some aspects of the literature of anthropology's 'recursive turn'. I expand on this analogy in Chapter 6, but for now I focus on two trends they identify in anthropological engagements with human rights: the first they call 'co-construction', and the second, 'denunciation'.

Co-construction, or 'giving voice', is the sympathetic approach taken by anthropologists interested in the 'experiential dimensions' (2005: 177) of what Joel Robbins has recently called 'the suffering subject' (2013). Focused, in the human rights sector, on narratives of violence and loss, 'giving voice', as Jean-Klein and Riles note, 'curiously became a kind of postmodern solution to the critiques of positivism on the one hand, and to the vilification of theory on the other (as in the conceit that one could get away from representational authority and epistemological debates and simply "listen to people's voices")' (2005: 177).

Denunciation, on the other hand, is what Jean-Klein and Riles identify as the critical approach taken by anthropologists when studying either situations of violence or oppression, and thus from a humanitarian perspective, or responses to such situations on the part of states or NGOs which are viewed with suspicion because of their 'formalized' or 'institutional' nature (2005: 180).

Both approaches could be applied to my ethnographic context. Interviews I conducted with LGBTQ couples who had succeeded, against enormous odds and in spite of the legal and political obstacles the Italian state put in their way, in adopting children or receiving fertility treatment abroad were deeply affecting, and if their narratives do not form a part of this particular project it is because there is not the space here to do them proper justice. Similarly, Italy's woefully inadequate record of securing and protecting the rights of its LGBTQ citizens (e.g. Mahony 2013), not to mention the homophobic and racist statements that the nation's elected representatives make on a regular basis (e.g. ANSA 2013), are targets of critique and denunciation so obvious that it barely requires stating.

Both approaches are also curiously similar, in some senses, to aspects of anthropology's recent 'recursive turn', though their respective advocates may not find the comparison entirely to their liking. The idea of 'giving voice' as a resolution to epistemological problems sounds not unlike the implicit promise of transparency to be found in variations of the 'follow the actors themselves' formula that inspires Latourian variants of the turn (Latour 2005), particularly in its suspicion of 'theory'. Though the projects of Latour and of the authors Jean-Klein and Riles have in mind (e.g. Zur 1996; Wilson 2003) are worlds apart in a number of ways – particularly in their relationship to politics – they are made strange bedfellows by their rhetorical antipathy for anything that intrudes upon the immediacy of ethnographic presentation. They share the perspective I described earlier as 'ethnographic foundationalism'.

A perhaps somewhat clearer parallel can be drawn between the approach Jean-Klein and Riles call 'denunciation' and the more politically-inspired variants of the 'recursive turn' (e.g. Blaser 2009, 2013; de la Cadena 2010; di Giminiani 2013; Salmond 2012; see also Lloyd 2011: 838; and Holbraad et al. 2014). As I have already noted, much of the turn's metaphysics are inspired by a critique of those they see as 'Euro-American' (Descartes being the most frequent shorthand target, e.g. Robertson 2011), and some emphasize this critique more than others. Probably the clearest example of this sort of position is to be found in some of Viveiros de Castro's writings, in which he is more or less explicit about his lack of interest in 'taking seriously' Western philosophy, and the politics that inspires this (e.g. 2011a; 2011b; 2013: 497).

The purpose of drawing out these parallels is to highlight the fact that the problems Jean-Klein and Riles identify with both 'co-construction' and 'denunciation' are also to be found in the 'recursive turn'. Firstly, both are duplicative; as Jean-Klein and Riles note,

> although anthropologists often claim observation and representation as their domains of expertise, for example, much human rights work consists also of fact-finding, reporting, analysis, and poetic evocation – even 'contextualisation' ... likewise, where anthropologists aspire to the role of expert critic of human rights

administration, communities of 'critical legal scholars' now invoke the same bodies of critical theory to produce highly nuanced, sophisticated analyses of the type anthropologists ideally hope to produce. (2005: 184)

This is absolutely true of my interlocutors (one group even conducted an 'ironic' survey of attitudes to masculinity). Of course, this is also true of 'recursive turn' anthropology, to the precise extent to which it succeeds in making the relationship between indigenous categories and anthropological ones recursive.

Furthermore, as Jean-Klein and Riles go on to argue, it should not be surprising that this kind of intentional duplication leads on to a consequent problem of iteration. Just like anthropological engagements with human rights – and indeed with activism (e.g. Low and Merry 2010; Merry 2008; Sanford and Angel-Ajani 2006; Turner 2006) – and despite their comparable professed emphases on innovation and contingency, recursive analyses are often remarkably homogenous, as Martin Holbraad himself has noted (2017), an issue I expand upon in Chapter 5.

I conclude this section with a final quotation from Jean-Klein and Riles that neatly summarizes both their position and the beginnings of my own: 'our larger point, then, is that if at times it seems that there is no difference between anthropological practice and human rights practice, then perhaps difference, like relevance, must be produced, as an effect, not simply found in the world' (2005: 188). Because of this same conviction that a difference between anthropology and its object is worth producing (or 'making'), for reasons Part Three will set out, my account will at least endeavour not to mirror the practices and categories of my interlocutors, either by 'giving voice' to their interpretations of Foucault or Butler, or by ventriloquizing their critiques of the Italian state, although it will undoubtedly fail at least occasionally in this endeavour. Crucially, though, what I add to Jean-Klein and Riles is that this conviction that difference must be produced is not merely an analytical one: it will be one of the central arguments of this book that the production of difference is an essential aspect of LGBTQ activism (see Chapters 4 and 6). So, bringing us back to the paradoxically recursive/non-recursive nature of this account, it is the production of difference, not difference itself, which is a found object here, and for that very reason, this account will aim to produce a difference between itself and its object.

Outline of Chapters

This book is divided into three parts, each containing two chapters. Part One describes some key aspects of the moral and political context of queer activism in Bologna, and introduces the issues of relatedness and difference with which the book will be concerned. Chapter 1 describes the recent political history of Bologna as a hotbed of left-wing activism, and highlights the frequency with which people self-designate as left-wing, regardless of the actual content of their political beliefs. It thus shows how the idea of 'left-wing' in Bologna does not function to homogenize a particular political community, but to connect radically different ideas that might otherwise fail to relate to one another through a homonym over the proper meaning of which people can disagree. Chapter 2 explores a similar relationship in regard to moral codes, in which it is possible to subscribe to ethical injunctions in such a way that the eventuality of their betrayal under certain conditions is already allowed for.

Part Two focuses in on the notions of identity and difference with which queer activism is concerned. Chapter 3 describes a set of dialogues between queer activists and a pro-LGBT liberal Catholic group, using them to explore some notions of difference at work amongst queer activists in Bologna and the ways in which these dialogues faltered with a failure to agree on how the groups in questions actually differed. Chapter 4, the culmination of the book's ethnographic portion, sets out its key ethnographic focus by showing how important but also problematical the production of difference is to activists through a series of key debates that took place in advance of the 2012 Italian national Pride week in Bologna. It shows how a belief in the virtue and necessity of performing difference from any form of fixed identity led activists repeatedly to reject attempts to unify them around either support of or objection to the city's official Pride celebrations. Yet it also shows how on occasions like the day of the parade itself, it was precisely this belief in the value of difference that did bring them together as a community.

Part Three turns from the problem of difference in queer activism to the problem of the alleged identity between theory and ethnography in anthropology. Chapter 5 makes this switch in registers as clear as possible, surveying some responses to the question of what form the relation between theory and ethnography should take, and showing how much contemporary reflection on the topic aims to collapse the distinction between the two, whilst in fact relying upon it. This forms the centrepiece of a critique of what I call 'ethnographic foundationalism', on the basis that it purports to absolve anthropologists from the need to reflect on the epistemological foundations of their claims. Thus, the chapter's move away from queer activism in Bologna and towards theoretical abstraction is a deliberate instance of its own argument. Chapter 6 returns to ethnographic concerns by showing how the problem of ethnographic foundationalism is in fact very similar to the problem of difference in queer activism. As an argument though, that clearly verges on ethnographic foundationalism itself, as it derives what force it has from a direct comparison of an analytical and an ethnographic question. The book thus concludes by breaking down that very comparison in order to ask whether anthropology could possess what queer activism refuses: its own essential identity.

Notes

1. At the time of my fieldwork, neither same-sex civil unions nor marriage were legal in Italy, and prior to 2012 the legal recognition of same-sex relationships was not a part of the platform of any major Italian political party. Civil unions have been recognized in the country since June 2016.
2. For successive overviews of 'Mediterranean' literature, see Davis (1977), Gilmore (1982) and Pitt-Rivers' (1977) volume on 'the politics of sex' as well as Herzfeld (1980, 1985) and Peristiany (1965) for examples of 'honour and shame'; for subsequent critiques of the 'Mediterranean' as a regional category see Herzfeld (1984), Pina-Cabral (1989), SERG (1981); for a more recent survey and the argument that 'Mediterranean anthropology' is undergoing a renaissance, see Albera (2006), and Ben-Yehoyada (2014).

PART I

1

Equivocal Locations

Bologna is known to its inhabitants – and to tourists – by a number of names: its three most well-known soubriquets are *la grassa* (the fat) for its culinary excellence; *la dotta* (the learned) for its university, the oldest in Europe; and, most pertinently to this book, *la rossa* (the red) for its traditional political proclivities (as well as for the colour of much of its historic architecture). It is in no small part because of this final aspect of the city's reputation that it has become, in recent decades, a Mecca for many in the Italian LGBTQ community; and it was with *la rossa* in mind that I selected Bologna as my field-site for a study of the ethics of LGBTQ activism.

In many ways, as I describe below, the city's reputation as *la rossa* is well deserved. It was extremely uncommon for me to hear people from any walk of life self-describe as anything other than 'left-wing'. Yet as I (predictably) discovered very shortly after my arrival, what people actually mean by this and similar terms is enormously varied, and frequently in contradiction with orthodox social science understandings of them. In this chapter I describe a number of ethnographic examples from my fieldwork of how being left-wing in the heartland of Italian left-wing politics can have a range of different (and sometimes surprising) meanings, such as being anti-immigrant, or pro-Catholic, or anti-gay marriage.

This ethnographic problem is an old one for Italianist ethnographers (e.g. Kertzer 1974, 1980; Pratt 1986; see also Però 2007: 19-20; see Holbraad 2014 on a similar paradox in Cuba), as I detail here, often with reference to communism and Catholicism, and has also resurfaced in more contemporary forms in discussions of the relationship between the left and immigration (Però 2005a; 2007) and neoliberalism (Muehlebach 2009, 2012), for example.

But it is also connected to conceptual issues of perennial concern in anthropology, ones related to those this book as a whole aims to address: what to do when an emic understanding of a concept looks very different to our own (where 'our own' may refer to Britain or the US, or to anthropological theory); and can the relationship between a topic of study (such as 'being red') and a field-site (such as 'Red Bologna') ever be anything but 'arbitrary' (Candea

2007) when it (unsurprisingly) transpires that the topic of study manifests itself in a myriad different ways in the field-site?

Below I outline a number of solutions to the apparent paradox of how being left-wing can mean so many different and surprising things in Bologna, some historical – with the aid of David Kertzer's seminal ethnographic study of Bologna (1980) – and some potential – through comparison with more recent work in the anthropology of politics on Italy by Però (2005a, 2005b, 2007) and Muehlebach (2009, 2012). I then advance my own argument, namely that it is not the paradox it appears to be: what seem to be incoherent understandings of the same concept are actually references to different objects (Holbraad 2014). It is precisely through a superficial ideological uniformity that real political differences are expressed – the 'red' in 'Red Bologna' is a homonym, with a multitude of different referents, and it is the differences between these referents, not the assertion of a common identity, that is often at issue when people self-describe as left-wing.

I conclude by arguing furthermore that the relationship between the 'field' as a location and the 'field' as a theoretical interest may productively be viewed in the same light: despite its sobriquet, 'Red Bologna', it transpired unsurprisingly, did not constitute a 'representative' field-site for the study of left-wing activism; but neither is it the case that ideas about what it means to be left-wing in anthropology bear no necessary relationship at all (Candea 2007) to the diverse ways in which it was understood ethnographically. Instead I suggest that in this case – just as what is interesting about being 'red' in 'Red Bologna' is not how everyone is 'left-wing', but how so many people are 'left-wing' and mean different things by this – what is interesting about the relationship between being left-wing as a concept in anthropology and being left-wing in Bologna is neither that they are equivalent nor entirely unconnected, but that they are related through their difference.

A Party for the Party

On a warm evening in September, in the company of two friends, Maria and Antonio, I took a crowded bus out beyond Bologna's northern limits to one of the biggest and most famous annual festivals in the country, known in the city as the *Festa dell'Unità*. Beginning shortly after the conclusion of World War II, the *Festa* takes place every year in towns and cities across Italy, and – particularly in the region in which Bologna is situated – sometimes even in the tiniest of villages. It is named in honour of the official newspaper of the Italian Communist Party (PCI), and, until the latter's dissolution in 1991, was organized by its local branches. Since that time it has continued to take place under the auspices of the PCI's variously named successors, and is currently known – at least officially – across most of the country as the *Festa Democratica*, after the contemporary incarnation of Italy's historic left, the Democratic Party (PD).

Not, however, in Bologna. Not only, Maria and Antonio explained to me on the bus, is Bologna one of the few places in the country in which the *Festa* continues to be known by its original (Communist) name, but it is also the largest version of the *Festa* in Italy. Lasting for two weeks, it attracts thousands of visitors both in the daytime and at night, and indeed on this particular evening we got off the bus and joined a very large crowd moving towards the entrance.

The crowd was composed of people of a remarkable variety of ages, from groups of teenage girls in brightly coloured padded jackets to elderly men wearing overcoats and fedoras, and as we entered it became clear that the *Festa* catered to a range of tastes: the first stalls were all commercial ones, selling local food and produce, clothes, and even cars from a nearby factory, whilst loudspeakers blared out hip hop music at every intersection. Somewhat surprised at the lack of party political content, I asked Antonio whether this is what the *Festa* had always been like; he told me that he was too young to give me a proper answer, but that a friend of Maria's we were due to meet knew all there was to know about its history, and he promised to introduce me.

As we moved deeper into the large park where the *Festa* was being held, we came to a series of tents offering a product that looked a little more like what I had expected: the symbol of the PD was everywhere, and a number of stands represented particular sections within it; there was a tent for female party members (empty), a tent for young members (empty), and a very large tent with a stage where I was told that debates would take place. Other associated political groups were also represented: several anti-mafia organizations were running a sequence of bars and handing out T-shirts, and a number of left-leaning newspapers had put up stalls as well.

We eventually reached a large marquee that had been converted into a makeshift bookstore, and here we met a group of friends Maria had known for years through her work at an NGO; most were at the *Festa* manning a stand for Amnesty International, but Giorgio, the man to whom Antonio had promised to introduce me, worked in one of the many restaurants staffed by volunteers. Large and in his late forties, Giorgio worked as a butcher in a co-operative in the centre of the city, and was also heavily involved in trades union activity. Like his father before him, he volunteered at the *Festa* every year without fail, and had been attending since he was a boy. The first thing he did when I was introduced to him as an anthropologist interested in the history of the *Festa* and its association with the left was to take out his mobile phone, give me his number, and tell me to call him then and there, which, although a little nonplussed, I proceeded to do; the stirring chorus of the 'Internationale' rang out at full volume. Gesturing at the speakers – still playing hip hop – with repugnance, he said: 'When I was a boy the only music you'd ever hear at the *Festa* was this' as he pointed to his mobile 'and "Bella Ciao" [the anthem of Italy's wartime partisans]. Now politics comes second to all the rest. Even here in Bologna'.

Why should it be particularly surprising that 'even here in Bologna', party politics comes second at a festival purportedly devoted to the propagation of a specific kind of political content? Because for Giorgio and others like him Bologna is not just Bologna but Bologna *la rossa*, 'the traditional showcase city of the Italian Left', as Però puts it (2005a: 835; see also 2007); they are proud of the fact that the *Festa*'s name remains tied to its Communist roots, and proud of the fact that it continues to attract the largest number of attendees of any of the equivalent *feste* in Italy, as well as a sufficient number of volunteers to keep the stalls manned throughout the day and night. Equally, they are saddened by what they perceive as a weakening of enthusiasm for old causes, and a slackening of ideological rigour.

From 1945 until the party's dissolution in 1991, the city was governed by a continuous succession of PCI administrations. David Kertzer, who studied Communist and Catholic activists in Bologna during the 1970s, describes how during that period 'Almost half of the entire national membership [of the PCI] is found in the Red Belt, composed of the regions of Emilia-Romagna, Toscana, Marche, and Umbria ... Bologna remains the most heavily Communist of the large cities. In the period 1968-76 almost 14 percent of the Bologna population were PCI members' (Kertzer 1980: 33). The PCI dissolved itself in 1991 after the so-called 'Bolognina turn', named for the suburb of the city in which it was first announced, thus putting Bologna in the (equivocal) position of having been both the PCI's pride and joy, and the site of its death throes (Kertzer 1996). The dominance of the left did not dissipate however. Apart from a brief five-year interval between 1999 and 2004, the successors of the PCI – first the Democratic Party of the Left (PDS), then the Left Democrats (DS), and currently the PD – seem to have inherited much of the city's loyalty, at least when it comes to local elections.

It is not the case, however, that all are content with the transition to post-Communism in Bologna. At the *Festa*, for example, many people would refer simply to 'the Party' interchangeably when speaking both of the old PCI and of the new PD. When I asked Giorgio what he thought about this however, he was vehement in denying any equivalency: his father, he told me, had taken off the hammer and sickle pendant he had always worn at the end of a chain when the PCI dissolved and was reconstituted as the PDS; he, on the other hand, still wears one proudly. 'I will never vote for the PD', he insisted, 'they're nothing like the PCI – they're full of Catholics'.

What this brief vignette illustrates is the problem with which this chapter will be principally concerned: despite the appearance of a remarkable degree of ideological uniformity in Bologna *la rossa*, what being left-wing actually means to people varies to a considerable degree. Being 'red' in Red Bologna, it transpires, is by no means as straightforward as it sounds.

What I will seek to suggest in this chapter is that despite the absence of a homogenous emic conception of what it means to be left-wing in Bologna, that does not make the city an 'arbitrary location' (Candea 2007) in the sense of lacking a relation to the topic under study (in this case, what it means to be a left-wing activist). Instead I propose to describe it as what I will call an 'equivocal location', a concept which seeks to express the fact that whilst there may be (and often is) a relationship between an anthropologist's field-site and a given analytical object, that relationship does not have to be one of equivalency or representation.

An Old Problem

It is, of course, difficult for an ethnographer to say for certain whether and how far Giorgio's laments reflect the reality of a genuinely radical transformation of the sort he describes: from a *Festa dell'Unità* focused entirely on party politics to one in which everything has become commercialized, and the ideals – as well as the music – of the 'Internationale' forgotten; from an Italian left in which the hammer and sickle reigned supreme and avowed anticlericalism of the sort Giorgio espoused was rife, to one in which a crucial faction – known as La Margherita – is a direct descendent of the Christian Democrats, the PCI's arch-nemesis, and whose Catholic social conservatism divides the party and has pulled it towards positions such as an opposition to gay marriage. The leader of this faction had paid a visit to Bologna and to the *Festa* shortly before my own, and upon her arrival had been showered with confetti by a group of protestors of my acquaintance.

We can however turn again to the work of Kertzer, who describes Communist rituals, including the *Festa*, in superb detail, for some idea of what they once were: 'Although the décor of the *festa* is eminently political', Kertzer writes,

> the manifest content is overwhelmingly non-political, a continuation of the traditional Church *festa* forms. Food and drink are the center of the *festa*; the largest area contains long dining tables seating 200 to 400 people where the traditional Bolognese delicacies are served along with great quantities of locally produced wine ... A variety of games of chance is offered, ranging from the cork-pull to the dart competition ... The political content of the Communist *festa* centers around a speech made in the middle of the weekend's festivities by a PCI official, usually from the Bologna provincial Party office. The speech is regarded by almost everyone as a mere formality, a concession to the official Party conception of the *festa* as a raiser of political consciousness. Few people in fact listen to the speech; the great majority continue to eat or play games of chance. (1980: 150–51; see also Kertzer 1974)

Apart from the absence of hip hop music, Kertzer's description of the PCI *festa* of the 1970s could apply equally well to the PD *festa* of 2012.

Undoubtedly there will have been many other differences; and my point here is not that Giorgio may be wrong or that his memories may be mistaken; what is more interesting about Giorgio's nostalgia for another way of being left-wing is that its deployment serves to differentiate his conceptions of what it means to be 'left-wing' in Bologna from those of others. Furthermore, such differences in ideas are not only a feature of contemporary Bolognese political life; Kertzer concludes the above description of the *Festa* with the following:

> The specifically political content of the Communist *festa*, in fact, has been largely delegated to the FGCI [the youth wing of the PCI], with the adults concentrating on the more traditional *festa* aspects. The youths, indeed, have taken on the role of defenders of the official political conception of the *festa*, in reaction to the practices they consider too similar to the traditional parish *feste*. The youths take it on themselves to organize political educational activities, such as photographic exhibits of Vietnam, of Italian substandard housing, of the war in Mozambique, and so on. They show anti-fascist movies, hold discussions on political topics at the *festa*, and run the only game booth having a political tinge: the dartboard contest [the targets are pictures of Richard Nixon]. In 1972, in line with their criticism of the non-political content of the Party *festa*, the FGCI youths called on the local Party leaders to close down the food, dance, and gaming facilities during the political speech. The Party leaders opposed this, saying that many people might drift away if compelled to attend the talk. (1980: 151–52)

In other words – and of course this ought not to surprise us – even during a period particularly marked by the dominance of the PCI amongst left-wing Italians, and especially so in Bologna, what it meant to be left-wing was still an object of dispute (for other such points see e.g. Hajek 2011).

Turning to Giorgio's oft-echoed criticism of the PD for allying with Catholic social conservatives and former Christian Democrats (whom Marco, an activist friend of mine, would refer to as the 'theo-cons'), this is also far from being an entirely novel phenomenon. Giorgio himself later told me that his father was a *cattocomunista*, or Catholic Communist – a tradition, I was told, that was born in Bologna – and indeed much of Kertzer's ethnography is devoted to precisely the question of how people in the city negotiated the competing claims of loyalty that issued from Church and Party, of which more later. The Catholic Communist explanatory framework is, as Kertzer notes (1980: 245), familiar to many Italians (including myself) who were raised on Giovanni Guareschi's stories of a little village in the Red Belt in which local priest Don Camillo and Communist Mayor Peppone battle ferociously for the affections of the populace, whilst in reality being united by their common interest in the welfare of the village; keeping the peace between them is a talking crucifix, a Christ who, though naturally the confidante of Don Camillo, sounds far more like the Christ of Liberation Theology than that of the official Church, and frequently sides with Peppone in their disputes.

Faenza (1959), whose work Kertzer discusses, provides perhaps the nearest thing to an ethnographic exposition of this idea. In his account of a small village in the Romagna, its inhabitants consistently vote for the PCI by overwhelming margins, yet also attend church on a regular basis, and are without exception baptized, married and buried with Catholic ceremonies. At the root of Faenza's explanation for this is the idea of 'belly communism', the notion that people subscribe to communist ideology because they feel it will serve their practical interests, without really comprehending it intellectually (Kertzer 1980: 247). I sometimes heard similar sentiments in Bologna. In fact, when I asked Giorgio how people in the city had reacted to the 'Bolognina turn' and the fall of the PCI, he said there had been no noticeable grief: 'People here are very flexible; it's typical of Bologna – go for what's good, not what's ideological'.

As Kertzer points out however, this model suffers from a number of flaws (1980: 247–48). It is not easily generalizable: neither in Kertzer's Bologna nor in mine was the overlap between the Catholic and Communist (or left-wing) worlds so significant as to justify the idea that there was no real emic distinction. Neither was it in any sense the case that people did not comprehend the divisions involved; indeed, although I will discuss in detail below further instances of an overlap between being left-wing and being Catholic, I would go as far as to say that it would be impossible to live in contemporary Bologna and fail to recognize the antagonistic relationship between the left and the Church, which Marco described as being one of 'open warfare'.

Although I will return to this problem later in this chapter, for now I want to set it aside temporarily and describe two more (somewhat unlikely) examples of nostalgia for the city's past glories as a bastion of the PCI in the fight against Christian Democracy, in which the idea of Bologna *la rossa* is further complicated.

Which 'Red'?

Running slightly late for an interview one day and unable to face the prospect of making my way to an out of town suburb on foot in the roasting August heat, I decided instead to take a taxi from a rank near to my apartment; the driver was in a voluble mood, and we soon began discussing the economic crisis and what he perceived to be the failures of the then government of Mario Monti, a technocrat appointed to steer Italy out of its recession. He was of the opinion that many of the austerity measures the Monti government was attempting to put in place would hit the country's workers the hardest whilst leaving the rich unscathed, and he lamented the failure of the PD to put up a fight in defending the interests of their voters. He told me, with the air of someone repeating an assertion he has made many times in his life, that there were two crucial things missing in left-wing Italian politics: the first, a real Communist party that would truly represent the interests of the workers; and the second, he explained, holding up – to my surprise – a small picture of the Madonna he kept on his dashboard, was the spirit of the Church, which should guide politicians in making the best choices for the Italian people. Brushing aside my hesitant suggestion that this seemed an unlikely combination of political aspirations, he insisted that there was no contradiction: 'Inside every communist there is a secret Catholic'.

Earlier on in my fieldwork I had been struck by a similar conversation, this time over *aperitivi* in a bar in the area in which I lived, one often frequented by my LGBTQ activist interlocutors. During the course of a quiet drink with a female friend, we were approached by a middle-aged man I had not seen before, but whom I would later spot occasionally at various assemblies and other bars with similar reputations. He immediately struck me as somewhat out of place, if only because his approach to us was patently connected to the less than furtive stares he had been directing towards my friend since we had arrived, behaviour that is – unsurprisingly – frowned upon in this particular environment. After grasping relatively swiftly that his advances were not going to be returned, he turned to me, introduced himself as Davide, and asked what I did for a living. After I had explained a little about my research, he remarked on what an excellent choice I had made in coming to Bologna, but lamented the changes that the city had undergone in recent decades, particularly the influx of immigrants, which, he claimed, had led to a rise in crime, high unemployment amongst Italians, and the presence of an increasing amount of litter in Bologna. I asked him whether he had a job, and he replied that he worked in a newspaper printing press, which aroused my curiosity as I had recently been discussing the demographics of newspaper consumption with Carlo, a friend who ran a newsagent.

Carlo had been instructing me on the political leanings and affiliations of the various dailies, and explaining the consumption habits of his customers: almost everyone bought *La Repubblica*, he told me, the main centre-left national paper, and many also bought *Il Resto del Carlino*, the most well-known local daily, which, whilst leaning to the right, had excellent coverage of the local sports teams. Some would buy *Corriere della Sera*, an established centre-right national. He sold few of the papers to the left of *La Reppublica*, and even fewer of those to the right of the *Corriere*.

So naturally I asked Davide, as an insider of sorts in the business, which paper he himself read, the response to which was *Il Giornale*, a newspaper which has been published by the Berlusconi family since the late 1970s, and is thus well to the right of many others, in addition to carrying the added stigma of being publicly associated with a man who is, for obvious reasons, anathema to many on the left in Italy. This admission, coupled with his earlier remarks regarding immigration, led me to wonder whether I might finally have met someone in the city who would style themselves openly as right-wing, and I proceeded to ask if this was the case.

Davide looked horrified at my suggestion, and immediately began to insist that, far from being right-wing, he was in fact left-wing. Furthermore, he claimed always to have voted for the PCI when they existed, and that if they were around today they would undoubtedly put a stop to the problem of immigration in Bologna. *Il Giornale* he read for the sports pages. When I asked him if he thought it was unusual for someone who thought of himself as left-wing to read a newspaper owned by the family of the figurehead of Italy's right-wing, he shook his head dismissively and told me that just because people do not admit to reading it does not mean that they do not do so.

These two cases were not isolated, but neither do they exemplify ubiquitous points of view. It should come as no surprise that many of those I met in Bologna who self-described as left-wing did not believe that the Catholic Church was a force for good in Italian politics; more often quite the opposite, in fact. Nor did a majority express anti-immigrant sentiment in the same breath as nostalgia for the PCI; indeed, many were active in pro-immigrant organizations.

But as Davide Però makes clear in his rich and detailed ethnographic studies of the relationship between the left and immigration in Bologna (e.g. 2005a; 2005b; 2007), that relationship cannot simply be taken for granted: as he notes in a statement that could equally well apply to LGBTQ rights and (reversed) to anticlericalism, 'the Left is often un-problematically assumed to be supportive or even representative of immigrants' (2005a: 833). In the same piece, Però describes the ways in which the sympathetic official rhetoric of the PDS in Bologna towards immigrants in the 1990s was often belied by the behaviour and discourse of its grassroots activists (2005a: 840–41), and how even when this was not the case, 'pro-refugee' politics was often 'ghettoizing, patronizing and infantilizing' (2005a: 843).

Però's work is a salutary critique of the gap between principles and practice within Italy's post-socialist left when it comes to dealing with immigration. Yet perhaps because of this critical impulse it tends to take for granted, for example, the fact that the principles of respect for cultural difference expressed in public self-representations of the PDS are or should be shared by all of its members. The gap it highlights may be worthy of critique if it is solely evidence of hypocrisy (though cf. Herzfeld 2009 and Heywood 2015 and below for discussions of moral flexibility in contemporary Italy); but it may just as well be evidence of a lack of uniformity about what the left's attitude to immigration should be. In which case the risk of critique is that it comes at the cost of ethnographic sensitivity (cf. Candea 2011b: 311). So unlike Però, my intention here is not to argue that because the assumption that being left-wing means being pro-immigration (and other similar assumptions) may not always be reflected in reality, being 'left-wing' in Bologna must therefore mean somehow falling short of what it really means to be 'left-wing'.

Nor, in describing these encounters, has my aim been to suggest, as Andrea Muehlebach has, that the left in Italy more broadly has become incorporated into a hegemonic 'neoliberal' political economy (2009; 2012; see also Heywood 2014) that has in some manner perverted its true goals and methods. Muehlebach writes perceptively of the contemporary Italian political landscape as one in which it is increasingly difficult conceptually to discern the difference between left and right (2009: 496). She describes a situation in which leftist practices of solidarity and support for others articulate in complex and often complicit fashion with the withdrawal of the welfare state. Thus, she argues, they have become paradoxically enrolled in a hegemonic neoliberalism capable of encompassing critiques of itself. Yet the conceptual or effectual indeterminacy of left and right she describes is not matched by a comparable ethnographic admixture. As she notes, her leftist subjects themselves see what they do as motivated by beliefs as distinct from 'neoliberalism' as it is possible to be (e.g. 2009: 497; 2012: 7). Her theoretical sense of what these terms mean, in other words, is somewhat different from the way in which they are understood by her subjects.

Both Muehlebach's and Però's approaches are sophisticated and valuable interventions in the anthropology of politics in Italy. But in responding to a problem that very much resembles the one I treat here, both proceed from certain assumptions about what it really means (or ought to mean) to be left-wing that ethnographic evidence puts into question. Both share a certain hermeneutics of suspicion towards what is asserted by their interlocutors to be left-wing, not uncommon in the anthropology of politics more broadly (cf. Candea 2011b), and an assumption that something has gone awry, as it were, when those assertions do not match up with what we think it ought to mean, or what it is represented as meaning in certain kinds of rhetoric.

Yet in the examples I have described so far we have encountered much disagreement over these meanings: in Giorgio's lament for the commercialization of the *Festa* and the disappearance from the political scene of the PCI; in Kertzer's Bologna of the 1970s, in which different factions within the PCI disputed the extent to which the *Festa* was appropriately political; and in the problem of Catholic Communism. In other words, what I wish to draw out here is the simple ethnographic fact that 'being red' in Red Bologna does not, in fact, mean any one thing at all.

What If There Is No Communism?

To return to Bologna, it should be clear from the discussions above that the meaning of being left-wing is not the same to Giorgio as it is to the many Catholic volunteers staffing the Party-sponsored restaurants at the *Festa*, and the many who have joined or vote for the PD since it merged with La Margherita. It also evidently means very different things to the taxi driver and to Davide, as well as to the vast majority of the activists with whom I worked, for whom the Church and even the faintest whiff of anti-immigrant rhetoric (let alone of Silvio Berlusconi) were anathema.

These last two examples are slightly more complicated than the first, however, because the equivocation they exemplify is particularly marked. Take the case of the driver, for example: his view of what is missing in the Italian political left is almost the inverse of Giorgio's (more Catholicism, rather than less) and as I have mentioned, of many of my activist interlocutors. But it is not just activists who imagine that Catholicism and Communism are antonyms:

entire books, such as Kertzer's (and see e.g. Berlinguer 1977; De Rosa 1966; Faenza 1959; Riccamboni 1976), have been written in an attempt to account for the intersections that exist between them; thus from a social scientific, etic and analytical perspective, these issues are perplexing, problems deemed requiring of a solution.

A range of explanatory frameworks present themselves in answer to this conundrum: we have already met and discarded one of them, namely the idea that people do not really comprehend the depth of the ideological distinctions at play. In the example of the driver, he is clearly not unaware that some (such as myself, in that particular instance) may see his position as surprising; and his insistence on a 'secret' Catholicism beneath a superficial Communism suggests an awareness of why such a Catholicism must be 'secret' in the first place.

Neither is the solution tentatively put forward by Kertzer completely satisfactory to the contemporary problem posed here. Kertzer argues that individuals may vote for the PCI in search of economic betterment, whilst looking to be buried in church to ensure spiritual salvation, thus obtaining 'the best of both worlds' (1980: 259). Such an explanation, couched in terms of 'strategies', whilst acknowledging people's awareness of theoretical norms – such as those which make Catholicism and Communism inconsistent – assumes that awareness must coincide with agreement, and that if people acknowledge inconsistency of this sort, yet behave as if it were not important, it must be because it serves a particular interest, be that material or spiritual. Even were we to accept Kertzer's argument, it is developed with reference to Catholicism and Communism, and it is not generalizable to comparable situations. It clearly falls short in the case of Davide, who gains no benefit of any form by espousing views which many – and certainly the majority in the locations he frequented – would consider to be as inconsistent with being left-wing as those of the Catholic Church. Finally, the hermeneutics of suspicion of Però and Muehlebach and political anthropology more broadly may be helpful in investigating the gap between appearance and reality in being left-wing, but it assumes that such a gap exists, rather than taking seriously the possibility that the gap may be between not appearance and reality but certain realities and others.

An alternative analytical strategy is available to us if we examine the question from the other side, as it were: the anthropology of religion has long had to cope with the fact that what, in anthropological analyses, have been called 'world religions' are in fact a collection of a remarkably diverse array of dogmas and practices, many of which do not easily accord with one another. Writing of this in relation to the anthropology of Buddhism, Cook et al. note

> People believing that behind the multifarious things Buddhists, Christians, or Muslims think and do there is in all cases and necessarily an original and authentic coherent system, does not in itself make this so. It is importantly possible that no such system exists, and that there is nothing which in this sense makes it true that particular beliefs or practices are or are not 'really' Buddhist, Christian, Islamic, or whatever. (Cook et al. 2009: 53; see also Asad 1986; Gellner 1990; Laidlaw 1995)

To transpose this to the dilemma we face here: it is not necessarily the case – and therefore should not be assumed in analysis – that there is one 'real' way of being left-wing in Bologna, and it is thus not the ethnographer's task to adjudicate on whether some – albeit strikingly odd – conceptions of what being left-wing means are anomalies, perversions or misunderstandings. Just as particularly common rituals or texts do not exhaust what it means to be Buddhist, neither do the opus of Marx, or the doctrine or rhetoric of the PCI or the PD exhaust what it means to be left-wing. Instead, in other words, of asking how it is that people can come to subscribe to contradictory systems of thought, the ethnographic fact of them doing so ought to lead us to discard, in this particular instance, the assumption that the systems in question are, in fact, quite as systematic as we thought.

In many ways the argument I make here is similar to one Holbraad makes in a recent (2014) paper on the ontology of revolution in Cuba. He resolves the 'late revolutionary paradox' – the apparent contradiction of people both defending and critiquing the Cuban revolution – through similar recourse to notions of homonymy and equivocation described below (2014: 370), by arguing that revolutionary discourse – as opposed to 'liberalism' – is inherently and ontologically absolute: 'relativisation of the Revolution – comparing it to an outside and finding it wanting – is fundamentally incoherent' (2014: 382), and thus when people speak of 'the Revolution' as having failed in some manner they are speaking about a different thing to that which they speak about (or act in relation to) when they pledge allegiance to 'the Revolution'.

The main, if minor, difference between this argument and my own is that I am unwilling to isolate a 'left-wing discourse' in Bologna, as Holbraad does for the revolution in Cuba – mainly through the writings of Ché Guevara and Fidel Castro (2014: 372–79) – and as Però does for immigration, and indeed less interested even were such a discourse to exist in the differences between it and the various things that people actually mean when they describe themselves as 'left-wing'. More interesting to my particular case are differences not between a certain kind of rhetoric and ethnographic understandings of it, but differences within those ethnographic understandings, and between them and what anthropologists understand by a concept.

What I would like to suggest is that just as there exists an equivocal relationship between varying uses of 'left-wing' in Bologna – that they refer to different objects – so there exists a similarly equivocal relationship between analytical concepts and ethnographic ones: in other words, the discrepancy between the ideas we as anthropologists have about what being left-wing might or should mean (exemplified for example in the work of Però and Muehlebach) and the (varied) understandings of it we find in the field is not a problem requiring resolution, but a productive feature of ethnography.

The notion of equivocation is premised on the fact that relations can be established across difference rather than simply similitude: it is a form of comparison that does not presume 'immediate translatability' (Viveiros de Castro

2004a: 4) (for example, that being left-wing in Bologna must mean what anthropologists like myself might assume it must – being pro-immigration, pro-LGBT rights, anticlerical, etc.) and 'which necessarily includes the anthropologist's discourse as one of its terms' (2004a: 5). Its purpose is not to uncover the common referent of superficially distinct representations or synonyms, but 'to avoid losing sight of the difference concealed within equivocal "homonyms"' (2004a: 7); or, as Holbraad eloquently puts it, 'the idea of homonymy allows us to conceptualise the otherwise blatant ethnographic observation that people can hold at the same time views that are so divergent as to verge on self-contradiction' (2014: 382).

It also allows us to conceptualize the similarly blatant observation that anthropological concepts are not the same as ethnographic ones: 'the equivocation is the limiting condition of every social relation, a condition that itself becomes superobjectified in the extreme case of so called interethnic or intercultural relations, where the language games diverge maximally. It goes without saying, this divergence includes the relation between anthropological discourse and native discourse' (Viveiros de Castro 2004a: 12). So my suggestion is that instead of adjusting anthropological concepts until they equate to ethnographic ones (which, as we will see, is a constitutive aspect of argument for a 'recursive' anthropology), we simply accept that the two mean different things.

In a similar vein, Cook et al.'s methodological injunction to 'assume no wholes' refers to what is fundamentally an empirical question: it asks us not to presuppose the existence, out there in the world, of a homogenous 'system' called Buddhism and instead to trace ethnographically the way in which people practise and enact what they refer to as 'Buddhism'. What it does not ask us to do is to dispose of 'Buddhism' as an analytical concept. The concept of Buddhism in anthropology has an extremely long history – of which I am largely unqualified to speak – developed (and developing) in relation to theological, philosophical and ethnographic discourses. But in spite of that last connection, it is, crucially, not substitutable for any particular local conception of Buddhism – although it may bear more of a resemblance to some than to others – let alone for Buddhism the 'world religion', if indeed such a thing exists. So it is more than possible to retain both the methodological asceticism that rescues us from the (non)problem of having to decide what is 'really' Buddhist (or left-wing) as well as the theoretical concept of Buddhism in anthropology with all of its particular heritage, so long as we keep that distance in mind. But what does such distance entail for the relationship between a topic of study and the ethnographic reality in which it is studied?

Locations and Boundaries

Cook et al.'s article is in fact an intervention in a now decades-old debate on the subject of how best to delimit the ethnographic field; and since this chapter began with a discussion of why Bologna made for such an apposite field-site for the investigation of LGBTQ activism, but has gone on, however, to complicate precisely those preconceptions about what it might mean to be 'red' in Red Bologna that I – and others before me – have held, it seems fitting to come full circle at this point and deal with some of the implications of this on the nature of the city as a locale for the study of being 'left-wing'. The connection between the analytical object under investigation and the site of the investigation seems suddenly a lot less clear than it had first appeared (at least to this inexperienced ethnographer); is Bologna then simply an 'arbitrary location' for the study of left-wing ethics (Candea 2007)?

Following George Marcus' call for an ethnography which would be attentive to the ways in which localities are connected to and by wider systems, the supposedly 'traditional' Malinowskian method of long-term immersion 'elsewhere' (Gupta and Ferguson 1997: 35) has been subjected to repeated critique for being unable to represent a world in which the inadequacy of a method which attempted to isolate 'cultural gardens' (Fabian 1983) unconnected to one another is clear. Yet recently the unbounded imaginary has come under fire. Candea (2007) has charged it with an 'implicit holism' in the sense that its proponents assume *a priori* the existence of 'whole systems' (Marcus and Fischer 1986: 91; Marcus 1999: 51) within which particular ethnographic situations are embedded. Thus, whilst eschewing one kind of holism – the notion that a given geographic area is contiguous with a given set of social or cultural forms – they assert another, namely that of 'the world system', 'globalization', 'trans-nationalism' or 'diaspora' (Candea 2007; Cook et al. 2009; Tsing 2000).

It is not my intention here to rescue multi-sited ethnography from this critique; it serves instead as an introduction to the alternatives posed by Candea and Cook et al., and to the manner in which their arguments intersect with the point I seek to make regarding the value of distinguishing between analysis and ethnography, and the implications that has on the selection of fieldwork locales.

Candea has highlighted the potential of the 'multi-sited imaginary' to identify and delimit a 'seamless reality' (2007: 170). Thus, in Fortun's account of the Bhopal disaster (2001) the object of the ethnography is assumed to be an endless web of connections yet the method of representing such connections is seen as capable of encapsulating them all. This exemplifies Candea's point about the 'new holism' (2007: 178) – a macrocosmic reproduction of the idea that a total account of a bounded culture is possible in 'traditional' ethnography. By identifying the field as a 'seamless reality' and refusing to delimit it, one actually implies at least the possibility of a total account of a 'world system'. With Candea's notion of the 'arbitrary location', on the other hand, the site is deliberately identified and delimited *a priori* by the researcher in a spirit of methodological asceticism which seeks to acknowledge the impossibility of total knowledge (2007: 180). The village of Crucetta, within its administrative boundaries, is chosen to be a 'window into complexity' (2007: 179).

Again however, it is important to distinguish between different kinds of delimitation, empirical and conceptual: 'Crucetta', as Candea's field-site, is bounded off from other entities (France, or Corsica, say); but for his account not to fall into the trap of equating the site with the object of study – as in 'traditional' ethnography – it cannot simultaneously be conceptually bounded. Hence its provision of a vista onto 'complexity': if an account could bound itself so completely – conceptually and empirically – as to have no recourse to a single reference to something outside of itself, if it could explain each and every concept in its own terms, and if it were not, in other words, 'implicitly holist' in the sense of referring to some concept distinct from the field itself, then it would be explicitly holist, extremely dull, and would take up as much space as Borges' one-to-one map of the world.

This is what Thornton calls the 'essential fiction' of ethnography (1988: 287), namely that we must occasionally make reference to ulterior entities we are unable to explain in their entirety. This does not have to imply the positing of 'macro-systems' or 'cultural formations'; the simple use of an abstract noun such as 'redness' or 'politics' is enough to make the implication. The 'fictions' of ethnography – concepts that we may not experience in the field – are essential, as Thornton argues, because they guarantee the 'facticity of "fact" ... they serve as the templates against which reality can be compared' (1988: 287).

Candea makes a similar argument regarding the utility of separating out (but not discarding) analytical concepts in a comparable paper on the notion of politics (2011b): suggesting that anthropologists have tended to neglect 'the political' as an ethnographic category in favour of a theoretically 'unbounded' understanding of it in which it is essentially ubiquitous (2011b: 310), Candea persuasively argues for a greater attention to the ways in which 'the political' – as well as 'the non-political' – is performed in the field. At first sight this very much resembles a straightforwardly empiricist account in which theoretical concepts are to be subordinated to ethnographic ones, and in which the task of the anthropologist is, at base, to 'just describe' (Latour 2005). A closer reading, however, reveals that

> for all the stated empiricism of the article and its argument from and for ethnography, it would be disingenuous to claim that there is 'no theory' here ... Indeed, the article deploys its ethnographic empiricism in order to articulate a theoretical argument ... the point is procedural: ethnographic empiricism and theoretical criticism are separate and operate on different planes. (Candea 2011b: 329)

Cook et al. similarly depart from Candea's notion of an 'arbitrary location' in arguing that rather than delimiting the field on the basis of arbitrary spatial boundaries, those boundaries should be incorporated within the field in order to allow for internal conceptual comparison. In fact, they argue, the un-sited field need bear no relation whatsoever to any geographical area and is instead informed by theoretical concerns (2009: 67).

Equivocal Locations

To recap then: we know that despite its soubriquet, the meaning of 'being red' in 'Red Bologna' is inherently equivocal. A range of individuals with a range of political perspectives describe themselves as left-wing, and in doing so make evident the fact that such terms are homonymous in this context: far from establishing a common identity possessed of uniform viewpoints on particular topics, it is precisely through the differences that these terms express that people relate. Thus, the fact that somebody believes that the essence of Communism is anticlericalism, and somebody else thinks that the spirits of Church and Party are really one and the same, is not evidence that one of them is simply mistaken; it is that being left-wing means two different things to both. But it is through the idiom of being left-wing that this difference emerges and can be expressed.

A perfect ethnographic exemplification of this is the *Festa dell'Unità* itself, a microcosmic version of what I will describe below as an equivocal location. Its name – just like that of Bologna *la rossa* – suggests a very catholic uniformity of perspective on left-wing politics in Italy, but as we have seen it is not and never has been a place where everybody agrees on what counts as left-wing and what does not. What it undoubtedly is, however, is a place where what does and does not count as left-wing is precisely what is up for discussion. Over the days and nights I visited the *Festa* I witnessed innumerable and passionate arguments, debates and disagreements over various questions. Positions taken on issues could be as widely divergent as those I have described here. But what held them together in the *Festa* – and the city more broadly, I suggest – was that they were invariably couched as if everybody sang from the same hymnbook (or copy of the 'Internationale'). It was thus not – unsurprisingly – that everybody shared the same conceptions of what it means to be left-wing; it was that it was precisely those differences in conceptions that were important, rather than, say, differences between right and left.

We also know that some of these conceptions of what it means to be left-wing are closer to the concept of being left-wing as it has been employed in anthropology and the social sciences. This is not the place for speculation as to why that might be the case, although one might well wonder whether the political proclivities of ethnographers have influenced their opinions on what ought and ought not to be counted as left-wing or otherwise (just as practitioners of Buddhism influenced analytical concepts of what was and was not properly 'Buddhist'; Cook et al. 2009: 52). The point I have sought to make is that the difference between some ethnographic understandings of what it means to be left-wing and those possessed by an anthropologist presents a problem only if one assumes that the latter correspond to a somehow 'truer' or more 'authentic' vision of being 'left-wing'. In other words, the existence of Catholic Communists may have been a concern for Party officials (and indeed for parish priests), but the only reason for it to be a problem for an anthropologist is if we share their conviction that there is only one (proper) way of being Communist (or Catholic).

But in a parallel example of equivocation, this realization does not have to entail the abandonment of 'left-wing' as an analytical category. Indeed, if we share Candea's concern for the value of being explicit about 'not knowing things' (2007: 181), it must not entail this, for it is precisely in the gap between anthropological concepts of what it means to be left-wing and those we find in the field, between the 'fictions' of analysis and the 'facts' of ethnography, that our lack of knowledge is revealed. 'Left-wing' as a concept in anthropology – just like any other concept, be it 'redness' or 'Buddhism' or 'politics' – is not the same as ethnographic manifestations of that concept, nor should it be; for as in the case of the emic equivocations over what it means to be 'red' in 'Red Bologna', 'the parties involved find themselves united by that which divides them, linked by that which separates them' (Viveiros de Castro 2004a: 17); thus rather than being the templates for comparison that Thornton suggests they are (1988: 287), anthropological concepts, I suggest, serve as templates for equivocation, 'an operation of differentiation – a production of difference – that connects the two discourses to the precise extent to which they are *not* saying the same thing' (Viveiros de Castro 2004a: 18, author's italics). So the moment in which the conceptual apparatus of anthropology is assimilated into a particular ethnographic mode of thought is not to be sought after, but to be perpetually put off.

This way of conceptualizing the relationship between analytical concepts and those we find in the field has implications, of course, for the way in which we choose where we work. At the outset of this chapter I noted that Bologna's reputation as *la rossa* led in part to my selection of it as a field-site. So it was never, like Candea's Crucetta, destined to be an entirely 'arbitrary location', a convenient but happenstance window onto a particular analytical concern. But by now it ought to be clear that what Bologna *la rossa* means to its inhabitants is far from as simple as my preconceptions may have suggested. So what kind of location is it?

It is what I suggest calling an 'equivocal location' for the two reasons outlined in this chapter, making its nature as an equivocal location itself somewhat equivocal: in a specifically ethnographic sense, Bologna presents an example of a city in which the kind of political distinctions one might find in any large urban area are expressed through contrasting interpretations of a superficial ideological uniformity (cf. Strathern 2004: 25); thus its nature as an equivocal location in this sense is an ethnographic reality, making it (by luck rather than design) an eminently suitable field-site for an examination focused both on what it means to be a left-wing activist and on the analytical concept of equivocation.

The second reason for my suggesting the notion of the equivocal location is an analytical one, in that it is an attempt to capture the relationship of difference that exists between anthropological concepts and ethnographic ones. In some ways this is far from original: as Candea notes, it was through Nuerland and the Trobriands that the political and Freud respectively came to mean what they do in anthropology (2007: 179); and in a number of senses the notion of an equivocal location is built on that of the arbitrary one. Like the latter, it 'serves as a "control" for a broader abstract object of study' and 'allows one to reflect on and rethink conceptual entities' (2007: 180).

But unlike an arbitrary location, in order to accomplish this task the equivocal location does not have to bear 'no *necessary* relation to the wider object of study' (2007: 180, author's italics). Because although the location may be chosen with a view to the examination of a particular topic, that presupposition of a relation between concept and reality does not imply the assumption of an equivalency between the two. Indeed, the notion of the field-site as an equivocal location brings out precisely the fact that it is the difference between analytical and empirical homonyms – whether 'politics', 'Buddhism' or 'redness' – that is the object of investigation. It expresses, in other words, in addition to the diversity in interpretation of concepts that one is likely to find in any field-site, both the differences that exist between conceptual entities and their empirical manifestations as well as the danger of assuming that such differences can be – or ought to be – papered over through translation or redefinition. An equivocal location is not so much a 'space which cuts through meaning', as Candea describes the arbitrary location, but a space in which it is precisely the meaning of 'meaning' that is put into question.

Conclusion

Not everyone in Bologna remembered its years of PCI rule with the fondness with which those I have described here did. Many of the younger generation of activists did not, of course, remember it at all, and some in the LGBTQ community recalled the Party's failure to ameliorate conditions for them substantially or heed their demands for rights.

In the entire course of fieldwork however I met only one person in the city who self-described as right-wing. This was no doubt due in part to the nature of the circles in which I moved whilst carrying out my research; yet I had a number of friends and acquaintances who were completely unconnected with any particular political movement, many of whom I met simply by virtue of sharing a neighbourhood with them, a small zone of the old city with a reputation for housing its oldest and most genteel families. They would happily talk politics with me, and many expressed opinions such as those described above regarding the Church or immigration; but all would react in very similar ways to Davide if asked whether they counted themselves as right-wing, or would vote for the People of Liberty (PdL), then the largest and most important of Italy's centre-right parties.

Except, that is, for my landlady, Antonella. When I first met her and learnt that she and her family had lived in the city for generations, I asked her whether and how much it had changed during the course of her lifetime; having heard such comments often enough before, I was not altogether surprised when she responded by telling me that life in Bologna had deteriorated considerably since she was a child, and that this was largely due to the large number of immigrants who had arrived from North Africa and Eastern Europe (half-English immigrants were apparently more acceptable). I was not at all prepared, however, for her to follow this comment by explaining that she considered herself 'a bit of a fascist' when it came to politics: 'Other people are too', she later explained to me, 'they just hide it'.

As we have already seen from her willingness to forgive her favourite musician for his homosexuality though, 'not being red' is just as complicated a category as its opposite, and can entail a similar variety of positions. I bring her up, however, not simply to reiterate the argument of this chapter only this time applied to a different kind of political identity; what I want to focus on instead is the qualification she adds to her self-description, which bears a considerable resemblance to the comments of Davide on people's refusal to admit to reading Berlusconi's newspaper and those of the taxi driver on Communists being 'secret' Catholics.

What these comments – and others like them that I will go on to describe – suggest is that not only is equivocation at work in different understandings of concepts across individuals, but that it may also be so within individuals' different understandings of concepts across different contexts, particularly in the case of public and private domains. This further complication of relationships of difference will be the subject of the next chapter.

Note

This chapter was originally published as P. Heywood (2015), 'Equivocal Locations: Being 'Red' in 'Red Bologna', *Journal of the Royal Anthropological Institute* 21: 855–71.

2

The Anthropology of (Double) Morality

In the previous chapter we met some of the ways in which the meaning of 'redness' in 'Red Bologna' is far from straightforward; we encountered examples of how being left-wing in fact meant very different things to different people. Thus, the idiom of being left-wing, though ubiquitous, was often the means by which people were able to differentiate themselves from others, rather than to identify with them; the notion of equivocation, and the attendant idea of homonymy, was helpful in conceptualizing the way in which being left-wing took on different meanings for different people. In this chapter, by contrast, I will explore some of the ways in which equivocation can function not only across different people, but also within people across different contexts, thus making clear, to paraphrase Candea, that not only are there always 'other people' within 'peoples', but sometimes within 'people' as well (2011a).

What we also met in the previous chapter, but did not explore, was a particular form of explanation that people provided for their different conceptions of what it means to be left-wing. In all the cases described earlier, the apparent difference between an individual's particular understanding of what being left-wing meant and the perceived beliefs of others was justified with reference to the idea of a further difference, namely that between the professions of others and their actual practice.

This idea – that people may claim to subscribe to a particular (ethical) principle, yet in fact breach it on a regular basis – was one I encountered remarkably often during the course of my fieldwork. There is, in fact, a particular expression in Italian that is used to refer to it, namely *doppia morale*. Literally translatable as 'double morality', its implications are interesting both from the perspective of the anthropology of ethics, and in terms of the concept of relating through difference, suggesting, as it does, a capacity to switch between differing understandings of the same moral code on the basis of context.

This chapter will begin by explaining some of the senses in which *doppia morale* is used, and by relating it to examples from the previous chapter. It will then provide some, more public, examples of the same idea, and will go on to explore ethnographically some of the ways in which the expression is used in the evaluation of practices of fidelity and infidelity amongst both activists and non-activists in Bologna. This arena is not only one in which examples of what people refer to as *doppia morale* abound, but also one which is pertinent to another theme of this book, namely that of 'fidelity to the field' in anthropology.

The aim of the chapter is twofold: firstly, and in line with the broader arguments outlined here, it suggests that the notion of equivocation can be helpful not only in understanding intra – as well as inter – cultural differences, but also in theorizing some of ways in which people can be different to themselves, so to speak; secondly, it will argue for the continued utility of the concept of 'moral codes' – and 'modes of subjectivation' – to the anthropology of ethics. Whilst a range of work has productively and successfully explored alternative explanatory frameworks for ethical action (e.g. Humphrey 1997; Zigon 2008; see also Englund 2008; Yan 2011), and work within other sub-disciplines of anthropology has long been similarly process-oriented (e.g. Mol 2002), here I will suggest that the notion of a 'moral code' may yet be of service to anthropologists, provided we abandon the idea that people's relationship with such codes will always be one of fidelity.

Double Morality

This chapter constitutes in part a study of ethics amongst LGBTQ activists in Bologna, but some of the cases it describes are, in a certain sense, cases of people failing to be ethical. That is, they are often examples of various ways in which people fail to live up to the ideals they set for themselves, the rules they desire to live by, and the moral beliefs they profess. Such behaviours, however, are ubiquitous features of ethical life. We are all familiar with politicians who steal from the public purse whilst extolling the virtues of honesty and integrity, or with religious leaders who preach chastity yet are themselves far from chaste. We know that such individuals often seek to disguise or conceal their sins: hypocrisy, as the saying goes, is the compliment vice pays to virtue. On a more quotidian level, we know that the moral goals and ideals we set for ourselves are often difficult – and in some cases impossible – to achieve, that ethical injunctions are not always followed to the letter, and that rules are sometimes broken.

Whether we consider such behaviour to be hypocrisy or simply falling short of virtue, whether it is concealed or out in the open, we certainly know that it happens. But does it constitute an appropriate object of study for an anthropology of ethics?

Undoubtedly there will be many people who consider the behaviour of corrupt politicians, lascivious priests or philandering husbands to be far removed from anything we might wish to term 'ethics'. In the normative sense of the word perhaps they are correct. But what I wish to suggest, following Laidlaw (2002), is that ethics as an analytical category in anthropology is about the description of the practices by which people constitute themselves as moral subjects, the ways in which they configure their relations to codes of conduct, to ideals and to goals, whatever these may look like: 'if the word "freedom" is reserved only for choices one approves, then it loses its meaning' (2002: 326). Therefore it must also be capable of taking into account how people break the codes of conduct to which they subscribe and fail to live up to their ideals and goals, for these are also, I argue, modes of relation: to fall short is to fall short of something in particular.

This is especially true in my field-site. As I will go on to describe below, a peculiar and distinctive facet of ethics in Bologna is a manner of relating to moral conventions that involves their occasional betrayal.[1] Once again, I make no claim that such behaviour is 'ethical' in any normative sense of the word; indeed, it is certainly not seen as in any sense virtuous by my interlocutors. Quite the opposite, in fact. For the LGBTQ activists I worked with – more so than for other Italians – it was despised. But what I do argue is that such behaviour is ethical in a descriptive sense, in so far as it constitutes putting oneself into a relation – of an unusual kind – with moral conventions.

What it also constitutes, I suggest, is another example of relating through difference. A consequence of subscribing to a given ethical injunction in such a way as to allow for the possibility of betraying it is that one becomes, as it were, different to oneself in relation to that injunction; this is not merely hypocrisy, or a simple gap between profession and practice, because, as I will argue, intrinsic to this mode of relation is the notion of the incomparability of different spheres of ethical life.

Federica was an Italian academic in her early thirties who had lived in the UK for over a decade before returning to Italy mid-way through the period of my fieldwork. She became involved in activism of various types – including LGBTQ varieties – relatively quickly, and since we knew one another through mutual friends we arranged to meet for a coffee one afternoon about a month after her return. I was interested in how she perceived Bologna, as a stranger to the city, with experience of politics in other parts of the country, and as someone who had lived abroad for a long period. It was immediately clear that she was more than content to be back home: in England, she said, there was too much concern for other people's opinions; one had to behave in such a way as to generate the correct sort of impression. She illustrated this with reference to an episode we had both recently witnessed: Alessia, a mutual friend, had been with us and others a few nights previously at one of the events of the week-long Gay Pride festivities in Bologna, of which more later. In tow was a visiting acquaintance from abroad who was staying with her in her flat; at a certain point in the evening he had become tired, and asked Alessia if they might return home, a request to which she had immediately acceded, though it was clear she was enjoying herself and the relatively rare opportunity to see all her friends together; in the face of their protestations, she insisted that she was perfectly happy to go home, and that she would see them all again soon.

To my English sensibilities, this appeared an excellent example of virtuous behaviour: a host who sacrificed her own pleasures for the sake of her guest. The evaluations of my activist friends were quite different, however: Laura and Federica were both very clear that this had not been the right thing to do. Alessia ought to have handed her guest the keys to her apartment and sent him home on his own, rather than sublimate her desires to a norm of politeness.

Over our subsequent coffee, Federica argued that the virtue of politeness is born from a concern with others' opinions of ourselves, and is thus an example of what she called 'mediated' – as opposed to 'direct' – communication. She told me that one of the reasons she was so happy to have returned from England is that in Italy there is far less concern with the former, and that in general people are far more straightforward in their communicative interactions.

This is, of course, a not uncommon observation – if not an outright cliché – regarding differences between the English and their southern European cousins (e.g. Smith 2010 [1759]: 272); and the clear and direct expression of inner thoughts and feelings was regarded as one of the chief virtues amongst the activists I knew. It interested me on this particular occasion however, as I had that morning been reading over my fieldnotes, and been struck by how frequently people in Bologna invoked the notion of 'hypocrisy' – or the related one of *doppia morale* – in explanations of behaviour. Indeed, I was sure I had never heard the word as often in England as I had in the six months I had by then spent in Italy. Surely a city in which spontaneity and directness are virtues should not also be one in which hypocrisy – a far more 'mediated' form of communication than politeness, one imagines – is so commonplace? I put this to Federica, but she waved her hand dismissively: 'Ah, that's just the Church' she said.

Federica's response is itself an example of the kind of imputations I was asking her about; whilst descriptions of hypocritical behaviour abound in Bologna, such behaviour is always that of somebody else, which makes sense in light of the importance attributed to directness. Indeed, such accusations can serve not merely as reprobation to another, but also as approbation of oneself in the face of criticism: thus, whilst I may have sinned, I have at least confessed; not so those others who are sinners like me but hide it behind a façade. And when honesty and straightforwardness are cardinal virtues, the act of hiding a sin may be worse than committing it in the first place, particularly because the imputation of hidden guilt to others leads by implication to the idea that the sin in question is probably so commonplace as to be hardly sinful at all (cf. Parry 2000). Such a sentiment is neatly encapsulated in the pragmatic expression '*fatta la legge, trovato l'inganno*', 'laws are made to have loopholes'.

This is evident if we look back at some of the discussions from the previous chapter. Note that the taxi driver, Davide and Antonella all explain the difference between their behaviour or opinions and those of others with reference to an imputed gap between profession and practice on the part of the latter. They all suggest that although no one else may admit to the particular deviation of which they themselves are guilty, that does not mean they are alone in being guilty of it.

The taxi driver claims that all communists are 'secretly' catholic too – they simply do not say so in public. So there is nothing strange at all in the fact of his being both; indeed, the only thing peculiar to him is the virtue of honesty in admitting being so. Likewise, Davide implies that *Il Giornale* has plenty of readers in Bologna; they simply do not share his courage in conceding it. Finally, Antonella excuses her self-description as a fascist on the basis that she is not alone in her beliefs, only in her straightforwardness about them.

My concern here is not with the veracity of such claims, but instead with their ubiquity. Beyond these particular examples and the question of ideological beliefs, public commentary on social and political issues in Italy is saturated with a lingering suspicion that nobody really means what they say. Indeed, often such suspicions are expressed as outright certainties (sometimes justifiably). This has also been the case historically: I have written elsewhere of the manner in which Italian politics of the 1960s and 1970s was perceived as a network, with culpability for atrocities perpetrated by right-wing and left-wing terrorists often attributed to the state, public protestations to the contrary notwithstanding (Heywood 2009).

Neither is this kind of suspicion confined to the manner in which people relate to the state: as in the example of Alessia and her guest, what might appear to be harmless (indeed, virtuous) instances of the concealment of desires were often seen by my activist interlocutors as first steps on the slippery slope into hypocrisy and dishonesty.

Such suspicions could sour friendships and ruin love affairs, and indeed occasionally both, as almost occurred in Laura's case, for example. Laura, whom we have met briefly already, was a close friend throughout the period of my fieldwork. Vivacious, charming, confident and outgoing, she could often be found at meetings or events or simply in one or other of the LGBTQ-friendly bars that dotted the city. Like many queer activists, she eschewed clothes or other accoutrements that she thought would mark her out as a lesbian (very short hair, piercings, a preponderance of leather) in favour of a more playful style: baggy but well-designed jeans, cropped but stylish hair, and red lipstick. She worked part-time, sporadically writing grant proposals for a local hospital, whilst doing the same kind of work – for free – for Betty&Books, one of the organizations within the Puta network, having graduated several years earlier from the University of Bologna.

Sex was of considerable importance to Laura, as it was to many queer activists I knew. Not only does sex have an obvious importance to gender and sexuality based activism, but sexual relationships are a key part of people's lives, and they sought, as many of us do, to conduct them in line with their ethical and political principles, for example those of polyamory (see below). Though I did know some people in long-term monogamous relationships, I knew a great many more who were not, and so such relationships were often dynamic and unstable, and thus a source of anxiety, joy, despair and a habitual topic of conversation. In other words, sex – with whom one had it, how one had it, whether one had it – was of deeply political, ethical and personal concern to many of the activists with whom I worked.

Laura, for her part, was in a polyamorous relationship with an American woman in her late twenties who lived with a male partner in the US, and whom I only met once. Laura's attachment to her evidently ran deep, and indeed I saw her greatly affected by this relationship in a number of ways over the course of my fieldwork. Because of the polyamorous nature of their relationship however, she was also involved with others, nearer to home, and it was to these that I was a closer witness. Again, as with many other queer activists I knew, some of her relationships were with people within or loosely associated with the LGBTQ activist community. These kinds of relationships meant that one's partner was likely to share with one some basic political and ethical beliefs, and were also no doubt to some extent a by-product of a comparatively small group of people regularly associating with one another.

The particular relationship I have in mind in this case was with Maria, who had taken me to visit the *Festa*. She did not self-define as lesbian, and before Laura, as far as I am aware, all of her relationships were with men. She was somewhat peripheral to the activist community in Bologna – a newcomer to the city who stayed only for a year, and who worked for an NGO. She was however a close friend of Federica's and thus often accompanied us to discussions and meetings.

Laura's confidence and self-possession deeply impressed Maria upon their first meeting and at some point they spent the night with one another. Laura, for her part, was rather smitten by Maria's evident kindness and generosity.

The relationship took a turn for the worse shortly afterwards however, as Maria – for reasons unrelated to Laura – wished to remain unattached and single. She explained this with what she considered to be clarity to Laura, and believed that Laura had understood. Laura, however, had not understood – the explanation was too polite, and not direct enough – and so continued her attempts at seduction, leading Maria to believe that Laura was not being sincere in her acceptance of Maria's desire to remain alone. Laura, for her part, had no sense that anything of the sort had been explained to her, and so began to see Maria as a hypocrite, someone who would smile and chat with her at social gatherings and then ignore her messages and fail to return her calls.

A more public instance of this is one I have already briefly described, namely that of the funeral of Lucio Dalla. A range of examples of what people referred to as 'hypocrisy' (*ipocrisia*) were on display on that occasion. Firstly there was that of Dalla himself; for reasons we cannot know but can guess at, he had never spoken publicly about his sexuality, which was an open secret; a number of my activist interlocutors criticized him for this, arguing that he set a terrible example for young gay Italians by refusing to come out, and by implying through this that homosexuality was something to be hidden. Secondly, there was the media's treatment of the issue, which largely ignored this question and depicted him as openly gay. And finally and most obviously of all, there was the Catholic Church. By far and away the most frequent target of accusations of hypocrisy, at least amongst my interlocutors, its behaviour with regard to Dalla's funeral was much remarked upon. It chose to accord him the honour of a service in the Basilica of Saint Petronius – one of the city's most important churches, located on its main square – and conducted by the local Bishop; during the course of the funeral, Dalla's partner was introduced as his 'collaborator'; and before communion began attendees were pointedly reminded that anybody in a state of 'mortal sin' must confess and receive absolution before being allowed to participate. As one journalist subsequently claimed, 'Dalla's funeral is one of the strongest examples of what it means to be gay in Italy: go to church, they'll give you a funeral and they'll bury you with all the rites, just as long as you don't admit you're gay'; or as another news article put it, this was an excellent example of 'the double morality [*doppia morale*] of the Church'.

This expression, peculiar to Italian, is used to denote the difference between appearance and reality in people's behaviour. After encountering it a few times in the first month of my fieldwork, I asked Laura to explain it to me in detail. Because of its etymology, I had assumed an appropriate English translation to be something akin to 'double standards'. This, Laura told me, was a mistake. *Doppia morale* was not about 'inconsistency across comparable circumstances' but about a disjuncture between what you practice and what you preach, and, according to her, contains within it the idea that the two are inherently incomparable: 'nobody's perfect', she said, explaining the idea to me, 'after all, we're Italian; the important thing is to do the bad stuff at home'. Its most common usage, she suggested, was in a religious context, the Church being the most obvious target for such accusations. But, she argued, interpersonal relationships were also an excellent example: one might speak of the 'double standards' of men when it came to their differing evaluations of male versus female infidelities; but one would speak of the *doppia morale* of affecting an attitude of love and faithfulness to your spouse in public and then cheating on them in private.

A comparison with the concept of hypocrisy (*ipocrisia*) may be helpful at this point. Clarifying the distinction for me, Laura explained that of course *doppia morale* and hypocrisy were linked, but that there was a certain difference in perspective involved. In fact, she explained, an accusation of *doppia morale* was always really an accusation of hypocrisy, or else a judgement on someone's failure properly to sustain *doppia morale*, because once the disjuncture between professed beliefs and private actions has surfaced, the issue has ceased – by definition – to be a matter of *doppia morale* precisely because that disjuncture has become public through the accusation. Therefore consequent judgement can only be delivered as a critique of hypocrisy – double standards – or of a failure to conceal adequately the private actions in question; and as she put it, 'getting caught is often the bigger sin'.[2]

Just as in Chapter 1 we encountered what appeared to be contradictory understandings of the meaning of being left-wing in 'Red Bologna' which were in fact equivocal ones lacking a common referent, the notion of *doppia morale* is thus not a description of inconsistent behaviour across comparable circumstances but across incomparable ones: it is, in other words, another example of equivocation, presupposing a relationship of difference with a moral code.

This presents an intriguing case for anthropologists interested in the study of ethics. It is of course a truism to note that people are not always faithful to the moral codes they espouse. For this and related reasons, such as ethnographic evidence that ethics in non-Western contexts often place little emphasis on the application of universal principles, some have been led to conclude that the concept of the 'moral code' is not of great value to the anthropology of ethics, in comparison with, say, the exemplar, or self-cultivation (e.g. Humphrey 1997; Zigon 2008; see also Englund 2008; Yan 2011). In a certain sense these arguments resemble others in different branches of the discipline (such as the anthropology of science) which have oriented themselves towards the study of process, rather than principle or ideals, on the basis that the former are rarely abided by and the latter are usually missed. Obvious examples are Actor Network Theory-inspired ethnographies, such as the work of Mol on a Dutch arteriosclerosis clinic, in which she declares that 'in the act, and only then and there, something is' (2002: 33), as she unravels the work her interlocutors do to isolate and identify the 'reality' of disease.

What this analytical framework misses however, as Cook points out, is that 'a gap between hope/intention and reality does not necessarily suggest a deviation from the religious system or a dysfunction of social organisation' (Cook 2010a: 261; see also Laidlaw 1995). Indeed, the very fact that it is a truism to note that people often fail to live up to ideals, whilst those ideals continue to endure, ought to tell us something about the prevalence and nature of such 'gaps'. Cook goes on to argue with regard to Buddhist ethics that 'It is in that dynamic tension between precept and practice that asceticism is really lived' (2010a: 261); in other words, intrinsic to the concept of a precept – at least in the case of Buddhist asceticism – is the idea that it will not always be faithfully followed. Clearly then, the fact that the relationship between actual behaviour and that dictated by a moral code is not one of complete correspondence should not lead us automatically to assume that we ought to discard the latter as irrelevant to the former.

In Cook's ethnography, the gap between precept and practice is largely a consequence of the near or complete impossibility of consistently adhering to the conventions in question (2010b). This is fundamental to the paradoxical nature of asceticism. *Doppia morale*, on the other hand, I suggest, is a manner of relating to moral codes in which one allows for the possibility of their transgression under certain circumstances. To illustrate the distinction, I now turn to another public Italian example of *doppia morale*, this one about as distant from Buddhist asceticism as it is possible to imagine.

The Man Who Screwed an Entire Country

It is unnecessary to point out the equivocation at the heart of the headline *The Economist* chose to front its 2011 report on the cause of the current financial crisis in Italy: 'the man who screwed an entire country'. The nation's former premier, as he himself has suggested on a number of occasions (Follain 2010; *The Daily Mail* 2011), is not what one would describe as a faithful man. In fact, Italy recently endured the 'unedifying spectacle' (*The Economist* 2011) of a criminal court deliberating on whether its Prime Minister indulged in one particularly felonious infidelity by paying for sex with a minor (see Molé 2013b for an anthropological analysis of 'Berlusconismo').

'I am pretty often faithful' as he himself has put it (Follain 2010). Given the obvious implication that there have been at least a few occasions on which he has been unfaithful, one might ask, as a number of non-Italian newspapers have done, why it took his former wife, Veronica Lario, nineteen years to ask him for a divorce. The answer, according to Lario's friend and biographer (Latella 2009), is that though she was aware of Berlusconi's indiscretions for at least the last ten years of their marriage, it was only in the final two that she came to regard them as unacceptable: at an awards ceremony in 2007, he declared to television presenter Mara Carfagna (later his Minister for Equal Opportunities) 'If I weren't married, I would marry you immediately' (Fisher 2007), occasioning Lario to take the unprecedented step of writing an open letter to the Italian press demanding a public apology from her husband (*La Repubblica* 2007). In the letter, she declared that in years past she 'chose not to leave space for marital conflicts, even when his behaviour created reasons to do so' but that on this occasion 'these are statements I consider damaging to my dignity'. The Italian press speculated on the likelihood of an upcoming divorce.

What they got instead was an open letter in return, signed by the Prime Minister, in which he begged Lario's forgiveness, describing the remarks as 'thoughtless quips', and praising his wife as 'the splendid person you are and have always been for me since the day we met and fell in love'. Lario accepted the apology and the couple appeared reconciled, although a subsequent episode (on this occasion involving an alleged affair with a minor) would result in yet another public rebuke from Lario, one which was this time met not with declarations of love but threats of legal action over defamation, and divorce proceedings (BBC 2009).

What appears to be at issue in this most public of private dramas is precisely the fact that it has spilled over into the wrong domain. It is not the practice of infidelity *per se* that has 'damaged' Lario's 'dignity', but its public nature. As with the earlier description of the difference between *doppia morale* and hypocrisy, the issue here is not a failure to follow a rule or live up to an ideal consistently, but a failure to do so in a particular context.[3] Thus, in the case of Dalla, the 'sin' of homosexuality will not prevent one from being accorded the rites of a Catholic funeral, as long as the sin remains un-avowed.

Similarly, Berlusconi's marital infidelities were indulged by Lario, up until the moment intimations of them were broadcast on national television.

Freedom and Moral Codes

The debate over the relevance or otherwise of moral codes to the analysis of ethics in anthropology is not merely a matter of sub-disciplinary semantics. It goes to the heart of a question that is fundamental to anthropology's attempts to grasp the nature of ethics, and by extension more broadly to the issue of what place we accord to reflection, judgement and freedom in human life. Is ethics simply a matter of doing as we are told, or is it only really possible in the absence of moral pedagogy?

Obviously, the history of answers to this question is as long as that of the discipline itself, and I will not attempt to trace it here. Instead, after an (extremely brief) introductory survey of the place of reflection and moral codes in the anthropology of ethics, I will turn to two contemporary treatments of this problem.

It is by now a truism to note, with Edel and Edel (2000 [1959]), Wolfram (1982), Parkin (1985), Pocock (1986), Howell (1997) and Laidlaw (2002), that at least until recently there has been no clearly identifiable subfield of 'the anthropology of ethics'. Equally widely acknowledged is the culpability of Durkheim in this regard, who, as Parkin notes, 'so conflated the moral with the social that ethnographers could not isolate for analysis those contemplative moments of moral reflexivity that ... so typify human activity and predicaments' (1985: 4–5). Alongside this blindness to the capacity of human beings to consider and weigh ethical alternatives, the Durkheimian understanding of society as a system of moral obligations simultaneously expanded the scope of 'the moral' so as to equate it with any manner of behaviour in relation to social norms, as well as reducing its immense complexity of meaning to the question of whether and how people follow, break, construct, bend and otherwise engage with rules and laws, implicit or explicit (see e.g. Fortes 1959; Scott 1977). As Laidlaw argues, whilst essentially Kantian in his emphasis on duties and obligations, Durkheim departed from Kant in one very important sense: the problem of moral reasoning disappears along with the individual's freedom to reflect on such duties and obligations, whose efficacy no longer depends on the practical will of the subject but on the proper functioning of society as a moral system (2002: 314; see also Pocock 1986: 8). Faubion highlights the 'objectivist fallacy' inherent in the equation here of the desirable with the normative, value with obligation, and of which 'the very definition of ethics as "codes of conduct" is already guilty' (2001a: 83–84; see also Csordas 2013: 535–36).

With the turn of the millennium however came a burgeoning interest in people's capacity to make moral choices on the basis of considered reflection, judgement and embodied practice. Taking their cue from Aristotelian and other forms of virtue ethics (e.g. MacIntyre 1981) and from Foucault's later writings on technologies of the self (e.g. 1985, 1986), authors such as Laidlaw (1995, 2002, 2014a), Faubion (2001a, 2001b, 2011), and Lambek (2000, 2010) all called for sustained enquiry into ethics as an autonomous field of anthropological analysis and into the practices by which individuals pursue virtuous ends and form themselves into moral subjects, and a number of authors have since taken up these themes. Nearly two decades later, the anthropology of ethics has carved out a place for itself within the discipline, and its object of concern is a great deal clearer and more specific than when 'morality' was just another word for 'society'.

All of which is not to say that the problem of how to treat subjects' relationships to conventions and codes has disappeared, especially as ethics is seen to permeate the 'ordinary' (Lambek 2010) even if it does so contingently (Lempert 2013). Robbins brings out very clearly the sense of unease that the idea of an anthropology of ethics – as it has come to be defined and is described above – can give rise to in anthropologists whose attraction to the discipline rests 'on the extent to which it has generally ... focussed on "unfreedom"' (2007: 294–95; see also Mattingly 2012: 162–63) and thus – implicitly or explicitly – on Durkheimian collectivist models of society. He defends this somewhat gloomy predilection as part of a necessary scepticism towards any form of implicit universalizing of 'Western common sense models of social action' (2007: 295). Yet, finding himself nevertheless in sympathy with the aims of Laidlaw (2002) and Lambek (2000), he attempts to reconcile the apparent opposition between approaches centred around rules and obligations and those which emphasize the capacity of the subject to make practical and ethical judgements.

Robbins argues that there is an inherent danger to arguments such as that of Carrithers (2005) which emphasize the fluidity and flexibility of cultural contexts, namely that in focusing on instances of possibility we will 'throw out the Durkheimian baby with the bathwater of too rigid models of cultural reproduction' and forget that there are situations in which possibilities give way to necessities (2007: 295). He further credits Laidlaw with this realization, and compares the description he goes on to give for moral life in Papua New Guinea – that it is composed of two 'spheres', and that within each sphere the moral is defined by sets of rules and obligations, but that between spheres a degree of ethical reflection is possible – with Laidlaw's understanding of freedom as being culturally conditioned (2002: 323).

Jarett Zigon critiques Robbins for his failure to allow for contestation within a sphere of value as well as between spheres, but does not dispute – indeed praises – the central premise of Robbins' argument, namely that spaces in which freedom can be exercised are constructed in different ways by particular cultures, again attributing the origin of this view to Laidlaw (2009a: 253; see also Robbins 2009 and Zigon 2007, 2009b; and see Beldo 2014: 265–66 for a similar reading).

It is not difficult to see the attraction of this kind of interpretation: it purports to allow one to combine a model in which morality is essentially deontological and consists of rule-following and another in which it is a matter of *phronesis* or self-formation, in which freedom and ethical choice have roles to play. The concept of *doppia morale* might appear, at first sight, to be an excellent example of this idea: it precisely articulates the difference between circumstances in which a moral convention is assumed to apply and those in which it does not. It might be read as enshrining the public sphere as an area of what Robbins terms 'unfreedom', in which homosexuality and infidelity are sins forbidden by given ethical injunctions as in the examples above, whilst the private sphere is that space in which personal judgement and individual values are permitted to supersede such conventions.

The problem with this kind of argument however is that it ends up subsuming 'freedom' into 'unfreedom' by reintroducing 'culture' as an overarching determinant in the notion of freedom as 'culturally constructed'. In other words, whilst as an Urapmin I may be allowed the capacity for a degree of ethical reflection when deciding whether to follow the rules of the Christian sphere of value or those of 'tradition' (Robbins 2007), this is only the case because Urapmin 'culture' has neglected to inform me what the correct choice is in this matter.

Quite apart from the fact that this tilts the balance between the two models in favour of morality as Durkheimian social norms, since it is the presence or absence of such norms that determines whether or not freedom is possible, this interpretation of Laidlaw's argument manages to accomplish exactly the reverse of what is claimed for it as a strength: both Zigon and Robbins praise Laidlaw for avoiding a 'naively Western', or 'secular-liberal' definition of freedom (Robbins 2007: 295; Zigon 2009a: 253), but the 'culturally constructed' freedom they then go on to describe turns out to be almost exactly equivalent to Berlin's 'negative freedom' and indeed to 'agency', since it operates only in the absence of constraint (for Laidlaw's critique of which see 2002: 323, 2014a: 108–9, and also 2014b: 500).[4]

What Laidlaw actually argues is not – as Zigon and Robbins do – that the space in which freedom can be exercised is 'culturally constructed', but that the manner in which freedom may be exercised will vary by particular contexts (2002: 323). It is not the case, in other words, that freedom means exercising choice in the absence of relations of power or social norms, but that the practices of freedom in which we engage in order to fashion ourselves into particular kinds of subjects are made on the basis of the particular models we find around us, not in opposition to them, or in their absence (cf. Clarke 2014 on the presence of ethics even in the 'extraordinary', as well as in the 'ordinary', and also Agrama 2010 on the ethics of the *fatwa*).

What I want to argue here is that despite the superficial resemblance between the concept of *doppia morale* and Robbins' notion of differing ethical spheres, the former, in fact, presents a particularly intriguing example of

Laidlaw's point: far from delineating a private sphere in which certain moral conventions are no longer relevant, the notion of *doppia morale* describes specific ways in which it is possible to relate to moral codes precisely by betraying them. One consequence of this argument is that it reinforces Robbins' point regarding the value of retaining 'moral codes' as an analytical category; without something to betray, betrayal has no meaning.

Rather than delineating different spheres of moral action, *doppia morale* is, I suggest, an example of what Foucault calls a 'mode of subjectivation':

> [Y]ou find in Isocrates a very interesting discourse … [t]here Nicocles, who was the ruler of Cyprus, explains why he has always been faithful to his wife: 'Because I am the king, and because as somebody who commands others, who rules others, I have to show that I am able to rule myself.' And you can see that this rule of faithfulness has nothing to do with the universal and Stoic formulation 'I have to be faithful to my wife because I am a human and rational being.' In the former case, it is because I am the king! And you can see that the way the same rule is accepted by Nicocles and by a Stoic is quite different. And that's what I call the mode d'assujettissement, the second aspect of ethics. (Foucault 2000: 264)

Note that a mode of subjectivation is not the same thing as a moral code; a moral code is the content of a set of rules which may well remain the same across what are otherwise different ethical systems. Instead, a mode of subjectivation is the way in which an individual subscribes to such a code: in the example of Nicocles and the Stoic, the injunction to be faithful to one's wife does not vary, but the manner in which they are 'invited or incited to recognise' (Foucault 2000: 264) that moral obligation differs. The Stoic is faithful to his wife because it is the rational thing to do and he is a rational being (see also Foucault 1986: 150–85); Nicocles, on the other hand, is faithful to his wife because it is the correct thing for him to do as a king. Foucault, in other words, is describing two different ways of recognizing a rule; what I want to suggest is that the notion of mode of subjectivation may also be useful in examining how people fail to live up to rules. *Doppia morale*, I argue, is a mode of subjectivation that is inherently equivocal; it establishes a relationship to a moral code which is not one of complete fidelity.

Infidelities

As I have noted, the most frequent targets of accusations of *doppia morale* are the Catholic Church and those who adhere to its values, undoubtedly because of the former's public inflexibility on a range of politically charged moral issues, coupled with widely-available evidence of the personal fallibilities of the latter. During a preliminary period of fieldwork focused particularly on the ethics of infidelity and romantic relationships, I encountered a number of Catholic men who exemplify this problem.

Giovanni, for example, was a thirty-five-year-old Catholic school teacher, and had been married for three years when I met him through a mutual acquaintance. In the first year of his marriage he had a six-month long affair with a colleague from work; it ended quietly and without consequences for him, and he had become a father shortly before our encounter. He seemed repentant when discussing his transgression, and insistent that it would not recur. He certainly considered it a sin of very serious consequence; but it was one he had yet to confess, either to his priest, or indeed to his wife. When I asked him why this was the case, he explained that he did not really feel responsible for his infidelity:

> my father cheated on my mother, and probably his father cheated on my grand-mother too ... when it happened to me it was like a force of nature, it just swept me away. I think there's something animal or biological about it for men – we can't always control it, but it's not really us ... it wasn't the part of me that my wife knows.

This is, in a sense, the inversion of the stoic argument described by Foucault, in which it is reason which impels man to be faithful; here instead it is nature which impels him to be unfaithful. The idiom of an 'animal' part to the self allows Giovanni to construct a relation to a moral convention in which its betrayal is a consequence of a distinct part of his nature, whilst another part of him remains subject to it, in a manner akin to Laidlaw's description of how re-conceiving the self in certain ways allows for alternative distributions of responsibility (Laidlaw 2010: 153; see also Lambek 2013). In other words, I suggest, it is an example of a mode of subjectivation to a rule which allows for the rule to be broken. This, in turn, makes it a further example of equivocation: in Giovanni's formulation, two different parts of himself relate to the same rule entirely differently.

Doppia morale is not only invoked in the context of religious ideals, however: I met Gianni in the same fieldwork period in which I met Giovanni; in his mid-twenties, Gianni studied at the University of Bologna in one of its extra-urban campuses, and was active in a local anarchist student group; he and his current partner are also polyamorists. Originating in California in the early 1990s, polyamory (also called 'ethical non-monogamy') involves intimate relationships with more than one partner simultaneously (for a comprehensive – if not independent – overview see Anapol 1997, 2010). Inspired in part by Marxist critiques of the nuclear family but also by a variety of sources, ranging from neo-Paganism to Bertrand Russell (see Russell 1970 [1929]), it was a common position to hold amongst the LGBTQ activists I met in Bologna.

As one of the movement's foundational texts makes clear, the most important aspect of the ethics of non-monogamy is honesty (Easton and Hardy 1997). Informed consent must be sought and obtained from all parties to the relationship for it to be anything more than common or garden infidelity. Indeed, as Laura would often tell me, non-monogamy was intrinsically a more honest and direct way of relating to people than was monogamy: the latter required the regular suppression and sacrifice of desires for the purported benefit of another, whilst the former – when it functioned correctly – promoted the open expression and discussion of them. This ethic of directness chimed with the more general tendency I have already noted for LGBTQ activists to value clarity and straightforwardness as cardinal virtues.

Much like their monogamous counterparts however, polyamorous relationships do not always function as they should. Gianni, for example, had regular sexual encounters outside of his relationships and unbeknownst to his partners. Similarly, a previous relationship of Laura's had ended amidst recriminations over the fact that her then girlfriend, Sara, was sleeping with other people; this was not, of course, a problem in itself: the problem was that Sara was doing so without informing Laura. Laura herself was accused of a similar sin when she failed immediately to inform a partner in a budding relationship that she was already dating someone else.

Gianni's explanation for his failure to tell the other parties to his relationship about his sexual experiences with other men was related to his antipathy towards rules in general:

> Rules and institutions are the problem with our society; whenever we try to fix something we do it institutionally, and with new rules ... but the new rules are just as bad as the old ones, and the new institutions too. We [he and his collective] stay as far away from rules as possible, and I try to do this in my relationship too.

So, whereas Giovanni's arguments regarding his nature as an Italian man inverted the stoic injunction to fidelity based upon reason, here Gianni takes the opposite position to Nicocles, for whom fidelity was a political decision by which he demonstrates his capacity for control; for Gianni, in contrast, it is infidelity which is the politically appropriate way in which to demonstrate a generalized antinomianism.

An opposition to rules and norms was not uncommon amongst my interlocutors, particularly students and younger activists. A common piece of graffito to be seen in Bologna is 'the law is illegal', a phrase which gestures to the May 1968 movement in France and its slogan that it is 'forbidden to forbid'. But, as Julian Bourg notes in the case of the latter (2007), Gianni's antinomianism is a paradox: it denies law whilst simultaneously asserting this denial as law. It also puts him in the same curious position as Giovanni in relation to a moral convention (in this case that of honesty in polyamorous relationships): that of subscribing to it whilst also contravening it.

Conclusion

What I have attempted to describe here is an important facet of the moral climate of LGBTQ activism in Bologna, a way of understanding one's relationship to ethical injunctions in which adherence to them is not always expected. The examples above, I argue, together with those described earlier, illustrate the way in which *doppia morale* may be helpfully conceptualized as a mode of subjectivation, albeit a particularly curious one: already inscribed in it is the possibility that conventions may be broken under certain circumstances. Such non-adherence is itself a form of relation, rule-breaking behaviour remaining defined by the rule in question.

What is the nature of a rule which does not always have to be followed? One might see in this a resemblance to theories of situational ethics, in which there are no universal laws (apart, in some variations, from the rather unclear injunction to 'love') and ethical judgements must be made on the basis of context. Or one might see simply an acknowledgement of the fact that a great many rules come with particular exceptions.

Neither of these explanations would quite do justice to the problem however, as both cases involve an explicit acknowledgement of the non-universal nature of moral codes. Whereas what is interesting about examples of *doppia morale* is that they cannot do this; the point of the concept is precisely that whilst failures to adhere to moral codes are at least implicitly condoned, they can only be so if properly hidden. Once the transgression is made explicit, it can no longer be a case of *doppia morale*.

Unlike, therefore, in Robbins' discussion of the Urapmin, Bolognese 'culture' does not circumscribe spaces in which rules do or do not apply;

Figure 2.1 'The law is illegal', a ubiquitous graffito in Bologna. This one adorned the building housing the University of Bologna's School of Jurisprudence. Photograph by Paolo Heywood.

doppia morale does not involve a negation of the universal applicability of moral conventions. What it does is provide for certain ways of relating to such conventions in which the possibility of their betrayal – in a certain form – is already allowed for.

Paradoxically, I argue that this in fact reinforces Robbins' point regarding the continued utility of the moral code as a category in the anthropological analysis of ethics; as I hope to have shown, even the most antinomian of behaviour can remained defined by its relationship to rules. This is not the same as saying that there is nothing to ethics or morality but codes of conduct; it is saying that the realization that this is not the case need not lead us to conclude the opposite, namely that only in the absence of such codes can there be ethical behaviour. This is also somewhat akin to Clarke's (2012) call for a renewed attention to rules in the anthropology of ethics, but unlike him I am not suggesting they constitute 'technologies of the self' (thus subsuming them back into what we usually refer to as ethics); instead I suggest that we can retain both the category of technologies of the self, and that of the moral code, as one object of such technologies.

What I also want to suggest here is that the presupposition of a distinction between the meaning of an ethical injunction in a public context and a private one intrinsic to the concept of *doppia morale* makes it an inherently equivocal one; the injunction to be faithful to one's spouse, for example, possesses differing degrees of moral force depending upon the situation. One way of breaking the rule is acceptable, whilst another is not.[5]

This is, in other words, a further instance of the broader focus of this book, namely relationships premised on difference. In the previous chapter I illustrated the presence of difference between people in Bologna in terms of different conceptions of what it means to be left-wing; here what I have tried to suggest is that not only are there always 'other people' within 'peoples' (Candea 2011a) but also sometimes within 'people' too (Simon 2009),[6] thus further complicating the quest for recursivity and 'ethnographic theory' in contemporary anthropology.

The purpose of this chapter has also been to illustrate further the related methodological problem, raised in the introduction, of how to be 'faithful' to a field-site in which unfaithfulness is a key trope, whether it be to ideologies, to people or to moral codes. As I will go on to argue later in this book, fidelity to the study of unfaithfulness as a form of relation requires a further equivocation, namely one over the fidelity or otherwise of theory to ethnography.

Notes

1. This chapter was originally published as P. Heywood (2015), 'Freedom in the Code: The Anthropology of (Double) Morality', *Anthropological Theory* 15: 200–17. I make no claim here regarding how generalizable my account of *doppia morale* may be throughout Italy (or indeed beyond – see Matysik 2008: 68) because any such claim, as both Mol

(2002) and Candea (2010a; 2010b) note, will be as arbitrary – or equivocal – as the boundaries of the 'culture' that it demarcates.

2. To be clear, this was her assessment of those guilty of *doppia morale*. Such people might see virtue in being 'good at' *doppia morale* by effectively concealing it, but obviously by definition therefore they would not acknowledge this themselves.

3. This is reminiscent of the Greek proverb quoted by Juliet du Boulay: 'God wants things covered up' (1974: 82).

4. Hence their references to freedom as 'choice' (e.g. Robbins 2007: 294; Zigon 2009a: 252).

5. Additionally, an element of what moral philosophers call 'moral luck' (Williams 1981) is involved in whether one's actions fall on the acceptable side or not, as one cannot know in advance or completely control whether or not one's sin will be discovered.

6. There is of course an extensive literature in anthropology and beyond on 'fragmented' selves (e.g. Ewing 1990; Jameson 1984), some of it also critical (e.g. Quinn 2006; Sökefeld 1999; Strauss 1997). My point here is less normative than either set in that I take it for granted that people may occasionally differ from themselves, so to speak, by behaving in apparently contradictory ways, but rather than infer from this any particular judgement about selfhood, I have sought in this chapter to illustrate how in some cases this may be less contradictory than it first appears (as in Holbraad 2014). I also add here that the possibility of such self-contradiction makes the project of recursivity yet more complex.

PART II

3

Agreeing to Disagree

The 2012 Pride in Bologna stretched over the course of more than a week of seminars, parades, meetings and celebrations. It included a wide range of LGBTQ groups with a diverse array of perspectives on what Pride ought to mean, and as such developed into a fascinating opportunity for me to observe some of the internal differences (often, as I will describe in the following chapter, over the nature of difference itself) within Bologna's LGBTQ activist community.

Yet in spite of the array of differences on display during Pride, there was a strong sense in which the various participating groups possessed a certain 'continuity of purpose' (Strathern 1987a) despite – or perhaps indeed because of, as I will argue in the next chapter – their concern for being different. This uniformity of concern with difference was particularly visible on the day of the Pride Parade, as I will describe.

Visible also that day, however, was a group who appeared different in a yet further sense, and the precise question of how and if indeed they were different is the object of this chapter. Amidst scantily-clad transgender activists, grandmothers demonstrating for the rights of their gay grandchildren, and an army of 'love soldiers' arrayed behind their giant pink velour tank, something a little odd – at least for that day – was taking place in one corner of the square from which the parade commenced. Standing alone and looking somewhat forlorn amongst a sea of rainbow banners was a statue of Padre Pio, a twentieth-century priest and saint of the Catholic Church. For several hours, groups of soon-to-be marchers had been draping themselves over him for photographs, or festooning him with anticlerical posters. At a certain point in the afternoon, however, a different set of banners appeared: 'We Are Church' these declared, held aloft by a small group of nervously smiling men and women along with others that testified to the presence of gay and lesbian Christians that day. As the banners went up there was a moment of tangible surprise from the surrounding crowd, punctuated by whispers and some giggling, but soon a smattering of applause broke out, and people began again to photograph Padre Pio, by now looking a little more dignified. Indeed, the group had deliberately chosen his statue as their meeting point, hoping as they did to find a place for the Church he symbolized in the march that day.

In a fairly obvious sense the activists I worked with shared some beliefs and opinions that the group I have just described did not. For various reasons, the institution of the Church is viewed with hostility, suspicion and occasionally outright hatred by many LGBTQ activists, who were thus unlikely to welcome

Figure 3.1: Padre Pio with We Are Church's banners below. Photograph by Paolo Heywood.

members of this group, no matter how different they may have appeared to be from their brothers and sisters in faith. In passionately subscribing to the Catholic faith, this group is 'different' in many senses from those I worked with in very specific ways: members of We Are Church do not share the atheism and anticlericalism that unites most of the latter. They set out with the explicit ambition of altering dynamics that exist within the Church, with which they are also often at odds. They thus exist, insofar as they seek to relate to what are commonly regarded as opposite poles of the political spectrum, in a state of ethical liminality of sorts, attempting, with occasional success, to initiate dialogue across deeply entrenched barricades (Mair 2014; see also MacIntyre 1981, 1998). What they are engaged in, I suggest, are what Mair calls 'ethical conversations across borders' (2014). Mair's formulation is intended to capture situations in which parties to a dialogue seek some common ground, whilst also respecting one another's differences. As I show in this chapter, the first concern – persuading the LGBTQ activist community that there was enough ground for a dialogue to be had – was an obvious one for We Are Church; as I also show, the second concern – of how to find common ground whilst also sustaining difference – became an important factor in the relationship between We Are Church and the activist community.

The ethnographic situation I describe however somewhat complicates the connection between these two concerns as Mair describes them. As I have noted, the basic and most fundamental problem for such dialogues appears to be how to find enough common ground in order not to be simply talking at cross purposes to one another, whilst not coming together closely enough that one tradition collapses into another. The problem with this formulation though, as I will show, is that it takes for granted the given nature of borders between traditions; sometimes they take work to maintain as well as to break down.

What this way of seeing the problem risks missing in other words, is that identity and difference can be – and in the case of queer activism clearly are – two sides of the same relational coin, and that succeeding too well at the first problem of ethical conversations risks failure at the second. No matter how distinct two groups may look, if difference is only ever a construction then work must be put in to making it. As I discuss in the next chapter, making a difference, in this sense, is what made many of the LGBTQ groups with whom I worked occasionally and in a very paradoxical sense the same: what they agreed upon was how they were different. This was their 'continuity of purpose'. In this chapter, by contrast, I explore a situation in which a quest for common ground hits a brick wall in the form of a failure to agree upon difference, making the two groups in question thus appear, in other important respects, too much the same. What they could not do, I will suggest, is 'agree to disagree', not in the straightforward sense of the phrase, but in the sense that what they failed to build and maintain was not so much common ground as difference.

We Are Church

I first met Domenico in a little ice cream shop half way between his apartment and mine, on a sunny afternoon in April. A journalist and blogger for a popular local daily newspaper, Domenico, in his mid-thirties and then engaged to be married, had a brisk air of efficiency about him, and barely waited for my questions before launching into a description of his organization. He described how We Are Church originated in Austria in 1995 following a paedophilia scandal amongst the clergy there; a liberal cardinal retired and was replaced by a conservative one who was himself involved in this scandal, but who swiftly resigned following an outcry from sections of the laity. Before he did however, the movement that had emerged in opposition to him produced a document titled 'An Appeal from the People of God' (We Are Church 2006) in which they used the platform they had achieved to make further demands of the Vatican, including the removal of the requirement of celibacy amongst the priesthood, an increased role in the Church for the laity, and communion for divorcees. This appeal, so Domenico told me with pride, was signed by millions of Catholics around the world, including 35,000 from Italy, and resulted in the formation of an umbrella organization, International Movement We Are Church, which included within it national organizations in, for example, Austria, Germany, France, Spain, Italy, Ireland, the USA and Mexico. The groups are particularly strong in Germany and Austria, Domenico told me, where the Church is relatively liberal, unlike in Italy, where the influence of the Vatican is very strong, although, he said, there had been steps forward, such as a meeting with a prominent Italian cardinal in 2008.

The branch in Emilia-Romagna was founded by Domenico and two others in 2005, one of whom was gay, and so from the very beginning concerned itself with sexuality in particular. Other groups occupied themselves with other issues: the one in Rome, for example, with Vatican rent. The other respect in which the Emilia-Romagna group was distinctive was in – despite its name – its emphasis on not being a Catholic association; that is, Domenico explained, they were an association of Catholics, rather than a group which put religion at the forefront of its identity (and also rather than being directly affiliated with the Church, as other prominent groups like Azione Cattolica and Communione Liberazione are). They have, he said, no desire whatsoever to be officially recognized by the Vatican, and they try to avoid organizing events that presuppose faith on the part of participants, such as Bible study groups or church services; they focus instead on meetings, presentations of books or films, and debates. At the 2012 Pride, in fact, they were to host two such events in cooperation with Cassero: the first would be the screening of a documentary on the experiences of parents with gay children, followed by a discussion with the director, a participant and two sympathetic priests, whilst the second would be a discussion with a theologian and author of a recent book on Catholicism and homosexuality. On We Are Church's position on homosexuality, Domenico was careful to begin by pointing out that the organization had not officially endorsed the idea of gay marriage, seeing this as a political issue for the state rather than a religious one. But it did take clear positions on ending discrimination within the Church, arguing regularly against pronouncements from the Vatican condemning homosexuality as a sin.

Much of the theological justification they employ for their positions is based on a distinction between dogma – articles of faith which are immutable, such as the immaculacy of Mary's conception, declared *ex cathedra* ('from the Chair'), and thus infallibly, by Pope Pius IX – and positions taken by the Church that may be subject to discussion. This sounds simple, and in some cases it is: the doctrine of the Immaculate Conception is what Domenico called a 'foundation of faith'; because it was made *ex cathedra* it is an example of an infallible statement by a pope. It is, however, one of only two such statements, and debate rages over the infallibility or otherwise of other kinds of pronouncements: John Paul II's declaration of 1994 (John Paul II 1994) which sought to end debate on the question of women priests was not made *ex cathedra*, and therefore We Are Church (and many other Catholics) does not consider it to constitute Church dogma. The position of the Church, however, is that in issuing the statement he was simply confirming a truth upheld by tradition (the history of the Church) and by the magisterium (the pope and bishops) and it is thus as infallible a statement as that made by Pius IX on the Immaculate Conception.

The Church, Domenico explained using an Italian expression, thinks it has the truth in its pocket. This puts it in confrontation with others: it believes homosexuality to be objectively, intrinsically wrong, and the LGBTQ community react (unsurprisingly) badly to this kind of condemnation. If, on the other hand, the historic Catholic injunction against homosexuality is seen not as dogma but simply a contingent dictum of the Church hierarchy, a space for dialogue opens up; and for Domenico, dogmatic principles of faith ought to include only those questions upon which the Church as a whole could agree.

Mair (2014) describes a similar practice of distinguishing between fundamental universal truths and local and contingent means of arriving at them in the case of Fo Guang Shan Buddhism. Fo Guang Shan's practitioners emphasize the objective and universal validity of certain truths and virtues, such as those of compassion and wisdom, and indeed seek to evangelize them (2014: 72). However, they combine this emphasis with the recognition that such virtues are always realized in particular forms, and conditioned by historical and cultural circumstances (2014: 73). What this allows them to do is to reject a straightforwardly relativist approach to values in favour of a pluralist stance in which universal values become concrete in diverse ways in diverse conditions. Similarly, whenever Domenico spoke about Catholic values – the universality of which he evidently believed in – he would speak of abstract principles (such as love, or tolerance, as I will describe below) that he might reasonably assume most of his interlocutors would share a belief in. For Domenico whether one loved someone of the same or the opposite sex was an irrelevance in terms of the actual virtue that such love embodied, a contingent realization of an abstract universal. Where the Vatican was mistaken, in his view, was in elevating the condemnation of homosexuality to be found in, for example, the Old Testament, to a similarly universal status, akin to dogma such as 'love they neighbour'; to the contrary, he argued, the Church's current position is a contingent dictum, the product of certain circumstances, and thus subject to change and to dialogue.

Another theological basis for We Are Church's understanding of Catholicism is the legacy of the Second Vatican Council; convened by Pope John XXIII (known often as 'Papa buono', or 'the good Pope' in Italy, and a hero to Domenico and many liberal Catholics) with the famously stated intention to 'let some fresh air into the Church', Vatican II reformed the Catholic liturgy by introducing masses in the vernacular, placed a higher emphasis on ecumenism and interfaith dialogue than had hitherto existed, and – importantly for Domenico – attempted to realign the Church's relationship to the world, from a vision of Rome as a bulwark of faith in an essentially sinful and evil environment, to a more positive engagement with matters temporal. As he put it to me, before Vatican II the Church was the enemy of the world; after, it was supposed to be a part of it.

As his 'supposed to' suggests however, the legacy of Vatican II remains in dispute; for Domenico, its promise went unfulfilled. John XXIII died before the Council finished its work, and his successor Paul VI reframed its purpose from 'updating' to 'renewing' the Church; the hoped-for reform of the Curia did not occur, with power becoming ever more centralized in the hands of the pope and his ministers; furthermore the new pope ignored the liberal majority on the Council and took unilateral action on the issues of contraception and priestly celibacy, issuing encyclicals which enshrined the Church's current positions.

We Are Church's position on Vatican II is not only distinct from that of the Church itself, but also from many other Italian Catholics who view the few reforms it did succeed in achieving as having distorted the Church's traditional positions. Although, as I outlined in my first chapter, Bologna is not a natural home for conservative Catholics, one does occasionally encounter such viewpoints; drinking coffee in my local bar one Sunday afternoon I met two of my neighbours, both observant Catholics, although in quite different ways: Simone was a retired lawyer in his sixties, quiet and dignified in his speech, whilst Alfredo was a construction worker in his late fifties, whom I had first met in our local barbershop, where his fervent views on religion often made him the butt of jokes. Both men having returned that day from Church, I decided to tell them a bit about my experiences with We Are Church to see how they would react to its ideas: Simone was diplomatically noncommittal on the subject of LGBTQ Catholics, but viewed positively the ambition of reforming the Church's positions on divorce and celibacy; Alfredo, on the other hand, saw the group as the epitome of all that was wrong with post-Vatican II Catholicism. Unknowingly exemplifying Domenico's critique of the

Church, he said that the truth is the truth and nothing can change that; Vatican II, he argued, had made no doctrinal pronouncements, and left everything it addressed more confused than it had been before; homosexuality and divorce were sins, he insisted, and not even the pope could change that.

Dialogues in Action (1)

The position that We Are Church takes with regard to the LGBTQ community is thus one that puts them at odds with more conservative understandings of Catholicism than that espoused in Vatican II, as well as with the official stance of the Church. More of a puzzle for this chapter however, is the precise nature of their relationship with the LGBTQ community itself. In order to explore this I will describe the two events that We Are Church organized in conjunction with Cassero, as each exemplifies a unique problem with regard to these kinds of moral dialogues.

The subject of the first event I will describe was a recently published book, *Omosessualitá*, by a respected Catholic theologian, Gianino Piana, in which he details some of the history of the relationship between homosexuality and Catholicism, and argues for an ethics in which the 'authenticity' of a romantic partnership is what is important, rather than the gender or orientation of the persons comprising it (Piana 2010). The structure of the evening was a live interview of Piana conducted onstage by Domenico, followed by a question and answer session.

Domenico opened the discussion by asking why Piana describes homosexuality as a 'complex' in the book; Piana began by clarifying that the views he describes in the book are his own, and are not those of the magisterium, before responding that the word 'complex' was necessary because homosexuality is a 'complex problem', composed of a variety of biological and psycho-cultural causes. He went on to note that although the Old Testament condemns it, what it refers to is very different to the contemporary understanding of the word, and that in the New Testament it is barely mentioned. Church tradition, he argued, has taken the stance it has because of the generally poor view in which sex for any purpose other than procreation has always been held, citing Augustine as an exemplar. Vatican II, he continued, following Domenico's line of argument to me, attempted to broaden the definition of the family so as to make it more than simply just 'a baby factory', and the increased importance of love laid open the possibility that a loving couple composed of members of the same sex might someday fall within the Church's category of 'the family'. After Vatican II, however, came the turn back to tradition, with homosexuality once again clearly defined as a sin. Finally, Domenico concluded the interview by asking about his subject's views on gay marriage: Piana responded that he was not personally against it, although he found some common ground with Massimo in querying why it should be that an institution undergoing such a crisis should be so desirable.

Upon my arrival I had recognized a number of faces in the audience as members of Cassero, and their presence was made more evident during the question and answer session, as a number of them prefixed their queries with statements such as 'I'm not a believer'; indeed, despite his efforts both to clarify that his views were not those of the magisterium, and to attempt a (for him and for Domenico, at least) sympathetic reading of homosexuality through Catholicism, Piana's visit to Cassero soon became an opportunity for some of its members to air some long-held grievances against the Church, and he thus often found himself either having to explain beliefs that he clearly did not hold, or simply to agree with the questioner, becoming, as Domenico often regretfully said of himself, a stand-in for the Church as a whole. He was repeatedly confronted about why the Vatican is so obsessed with matters of sexuality ('shouldn't they care more about murder and genocide?') and why the Church's message of Christian love did not extend to the LGBTQ community ('Jesus didn't condemn women and gay people, did he?'), and he looked increasingly bemused as he seemingly struggled between the professorial inclination to explain the complexity of such issues to a lay audience, and a reluctance to appear to be defending views that were not his own and were unlikely ever to be well-taken in this particular context. The evening concluded on a relatively positive note, however, as Domenico intervened to ask a final question about Piana's views on Pride and We Are Church's participation: Piana eagerly took the opportunity to say that he believed Pride to be a very necessary thing, and that he was pleased that a Catholic group would be there in solidarity.

I lost Domenico amongst the audience that night, but caught up with him again a couple of weeks later and he revealed his disappointment at the treatment the speaker had received; people in the LGBTQ community, he felt, sometimes treated him simply as a representative of Catholicism, rather than as an individual with his own views. The problem was that people at Cassero equated the Church with the Vatican, and, understandably, they hate the Vatican; but this, he added, only helps you to fight, it does not help you to enter into a dialogue. He, instead, tries to find points of convergence, rather than differences, in values such as equality and respect.

This was also evident on the day of the Pride march itself. At the parade, the hostility of many in the LGBTQ community to Catholicism was on full display: as I described in the introduction to this chapter, the statue of Padre Pio in the square in which the parade commenced was gleefully festooned with rainbow flags, banners and posters bearing anticlerical slogans. Shortly before the procession was due to depart, Domenico and some of his colleagues from We Are Church arrived, taking up a position in front of the statue, and proudly, although with a hint of defiance, unfurling banners decorated with the group's name, and slogans in support of gay Christian men and women. The crowd of young people around them whispered and tittered to one another, but soon began applauding and taking photographs. As more and more of my friends and interlocutors arrived I lost track of them, but saw them again later in the day marching with their banners held up in front of them, and with the same air of pride tinged with self-consciousness, an island of faith in the midst of a world that had largely rejected it. A group nearby marched with a sign on which was painted 'yesterday the inquisition, today homophobia'.

Domenico had a problem, namely that his attempts at initiating dialogue were foundering because his LGBTQ interlocutors were identifying him and his group too closely with the Vatican. Instead of seeing the affinities he was trying to highlight – such as a respect for 'authentic' relationships, or a belief in love, which I will discuss with regard to the second event – they were focusing on their differences with an institution from which he himself differed.

At the time, I was convinced by Domenico's account of the problem. But later I came to think that perhaps we had both misunderstood it. What I came to realize after the second event, as I describe below, is that whilst finding affinities is undoubtedly a crucial problem in a conversation involving two groups with quite distinct values, those affinities cannot solely concern things about which they agree; paradoxically, they must also find and sustain affinities over exactly what it is that makes them different. In other words, what they had to do was to agree to disagree.

What we tend to signal when we use that phrase is the conclusion of a conversation in the face of insuperable difficulties. One agrees to disagree with a person when one recognizes that certain differences of opinion will never be overcome. In this case by contrast I suggest that it functions as the precondition, rather than conclusion, of the kind of conversation with which this chapter is concerned. Without agreement on how exactly it is that the parties in question differ, the conversation becomes of a different nature to that which we have so far been describing, and, as I show below, of a great deal less interest to at least one of those parties. In describing this as 'agreeing to disagree' my intention is to emphasize the point that just as common ground cannot always be found but sometimes must be built, so the same is true of difference (especially in the context of LGBTQ activism, in which the production of difference is of such crucial importance). Conversations across borders (Mair 2014), in other words, must also be conversations about borders to the extent that the borders involved are rarely if ever found objects in the world but are instead outcomes of the conversation in question.

Dialogues in Action (2)

The second of the Pride events was the presentation of a short documentary on gay Catholic parents, followed by a question and answer session with the audience. Around thirty people were present, and the crowd was substantially different to the kinds of faces I usually saw in Cassero's main event room (which was also their disco): there were few people under thirty present, and instead of being a sea of t-shirts and jeans, the room was instead filled with smartly attired men and women in dresses or shirts and trousers, many of whom looked to be over fifty.

On the stage, Domenico and some technicians from Cassero had set up a projector screen and five chairs: two of them were occupied by men in the familiar black suits and white collars of priests, and two others by middle-aged women, one the director of the documentary, and the other one of the two parents featured in it. Of the two priests, the first was Don Claudio, an elderly man in charge of a parish very close to Cassero; kindly and genial, he had been present earlier that evening with us, spending much of the time playing with the baby of a friend of Domenico's, Daniella (when it refused to look at him, he joked that it had already turned anticlerical). In previous years, he had run a service of remembrance for victims of homophobic violence, and also hosted the city's only all-gay choir, to the ire of his immediate superiors; his defences of such actions were a (somewhat mischievous sounding) denial that they constituted him taking a different position to the Church (on the remembrance service: 'all I did was listen to a prayer'; on the choir: 'I just offered them a room. They're gay, it doesn't mean they sing differently') and an insistence that he did not require the Curia's permission to do what he wanted in his own parish (Scheggia 2009). The other priest, Don Romano, was a younger man, in his late forties, and from Foggia, where he worked closely with an LGBT rights group in that region; he had also won plaudits from many liberal Catholics by criticizing the Church's standing on priestly celibacy and homosexuality in an open letter to his bishop.

The short film, which began around 9.30 PM, was titled (echoing Piana's thesis) 'Authentic Love' and was made up of a series of interviews with two mothers of gay sons, one of whom had recently died of AIDS. Its purpose, as the director, Irene, subsequently explained, was to bring out into the open something long regarded as 'secret': the coincidence of faith and homosexuality. The two mothers interviewed were Catholic, and spoke of their initial guilt over whether any aspect of their parenting might have been indirectly responsible for their children's homosexuality; this feeling however was soon superseded by the eponymous 'authentic love' that they held for their children, resulting in both deciding to be as open as possible about their children's sexuality, and to treat it with pride, rather than shame. As one of the women put it, the Church hierarchy had 'traduced' Jesus's message of love for all, and as the director subsequently claimed in the discussion which followed, 'guilt comes from the Church hierarchy – but the Church and its hierarchy are not the same thing: God loves everyone'. A particularly striking aspect of the film was its concluding interview with an elderly (now deceased) Livornese priest, who declared the Church to be misogynist and sexophobic. Sexuality, he argued forcefully, was a gift from God and there could be no immorality in it; 'do we really believe Jesus would condemn a homosexual if he met one?', he asked rhetorically, before concluding that the material of the marriage sacrament is love, and that where there is love, no one has the power to withhold marriage.

A brief discussion between those on the stage followed, in which the director and the woman who had appeared in the film explained the purpose behind it, arguing that religious parents of gay children have no voice in contemporary Italy. Don Romano described how an encounter with a young boy in his parish, whose distress at being told that his desires were 'against nature' resulted in an eating disorder, had led him to rethink what he had learnt at his seminary. But the Church as a whole, he argued, is too large an entity to change quickly: in an interestingly sociological justification for its attitudes to homosexuality, he suggested that the Church must cater to opinions that range from those to be found in Bologna to those in a Papua New Guinean village, and that at the moment the majority of the world's Catholics were not yet as enlightened as those at the meeting that night.

The first two questioners (an elderly man and a woman of a similar age) asked the priests about their positions on gay marriage and reproductive rights, giving approving nods when both refused to support them explicitly. The third question came from Daniella, sat directly behind me, and complicated the apparent affinity with the LGBTQ community that We Are Church was trying to elicit from the idea of 'love': didn't the speakers think, she asked, that the gay community needed to promote fidelity more than it did (especially in light of the risks to health involved)? Love, she said, is not the same as sex, which is what some in the community seem to think. By the time she had concluded I was squirming uncomfortably in my seat and awaiting what I assumed would be a chorus of disapproval from other audience members: though many members of Cassero – as opposed to more radical groups – are pro-marriage rights, many of them do not share the view Daniella was expounding regarding the benefits of monogamy over a more liberal understanding of love; at the same time, neither do they appreciate the promulgation of the stereotype that gay men and women are more promiscuous than their straight counterparts.

The backlash I awaited did not materialize however; the reason for this surprising passivity became obvious when I looked around properly and noticed again that almost everyone in the audience was in their fifties or sixties, well-dressed, and indeed looking nothing like the kinds of people I usually met in Cassero. Nor did I recognize any faces. There were, in fact, almost no LGBTQ activists present; and if there is one thing that constitutes a definitive obstacle to a conversation, it is the absence of one of the parties.

The reason for this was suggested to me after the event, when I bumped into Rocco, a friendly bald man in his forties who ran Cassero's health section, and was also an acquaintance of Domenico. Though he was usually hesitant when beginning conversations, once they were started it was almost impossible to get Rocco to stop talking, and I found myself, half an hour later, still standing in the evening heat outside the building, as he updated me on his life and on his impressions of We Are Church. He had attended the debate with Piana, and I asked him why he thought that almost nobody from Cassero had come to this event. 'Look,' he said, 'I like Domenico and I'm really glad about what he's trying to do, but this is just a band aid. Noi Siamo Chiesa are a tiny minority, and even some of its members don't share Domenico's openness [this impression would have no doubt been reinforced had he heard Daniella's question]. They're not representative enough to make a difference'.

Are 'We' Church?

How successful were Domenico and We Are Church in communicating across the ethical boundaries of the LGBTQ community and the Church (Mair 2014; MacIntyre 1981)? Did they succeed in 'making a difference' by finding the 'points of convergence' that Domenico highlights?

Points of convergence may not be as straightforward as they appear: the events described above could be counter-productive in terms of building bridges, because they could potentially reveal deep-seated differences in ethical outlooks, as well as or instead of convergences. Daniella's comment about the difference between love and sex underscored how distinct are the perspectives of a liberal (but observant) Catholic and polyamorists like Laura and many I met in the LBGTQ community; there is more to Catholic morality than how it accounts for homosexuality, and many in 'Red' Bologna's LGBTQ community take exception to other aspects of it as well.

Other responses, however, were more positive. Gaia, for example, whom we will meet again in the next chapter, held them in high esteem, and would often cite them as exemplars of notable successes of the LGBTQ movement. 'It's true that very anticlerical people don't trust them, but I do, and admire them very much', she told me. They represent exemplars, she explained, in the sense that they embody the values of equality and respect that the Church and the LGBTQ community should have in common. This is particularly true, she said, because they are not an LGBTQ group themselves, and defend the rights of the community not out of self-interest but on the basis of Christian principles like love and tolerance: 'they demonstrate that the Church is not just an institution'.

Caroline Humphrey, and, more recently, Joel Robbins, have both discussed the notion of the exemplar as an alternative to moral systems in which hard and fast rules form the basis of ethical judgements (Humphrey 1997; Robbins forthcoming). As Robbins puts it in his description of Humphrey's argument about exemplars in Mongolia, 'having long been subject to the play of shifting political powers that each define and enforce the rules in their own way, Mongols also evidence an informed cynicism about the worth of such rules as guides for life ... [and] instead pin their moral hopes on finding exemplary teachers' (forthcoming: 2).

J.E. Tiles, in his work on cross-cultural ethics, has identified the sharing of exemplary models as one way in which ethical dialogues between different communities may take place (2000). This is particularly apposite in the case of

LGBTQ activists and the Church. Behaviours in relation to rules amongst LGBTQ activists are ambivalent to say the least (see Chapter 2), and the case of We Are Church's interaction with activists suggests that coming together around shared exemplary values is far more likely to be successful than doing so through a set of rules: in addition to a prevailing antinomianism, the fact that there exist so many differences within and between LGBTQ activist groups over values makes a reliance on rules as difficult as it is in Humphrey's Mongolian context. This becomes only truer when dealing with the Catholic Church. The Church's tendency towards making absolutist and universal moral judgements of behaviours makes it a frequent target of accusations of hypocrisy, as I noted in Chapter 2; it is also the most obvious obstacle to conciliation with LGBTQ groups, both because of its form (in opposition to their suspicion of absolutism and universals) and, of course, because of its content (because some of those absolute rules are injunctions against homosexuality). As I have described, Domenico and We Are Church go to some lengths to avoid sounding like this; his refusal to use the word 'truth' and their insistence that the Church's condemnation of LGBTQ lifestyles is a matter of historical circumstance rather than moral dogma are both instances of an attempt to shift the nature of their dialogue with the community from one over the existence or non-existence of certain moral codes to one in which they can embody certain values that are at least in principle shared (respect, love, tolerance). Indeed, the very act of attempting to initiate dialogue on an equal footing is exemplary of these values in a way in which most Church engagements with the community are not, as they do not simply consist of condemnation from the pulpit.

Thus, insofar as We Are Church succeeds in 'making a difference', it is through attempting to bridge the gap between 'is' and 'ought' that many perceive to exist when it comes to Church teachings: many in the LGBTQ community are not at all unsympathetic to the spiritual aspects of Christianity, and Domenico, We Are Church, and people such as the mothers depicted in Irene's documentary are all evidence for the fact that there are Catholics who believe that the Church's attitude towards homosexuality contradicts its core teachings. We Are Church, I argue, seeks to narrow the distinction between facts and values: as with accusations of *doppia morale*, Catholics such as Irene's interview subjects attach their loyalties to the ideals of the religion, rather than the actual manner in which they are (not) instantiated by what they refer to as 'the hierarchy'. We Are Church seeks to put these ideals into practice, and in doing so, exemplifies a shared ethical model. This distinction between 'hierarchy' and faith maps neatly on to that delineated between dogma and dictum, with the former representing the (to them, unfounded) condemnation of homosexuality by the official Church, and the latter standing for Catholicism's true precepts of love and tolerance, embodied by the laity.

But succeeding in making a difference in this sense leads to the most serious obstacle to their 'making a difference' in a broader sense – indifference; the second event that We Are Church organized in particular was sparsely attended even by their hosts, Cassero, to say nothing of the wider LGBTQ community. When I tried to describe the group to friends and interlocutors from other, more radical LGBTQ groups, the most common response would be raised eyebrows and mirth at the idea of their naivety in thinking they could either change the Church or change the LBGTQ community's attitude to it. There was certainly no widespread inclination to engage with them, as many people felt (understandably) that a Church which regularly condemned their lifestyles from the pulpit deserved no such thing.

But the problem was not simply indifference in the straightforward sense of the word. In fact, I suggest, the indifference to We Are Church, in the obvious sense, of much of Bologna's LGBTQ community was a consequence of another kind of indifference – sameness.

Of course, demonstrating the affinities the two groups may (or may not) have shared over love or authenticity was an important part of their moral dialogue, as was We Are Church distancing itself from Vatican homophobia. But the better it accomplished this the less it actually looked like a distinct ethical tradition. The more people like Rocco felt that its positions on issues like homosexuality were closer to his own than that of the Church (as he understood that word) the less it appeared to be an interesting conversation partner and the more it seemed like a fringe group that was unrepresentative of the institution of which it claimed to be a part.

But We Are Church claimed to be more than a part of that institution. Its very name, indeed, points to this: 'We Are Church' should be understood as an attempt at a performative statement, literally seeking to 'make a difference' between the idea of the Church as 'hierarchy', magisterium, the Vatican, and that of the Church as a community of lay believers with differing views on a number of key issues. Because in an important sense it is not its views on subjects such as homosexuality that are the object of ethical communication with the LBGTQ community: the meetings organized by the members of We Are Church and their presence at Pride makes no secret of their position on this issue; and, of course, most LGBTQ activists find it neither surprising nor shocking – nor indeed particularly worthy of praise – that people should acknowledge their lifestyles as acceptable ways of being. What they do need convincing of, however, as evidenced by the discussions above, is that Domenico and We Are Church are anything other than a minority opinion in an otherwise highly centralized and dogmatic religious institution. They need convincing, in other words, that 'Church' does not only refer to the orthodoxy of the Vatican, but can also encompass more liberal interpretations of Catholic theology such as that of the 'We' in 'We Are Church'; and it was upon this claim – that We Are Church have both affinities and significant enough differences with the LGBTQ community to constitute interesting conversation partners – that their attempt to start a moral dialogue faltered.[1] In other words, by 'making a difference' through finding common ground, they failed to 'make a difference' precisely by 'making difference' between themselves and their interlocutors.

Domenico himself suggested this to me when he and his friends took me for a coffee just before the Pride march; there he told me that not only was he happy to be present that day, but that he felt that it was his duty to come and make a statement. When I asked about how the multitude of anti-Catholic banners made him feel, he told me that they made him sad, as a lot of what they said about the homophobia of the Vatican was true; what they did not understand was that the Church was more than the Vatican – as his group's name suggested, the real Church was the people, people like him, who were there to support Pride.

Conclusion

We Are Church's efforts to build common ground and to find affinities or identities with its LGBTQ activist interlocutors were well-intentioned and important; they were also successful. Too successful, in fact, because what they eclipsed was the importance to this kind of conversation of not only constructing identity but also of constructing difference. We Are Church sought to demonstrate an essentially ambiguous and partial relationship to the Church; on the one hand, it distanced itself from the Church's dogmatism and intransigence; on the other it tried to represent the Church, to exemplify a way of being part of the Church without suffering from these problems. But the danger of succeeding at the first is to fail in the second: the more it convinced its interlocutors of its only partial fidelity to Catholicism, the more it risked the latter perceiving it as irrelevant and marginal to the Church as a whole. As far as its LGBTQ activist interlocutors were concerned, in other words, it was not different enough from them to constitute a valuable conversation partner. What the conversation lacked was not affinity alone, but affinity over difference, or, as I have termed it, 'agreeing to disagree'.

The case study presented in the next chapter, by contrast, demonstrates the inverse of this point: its central claim (and the basis for subsequent ones which follow in later chapters) is that the anti-identitarian concern for the production of difference on the part of queer activism in Bologna becomes simultaneously the construction of its own identity.

Notes

This chapter was originally published as P. Heywood (2015), 'Agreeing to Disagree: LGBTQ Activism and the Church in Italy', *HAU: Journal of Ethnographic Theory* 5(2): 325–44.

1. As a speech act, in other words, their name failed to meet its felicity conditions, at least from the perspective of the LGBTQ activist community, for whom they simply were not the Church.

4

Different Differences

Laura, Alessia and I were having a drink with Marco one evening in May when the subject of 'community' arose; in the midst of a wide-ranging discussion about the values and morals of LGBTQ activists in Bologna, Marco declared that there was no 'LGBTQ community' in the city, but instead a series of fractured and diverse groups of people who share certain values, but do not share a great many others. Marco's activism reflected this problem: he worked occasionally with a number of groups (including Movimento Identità Transessuale – see below) but preferred not to commit himself completely to any one aspect of the movement. 'PCI ideology was very important to Italians, because we need something to have faith in', he put it on another occasion, 'the problem of the left today is that there is nothing unifying to have faith in ... every group has its own little faith'. These 'little faiths', and the interactions between them, will be the subject of this chapter and the next.

In Part One I introduced some aspects of the political and ethical context in which this study is situated. Chapter 1 complicated the picture of Bologna as a utopia for LGBTQ activists by discussing some of the ways in which being left-wing can mean very different things to different people; the status of the city and its relationship to the (loosely defined) LGBTQ community will re-emerge in this chapter as I describe some of the debates which surrounded the Pride festival that took place there in 2012, as will the notion of *doppia morale*, the concept described in Chapter 2.

The main aim of this chapter, however, is to provide a description of a tension that is fundamental to queer activism in Bologna. It will describe a set of key debates that took place in 2012 over the staging that year of Italy's national Pride festival in the city, debates which revolved around the meaning and value of difference. Such differences over difference cause serious fractures and fissures within what might otherwise be seen as a 'community' of activists; but they are also constitutive of what it means to be a queer activist in Bologna. To be such means to believe that difference is something that needs to be made – both in the obvious clichéd sense of the term, but also in the philosophical sense of difference as performed or constructed. It is this fundamental belief that makes many queer activists resistant to attempts to enrol them into larger groups or into Manichean political battles against a particular other.

But it is precisely insofar as this belief in 'making a difference' defines what it means to be a queer activist in the city that something like a queer identity emerges. 'Making a difference' is what makes them different from one another, because such difference must be constantly produced, but it is also what makes them the same, because others are perceived not to share this understanding of difference. This identity is particularly visible at moments like the Pride festival, when the queer activist community is in evidence precisely insofar as people go out of their way to perform difference, both from one another, and also from those who understand their identities as fixed.

Hence the tension that this chapter describes: in contrast to examples of what anthropologists often call 'strategic essentialism', in which identity is foregrounded but only because it is really being performed, the logic I describe here is what might be termed 'strategic anti-essentialism';[1] a 'politics of difference' is foregrounded, but has the effect of producing a certain kind of identity politics.

A Divided Community

One warm evening in spring, around thirty to forty people gathered in a bar on the north side of the city often frequented by my interlocutors. The atmosphere was somewhat more tense than usual, with several small groups of people talking quietly at individual tables, rather than the loud and disorganized kind of socializing that usually preceded a meeting. An impromptu stage was set up, and a projector screen unveiled. I arrived, as usual, on time, and thus around forty minutes before the meeting would eventually start. Laura had taken me to a workshop the previous day, and as I entered the bar I recognized a number of the participants, who smiled or nodded in greeting. I walked through to the back room and was about to take a seat on my own when I heard Laura call my name; she was sat with Angela and Gabriella, both of whom had also been at the workshop yesterday, but whom I had not yet properly met. Students in their mid to late twenties, they were part of a project that Laura was coordinating on behalf of her group, Betty&Books/SexyShock, to send young people to Romania to raise awareness of LGBTQ issues there, as well as also being members of a feminist collective.

Gradually, the space filled up with people more attuned to the temporality of Italian activism than me, and it became evident that a range of groups were to be represented at this meeting: occupying the stage as they waited to begin were the two speakers for the evening, Marina and Massimo, leading members of an occupied space (*centro sociale*) not far from where I lived, itself home to at least three different collectives.[2] Some of the city's most famous *centri sociali* – such as XM24, a former outdoor market, and TPO (Teatro Polyvalente Occupato) from which SexyShock first emerged – were represented; Laura and a number of others from SexyShock (of which Betty&Books was the commercial arm) were present, as were women from the feminist collective of which Angela was a member. Most intriguing of all was the presence of Gaia, whom we met briefly in the last chapter, a well-known activist from Agedo, a national organization which aims to support young LGBTQ people in difficult domestic situations, as well as their parents. It also lobbies vociferously for marriage and adoption/fertility rights, along with the largest and oldest LGBTQ organization in both Italy and Bologna, Arcigay. Representatives from the latter were notably absent from the meeting, and so, it became clear, Gaia was assumed to be speaking for them.

Angela – like Laura – had previously worked for Arcigay before becoming – also like Laura – disillusioned with its methods and ideals. She had tried, she later explained to me, to open up channels between Arcigay and some of the other groups in Bologna, without success, because they were, she told me, too 'radically different'; her association with the former made many of the people she sought to engage immediately suspicious. Since leaving Arcigay, she told me, she hadn't really settled into a new group, although she liked the relaxed atmosphere at Betty&Books; there was too much competition between the majority of the groups, she felt, and she did not wish to become absorbed into it. You are obliged in many groups, she said, to embrace everything wholeheartedly, otherwise they assume something is wrong with you. You can see this even in the styles of dress of many activists: to be a lesbian means short hair and punk clothes; one of the reasons she appreciated Betty&Books so much was their refusal to conform to these implicit codes. Her bisexuality, she told me, had also been a significant problem for her amongst some parts of the lesbian community in the city; going to bed with a man, she said, was seen as politically incomprehensible. She was even told by one eminent lesbian activist that what she did in her bedroom was her business, as long she hid her bisexuality in public (an example, she explained, of *doppia morale*).

The presence of Gaia was intriguing because the meeting's purpose was to discuss the upcoming national Pride celebrations which were due to take place in June in the city, for the second time since 2008. Gay Pride, as an international phenomenon, has its origins in the Stonewall riots of 1968 which followed a police raid on a bar which catered to the gay and transgender community in New York. In Italy, the first public demonstration in favour of gay rights was held in 1972, and the first official Pride (organized by Arcigay) was held in 1994. In 2012 – and not for the first time in the movement's history – Pride had become a bone of contention between groups of activists with very different agendas.

That evening's meeting – titled 'The Revolution is not a Wedding Breakfast' – was organized by the Puta Network, an umbrella group led, to all intents and purposes, by Marina and Massimo. Marina was in her late twenties, slight, and with her hair cut very short. She had recently graduated from the city's university, and was now working for a local government helpline, whilst trying to have her undergraduate dissertation published and working for the Puta Network in her spare time. She was earnest in a slightly nervous fashion, and had a habit of biting her fingernails seemingly un-selfconsciously. Massimo was the other founder, a handsome gay man of indeterminate age – he looked to be in his early forties, but it was often insinuated to me that he was older – who also worked for the local government, though in a permanent, and thus very privileged, position. Highly charismatic, he spoke with a relaxed, if slightly affected drawl that would speed up into staccato when he became agitated, and was very clearly the driving force behind the network. Though the latter was itself internally fractured, it did loosely cohere in its opposition to what was often termed the 'institutionalized' part of the LGBTQ movement, emblematic of which was Arcigay, and its base in Bologna, known as Cassero.

Cassero, for many LGBTQ activists in Bologna, symbolized an aspect of the movement that had forgotten its roots in the rejection of normativity and authority that Stonewall meant to them. Needless to say, Stonewall has been interpreted in various ways by differing sorts of people: the eponymous British gay rights charity, for example, would not recognize in it the idea of a 'rejection of normativity'. But for many in the Puta Network – certainly for Marina and Massimo – and for the absent allies they would seek that night to enrol in their cause, this is precisely what it stands for: a refusal to conform and a direct attack on authority (of any form).

Laura and others would often tell me that nowadays Cassero, supported by local government and structured like a corporation, is nothing more than a disco, with the money it receives from entry to its nightclub dominating more 'political' concerns. Its campaigns in favour of marriage and adoption/fertility rights also alienated many queer activists, who felt that the institutions of marriage and the family ought to be prime targets of the movement's critique, not ambitions in its struggle. Likewise, activists associated with Cassero would often speak scornfully of '*antagonisti*', those they believed to be on the fringes of the movement who were more interested in protest for protest's sake than in achieving any real progress.

This stark distinction was particularly evident with regard to Pride. I was introduced to the various disputes over what it meant, where it should be, who should participate, and how it should be structured, from the very first week of my fieldwork, and this meeting was only one intervention in a debate that had been ongoing for more than a year. Somewhat paradoxically, the organizers had upset many of the more radical activists in the city from the outset by deciding that it should take place in Bologna. This decision, I was told, was a consequence of internal disputes within Arcigay over which local chapter wielded the most power: 2012 was the thirtieth anniversary of Cassero's founding, and, it was alleged, holding the national Pride celebrations in

Bologna provided its leadership with the opportunity to showcase their successes, after a previous attempt to celebrate its twenty-fifth anniversary in 2007 had run into opposition from Rome. It would also, some ungenerously suggested, fill the coffers of Cassero's disco. Precisely because of the movement's success in Bologna however, most of the people present at the meeting that night believed the choice was mistaken: why hold a political demonstration or a protest march, they reasoned, in a city that was already an 'island utopia' for the community? That is not, of course, everybody's definition of Pride: for many – such as some in Cassero – it is precisely the opposite, a party to which everybody, gay or straight, is invited, and its success is measured in how far it dissolves the distinction between participants and spectators. But for most of those present at this meeting, Pride was about making a difference in a different way – by making difference visible against a background of normalcy, as well as by calling attention to what they saw as deep-seated economic and social injustices in Italy. For them, the decision to hold Pride in Bologna was taken as yet further evidence for the fact that Cassero did not, in fact, consider it to be a political demonstration, but merely an opportunity to celebrate itself. In addition, there was already a degree of bad blood between the groups following the national Pride held in Bologna in 2008, during which an activist who had crossed security barriers in order to unfurl a banner critical of the commercial aspects of Pride had been arrested, apparently at the direction of the Cassero leadership.

Sara, the recently elected Vice-President of Cassero, denied to me that the choice of Bologna was determined by the thirtieth anniversary celebrations. Instead, she argued, Bologna was put forward precisely because, at a moment of crisis for the movement in which there was so much division and disagreement, a Pride for which everyone could pull together might serve as a broader call to unity, and that this was most likely happen in a city like Bologna.

On this particular evening, however, it did not look likely at all. Indeed, precisely because the city played host to such a diverse array of groups and organizations, satisfying each of them was going to prove no easy task. Prior to my arrival in Italy, Marina had told me, Cassero had been trying to co-opt their network into participating in an official capacity, overtures which had so far been rejected; indeed, there had even been talk of a boycott.

Another significant factor in the opposition to the 2012 Pride amongst many of my interlocutors was the way in which it was structured and designed. Pride, I was often told, 'is not just a party'. In organizing this meeting, Marina told me, their aim was to try to bring 'actual political content' to Pride, such as connecting it to Italy's economic crisis, and the problems of unemployment and precarity affecting many of the nation's younger generation (see e.g. Molé 2010, 2012a, 2012b, 2013a; Pipyrou 2014), as well as the 'Occupy' movement. Cassero came under fire not only for being insufficiently political however, but also for being political in the wrong way. Thirty years after its birth, Massimo declared at a subsequent meeting, it was now a pseudo-movement; no longer in its radical adolescence, it was instead an adult and hence had become pathologically concerned with marriage, children and authority. It had declared this year's Pride a 'family Pride', much to Massimo's chagrin; 'the family', he declared, 'has always been something we've critiqued as an object that perpetuates normativity ... Cassero's political project is one of reaction: they're saying "we want to be like you"'. For Massimo and many of those involved with like-minded groups, the object of the movement ought to be the foundation of new modes of relation, not its subsumption into a society that had long rejected it. The 'integrative movement', as he called it, has failed, he said, so LGBTQ activism needs a focus that will not simply reproduce heterosexual norms. For him, this focus should be the broader problems of economic crisis and precarity.

All of which is not to suggest that the only division within the LGBTQ movement was that between Cassero and those at the meeting that evening. Indeed, the groups present that night were far from unanimous in their opinions on what to do about the problem of Pride. Neither were all the members of Marina and Massimo's network. Laura, for example, would often criticize what she saw as Massimo's obsession with Pride, arguing that it was stereotypical of what people meant when they referred to '*antagonisti*'. Employing his own vocabulary, she called it a 'politics of reaction', because it was entirely dependent on the 'mainstream' of the movement. Everything the network did was constructed in opposition to Cassero. She cited the example of a mass kiss-in Cassero had staged on Valentine's Day in anticipation of Pride. The network had been vocal in its opposition to it, purely because it was tenuously linked, via Cassero, with the struggle for marriage rights; what was next, she asked ironically, beating up gay people because Cassero opposed homophobic violence? She was also often critical of Massimo himself for what she perceived as his desire to take charge. The rhetoric surrounding the foundation of the network was that it was a loosely-defined and democratic association of like-minded groups, yet in practice, she pointed out, Massimo acted like he was its leader; he would use meetings as an opportunity to build consensus around his own point of view, rather than retaining the diversity of the various groups affiliated to the network. For all his talk of fluidity and flexibility, she claimed, what Massimo really wanted was to fix the network in his own image. Indeed, prior to the meeting of that night, Marina and Massimo had presented a manifesto to some representatives of the various groups in the network at a private meeting and had, according to Laura, been taken aback by the degree of opposition they encountered: for many of the network's members, a manifesto suggested a uniformity that did not exist. It was also, Laura highlighted, ironic that the only person with enough time on their hands – i.e. not struggling to survive in a string of part-time jobs – actually to write a manifesto about precarity and economic struggle was the only person with a permanent contract and a safe job with local government: Massimo.

Over a coffee a few days before the big spring meeting, Marina had defended the network – and, by implication, her and Massimo's implicit leadership of it

– from some of Laura's charges. 'The aim of the network', she told me, 'is to create a form of LGBTQ politics that is not just about recognition', one, she explained, echoing Massimo, that is not about saying 'we want to be like you', or 'we want to get married like you'. The groups that formed the network had often cooperated on these kinds of issues before, raising money and organizing events in spaces in which these ideas could be put into action (so not Cassero, she clarified). Generally, she said, the groups have a good relationship with one another, but not, she admitted, all the time. At that particular moment, she said, a degree of tension existed because everybody was finding it hard simply to survive, let alone to commit to activism. Referring to the same meeting Laura described above, she said there had been some issues about this recently. There was also, she conceded, not a great deal in common amongst the various groups within the network: some were queer feminists, whilst others were more commercial, and yet more were anarchists whose only interest was in practical action. MIT's involvement was still more complicated, given that it was an official institution and also a member of Cassero's Pride committee.

That evening at the Pride meeting, all of these groups and still more had come together to discuss what for many in the LGBTQ community is the most important event of the year. Precisely at issue that night however, as I hope I have made clear, was to what extent there was in fact such a thing as the LGBTQ community.

Butler in Bologna

By the time Marina got up to speak and officially open the discussion, the large back room of the bar was standing room only, with an unusually substantial group of people present. The focus of the meeting, Marina told us, was Pride, as we all knew, but it was not the Pride that Cassero would be organizing that June; it was instead 'real Pride', a more original, authentic and truer representation of what Pride should mean for us. It would put Pride (back) into the context of broader issues at stake in contemporary global politics, like the occupy movement, neoliberalism and economic crisis, through a series of video presentations and a subsequent discussion.[3]

The first video, she explained, would be an interview with Silvia Rivera, the American transgender rights activist, who had been present at the Stonewall Inn on the night of the 1968 riots. Rivera, in many ways, is emblematic of the issues that Marina and Massimo wanted to raise that night: though celebrated since her death in 2002 by many in the American LGBTQ community, her career as an activist was not without controversy. Her relationship to Cassero-like institutions (such as the Gay Activists Alliance) was strained at best, and she often fought publicly against what she saw as the 'mainstream' of the movement, and its tendency to exclude and marginalize transgender activists (see e.g. Retzloff 2007). This interview, Marina claimed, would help us to critique the idea of a non-radical Pride, in which 'real difference' is not properly displayed; sure enough, the focus of the interview was Rivera's memories of Stonewall, particularly on the violent aspects of the riot, and in it she argued that many in the gay community fail to understand what Stonewall really meant because they lack respect for what she called 'radical difference'.

After two more video presentations – both of Judith Butler, one in which she refused a prize from the organizers of a Christopher Street Day parade in Berlin and accused them of racism, and another of her speaking at an Occupy event in Washington – Massimo concluded their introduction by emphasizing that these videos were evidence for the fact that Pride is an intrinsically radical event, and that it ought to relate to wider issues of economic inequality.

Butler is an idol to many in the community, particularly those – such as Massimo and Marina – who feel that the 'mainstream' LGBTQ movement is no longer sufficiently radical in its politics. Her speech in the first video exemplified an approach to authority with which they feel a great deal of sympathy: the Berlin Christopher Street Day parade is one of the largest LGBTQ events in Europe, and has long been the target of critique for being too commercial and for being patronized by local and national politicians (e.g. Schwab 2005); in her refusal of the organizers' award, Butler claimed that 'some of the organizers made explicitly racist statements or did not dissociate themselves from them' (Butler 2010). After citing the names of groups whom she believed were more deserving of recognition because of their involvement in anti-racism LGBTQ campaigns, Butler closed by noting that all of them were members of an 'alternative' Christopher Street Day group that, 'as opposed to the commercial CSD', did not change the date of its parade in deference to a World Cup football match that was taking place in the city at the same time.

When Massimo had concluded the presentation, he opened the floor to discussion. After a somewhat awkward silence, Gaia got up and walked to the stage, taking the microphone from Marina. In her early sixties, Gaia cuts an imposingly matriarchal figure, and has long been a well-known fixture in the city's LGBTQ community. Gaia has also been an outspoken proponent of gay marriage and adoption rights. That evening she was the only person in the room with a seat on Cassero's official Pride committee, and she began her intervention by making it clear that she was speaking in that capacity. LGBTQ activism, she said, will always be complicated; there will always be political struggles internal to the movement, especially over big events such as Pride. But, she argued, in the end Pride is a space in which to put forward demands – such as anti-discrimination and anti-homophobia laws, one of Cassero's least controversial political objectives. She concluded by highlighting the fact that the 2012 Pride would be dedicated to the memory of Marcella di Folco, the beloved former President of MIT, the transgender rights organization. As a man, di Folco was an actor and had worked with a number of well-known directors including Federico Fellini and Roberto Rossellini; after undergoing a sex change operation in 1980, she became one of the founding members of MIT, and from 1988 until her death in 2010 was its President, as well as a local councillor in Bologna. In gesturing to her, Gaia was calling upon the memory of a unifying figure in the movement, and directly followed this invocation by declaring that 'in the end, we all ask for the same thing', that what ought to be of interest is not internal political struggles but what will bring us forward: rights.

However, even as Gaia was speaking, it became clear that Massimo was not going to allow her speech to pass uncommented on; visibly disagreeing with her call to unity, he began to speak as soon as she had concluded: after a brief genuflection to di Folco, and an acknowledgement that he and Gaia might perhaps agree on some things, he said that it was absolutely not true that 'we all want the same thing', and that not everyone cast the struggle in terms of rights (see e.g. Berlant and Warner 1998; Rahman and Jackson 1997). 'Not everyone here', he said gesturing to the crowd, 'wanted this Pride to happen in Bologna, and many of us thought it could be more useful elsewhere'; 'but', he continued, 'this Pride is wounded, not dead'. The mainstream movement, however, he claimed, no longer has anything to say about 'real difference', and this was exactly what was needed. Gaia shook her head sadly, and went back to her seat.

In a subsequent interview, Gaia explained her perspective on the movement's divisions; they made her very unhappy, she said, particularly because she did not believe them to be the result of real political differences. Instead, she argued, they emerged out of the desire of some individuals – often men, she noted – to be leaders, and from the kinds of internal power struggles that characterize parliamentary politics in Italy. She understood that the *antagonisti* did not care about getting married; neither did she, but she would still fight for someone else's right to have the choice. Getting bogged down over such things meant that the movement would struggle to achieve its aims, which she saw as full civil rights and an end to discrimination.

Later that week I met up with Laura again, and we talked a little about her impressions of the meeting; it was, she felt, a demonstration of some of the problems of Marina and Massimo's network, in the sense that despite the rhetoric of democracy and an equal voice for all, the evening was hardly very participative, with almost all the talking done by Marina and Massimo. And whilst she said that she disagreed with Gaia about what the movement has in common – it may have some common aims, she acknowledged, but it does not have common methods of realizing them – the fact that Gaia was the only representative from Cassero made the entire debate extremely one-sided. Massimo, she added, had no right to talk so loftily about difference, when what he really wanted was conformity to his own obsession with transgression.

The disagreements described in the meeting above are not, of course, unique to this particular context. Naisargi Dave (2011, 2012), for example, describes a set of very similar dynamics amongst Indian lesbian activists regarding choices over what kinds of identity to present publicly, how 'political' to be, and what sort of relationship to have with institutions such as NGOs and local government. One group she describes eschews the word 'lesbian' in favour of a 'more authentic, more Indian sexual subjectivity for those women who needed a safe space of anonymity and social exploration, rather than a Westernized politics of identity' and 'sought its inclusion in society through the trope of innocence, replacing the lesbian as a sexual activist with the Indian same-sex desiring (but not acting) woman as a thing of and in danger. Another 'sought its – and India's – place within a transnational politics and market of lesbian identification' and thus 'devalued desire and feeling and emphasized the importance of political competence and dialogue'. Yet another 'rejected funding in an attempt to be autonomous of market-driven agendas' and 'thought itself open to everyone, regardless of sex, gender, and sexuality' (2012: 91).

Perhaps a closer analogy is to be found in the seminal ethnography of lesbian feminist groups in London by Sarah Green (1997). Green vividly describes how the emergence of a 'politics of difference' in contrast to 'identity politics' in the late 1980s led the lesbian 'community' to become increasingly fractured. Green depicts the conflicts that took place between radical feminists and those they termed (pejoratively) 'libertarian feminists' over subjects like sadomasochism and pornography. Whilst both groups concurred – at least in theory – that gender and sexual identities were constructed, for the former there remained an idea that beneath the subject constructed by heteropatriarchy there existed a more 'authentic', 'real' identity, whilst for the latter all forms of difference were constructed, and there was nothing 'more real' to excavate beneath such constructions – they were constructivists *stricto sensu*, in Candea's terms (n.d.: 6). For radical feminists, that residue of an authentic female identity 'meant all women had something in common, which could serve as the basis for forming a community. The "politics of difference" cast considerable doubt on that assumption: all identities are constructions' (Green 1997: 98).

'[T]hat somewhat shadowy word that appears to mean everything and nothing', is how Green describes difference (1997: 163). As I have noted already, difference is a common concern for both anthropologists and LGBTQ activists. Indeed, the transition Green describes as taking place amongst London-based lesbian activists, from an identity politics based largely around a binary and fixed concept of gender to a politics of difference in which the latter is constructed and ubiquitous, was not of course unique to them. On the one hand, it was playing out in the pages of academic journals and newspapers in the feminist 'sex wars' of the 1980s (see e.g. Rubin 1984). More broadly, difference, as she goes on to point out, was 'also a central term in postmodernist debate' (Green 1997: 163). Indeed, one of the things that should make her ethnography of such interest to contemporary anthropological debates about difference is that in it one can see a microcosmic version of debates that were – and to some extent are – ongoing in the discipline, as well as the recursive influence of anthropology on European thought regarding gender and sexuality. As she makes clear, it was at least in part ethnographic insights about different ways of thinking about categories like 'woman' and 'lesbian' that led to the critique of their 'authenticity' and use in a rigid and fixed manner.

I say that influence was recursive because at the same moment that anthropology was impacting upon Green's interlocutors' understandings of identity and difference, the discipline itself was undergoing a similar shift, itself affected by the postmodern turn to deconstruction. Throughout the late 1970s and 1980s, and drawing on the broader philosophical movement of post-structuralism, a disciplinary orthodoxy developed to wit that identity and difference are only ever relational and constructed (for a brief overview see Candea n.d.: 4). This is evident, for example, in reviews of literature on the subject of gender and sexuality in anthropology by Weston (1993), Morris (1995), and Boellstorff (2007).

That proposition is also – largely speaking – hegemonic, at least at the level of rhetoric, amongst queer activists of the sort with whom I worked. Indeed, it is intrinsic to the very concept of 'queer', which, had it been in use at the time of Green's fieldwork, might perhaps have been how her 'libertarian feminists' would have self-described. Coined by Teresa de Lauretis at a conference in 1990 (De Lauretis 1991), and popularized through the work of, amongst others, Judith Butler, 'queer' carries with it the same repudiation of fixed identity categories that animated the opponents of radical feminism in the 1980s, along with the same valorization of identity 'play', through sadomasochism, for example (see also van de Port 2012). It was a ubiquitous term throughout the period of my fieldwork.

Yet, as the opening sections of this chapter make clear (and see also Sullivan-Blum 2006; van de Port 2012), there are often differences, as it were, over difference within Bologna's LGBTQ community. Indeed, it is differences over difference that put its status as a community occasionally in doubt. Is the purpose of LGBTQ activism, as the title of a conference Laura often referenced derogatively goes, 'all different, all equal'? Or is it to uncover and promote the 'radical difference' that Massimo referred too? Similarly, as I will go on to suggest in later chapters, although the basic metaphysical premise of difference as a relation continues to underpin anthropological studies of topics related to identity, such as gender, sexuality or ethnicity, it has not been without its critics, particularly within the last decade.

Difference Politics

As I have suggested, LGBTQ activism in Bologna is, I argue, about 'making difference'. But it is so in a broader sense than that suggested by the cliché. Clearly it is to some extent about making some alteration to the current state of affairs in Italy with regard to the status of a number of social, political and economic issues. But it is also about something more.

As I noted earlier, a fundamental insight of post-'writing culture' anthropology is that difference is not a found object in the world, but the product of a process of performance or construction, whether that process takes place purely on the part of those we study, or, as in some American variants, in dialogue with the ethnographer. That insight, as I will argue later, persists today, in spite of the occasional critique.

What I describe here, on the other hand, is a case in which it is precisely the constructed nature of difference that is a found object in the world. I will explore the implications of this for anthropological theorizing on difference below, but for the moment I want to draw out exactly what this means.

The battle that Green describes taking place in London in the 1980s is still ongoing in some areas. In Constance Sullivan-Blum's work on the polarized nature of debate on gay marriage in the United States in the early 2000s for example, a fascinating contrast is visible between some advocates of gay marriage who cast homosexuality as given by God or nature, and some evangelical opponents who see it as a choice (2006; and see van de Port 2012: 865). Writing in the 1990s, Rahman and Jackson identify a similar tendency on the part of large gay rights organizations to essentialism in their activism (1997). Both however are also exemplars of how widespread the turn to 'queer theory' had become by the early 2000s, as both find in a repudiation of fixed identities a solution to their respective 'problems'.

The same was largely true in my field-site, particularly amongst the younger generation of activists with whom I worked, of whom almost all would self-identify as queer. Cassero as an institution was somewhat ambiguous on the topic. The website of Arcigay, for example, describes Pride as 'an affirmation of our differences, and of all difference' (Arcigay 2013), and its constitution pledges to struggle for 'the equality of all individuals, with full respect for and valorization of the diversity and difference of every individual' (Cassero 2010), in language that at least implicitly suggests a certain form of essentialism.

The activists upon whom this book is focused, however, as I have said, were committed to an anti-essentialist understanding of gender and sexuality; and yet, as I have also noted, the community could occasionally seem fractured and deeply divided.

To explain this, an analogy with Simon Harrison's work may be helpful. Harrison, in a series of wide-ranging reflections, describes how, paradoxically, in their assertions of their distinctiveness, communities often draw on similar kinds of explanations (2003, 2006). Thus, he notes that in Schneider's work on understandings of ethnicity in America, Jewish-Americans and Irish-Americans both ascribe their differences from others to the influence of the Jewish or Irish mother; hence in their understandings of their distinctiveness, 'they were indistinguishable' (2003: 344).

A similar dynamic was at play, I suggest, amongst queer activists in Bologna, although in a somewhat more complex fashion. What they shared was a common understanding of the origins and nature of their difference – both from one another, and from the wider world – not as given, but in processes of performance or construction. Where they differed was precisely in the effects of such processes – the differences they produced. Unlike in the example from Schneider however, this tension between difference and identity is not incidental but intrinsic to the logic involved, hence the added layer of complexity: Harrison famously uses such examples to argue that beneath difference there is usually an underlying denied resemblance (for a critique see Strathern 2011). It is impossible to draw such a conclusion from my own material however, given that what is agreed upon amongst my interlocutors is that there can be no such thing as underlying resemblances.

To summarize, the problem runs as follows: how can you build a community out of people who see difference as ubiquitous and understand their activism to involve the constant enactment of such difference?

This is the problem, in different forms, faced by both Cassero and Massimo: the former, as Sara described, chose Bologna as a site for the Pride of 2012 in order to find something that would unite a movement riven with division and disagreement; yet in their attempt to do so they – predictably – caused yet more division and disagreement on the part of people like Massimo who felt that this 'unity' came at the cost of promoting 'real difference'. Recall also his comments regarding Cassero's 'politics of reaction', and the critiques he and Marina made of its purported desire to subsume LGBTQ identity into 'normality'. But at the same time Massimo himself was seeking to build some form of consensus around his own position: the very notion of 'real' or 'radical' difference suggests a fixed identity to which he hoped those at the meeting might subscribe. But in a microcosm of his own disagreement with Cassero, he found himself accused by Laura and others of smothering debate and alternative positions, in spite of his rhetoric about building a democratic network, or having his motives questioned by people like Gaia. Similarly, Laura's accusations regarding his own 'politics of reaction' highlight the way in which he appeared to privilege one kind of difference – that between his own 'real' difference and that exemplified by Cassero – over all others. When 'making a difference' – in the literal sense of permanently enacting a difference that is understood to be ubiquitous – is what defines your identity, then it is unsurprisingly difficult to solidify that identity at any kind of communitarian level.

As readers will notice however, that last sentence is a paradox: in suggesting that 'making a difference', in the sense of understanding difference as produced and producing that difference, is what defines queer activism in Bologna I have of course slipped into the language of identity politics. But that is precisely the tension I am seeking to draw out: Massimo, the young activists of Cassero like Sara, and all those at the meeting who disagreed with one or both, do share a common understanding of difference, and it is precisely this common understanding that does allow them to emerge occasionally as a community, in opposition to those who do not understand difference in this way. In other words, insofar as there exists a solution to the problem of how to build a community around the idea of difference as ubiquitous, it creates a new problem: how to reconcile the existence of such a community with the central tenet that actually holds it together, namely that difference is produced and produced all the time. A belief in 'making a difference' as what 'makes them different' from one another is also what makes them the same.

Strategic Anti-Essentialism

This becomes clearer if we examine the events of Pride itself. Pride, of course, did take place in Bologna in 2012, despite the concerns of many LGBTQ activists; and despite their opposition to its location and to its theme and lack of appropriate political content, many of them participated in the march. Marina and Massimo led a troop of activists – dressed distinctively but not uniformly in ragged style – playing musical instruments and draped in homemade banners calling for an end to economic precarity. Though it may not have been 'different' enough for their tastes, Pride was – unsurprisingly – a showcase of

Figure 4.1. 'Surrender to love'. Photograph by Paolo Heywood.

difference in many respects: there was a cardboard tank decorated with pink velour and a sign that said 'surrender to love', and the city's Mayor, who spoke in favour of civil unions on the main stage shortly after Gaia. That year's Pride was also different from earlier years, as the money that would normally have been devoted to floats had instead been sent in aid to the victims of an earthquake that had recently struck the region.

The big day itself, preceded by weeks of events, meetings and parties, began at around 2 PM at Porta Saragozza, one of the city's old medieval gates. Arrayed on a grassed area around it in preparation for the march were an enormous range of groups with a variety of different costumes and banners. There was, I was a little surprised to note, a large police presence, although this seemed to dissipate as the march began and I saw fewer and fewer men in uniform (of that variety, anyway) as the day went on. Uniforms, or costumes, of different sorts were ubiquitous however, and in the march's early stages it was easy enough to tell who was a spectator and who was a participant partly because most of the former were in matching t-shirts or other forms of clothing, and partly because a fairly firm dividing line between the parade on the road and viewers on the pavement was maintained.

By the time we arrived in the main square however, at around 7 PM, the physical divisions between marchers and those observing had long since dissipated. The piazza was completely packed, and it was a struggle to get anywhere near the stage, where Gaia had just finished speaking. After the mayor's speech, we made our way through the crowds to the nearby Piazza Verdi, a regular hang-out for activists and students, and the starting point for some of the evening's festivities. A number of outdoor bars had been set up in addition to the usual indoor ones, and the square was covered by tables full of people eating and drinking. Though earlier there had been some families in evidence along the parade route, by this point, around 9 PM, only young people were present, and already talk of subdivisions between the groups had begun. Cassero, for example, had organized a large party to take place in a park a little way outside the centre. As Federica, Maria, Laura, Alessia and the rest of the group I was with discussed whether or not to go (there was predictably little enthusiasm), a nearby man in dreadlocks (whom Laura later identified to me as another disgruntled former member of Cassero) interrupted us to describe his visions of Cassero higher-ups gleefully rubbing their hands at all the money they would be making tonight, which was greeted with general merriment and approval. In the end I followed the majority of my regular interlocutors to another location, where Massimo had organized one of a number of 'alternative' Pride parties.

To what extent was it possible to identify and delimit an LGBTQ 'community' of any form during this Pride? Clearly in part it was an opportunity for a range of groups and individuals that broadly interest themselves in LGBTQ-related activism to come together physically for a day and to demonstrate – in spite of their differences – a degree of unity, as Cassero wished. But unity in the face of what? If something like a community was more or less stable, though momentarily, what formed its borders?

In terms of its beginning and end, the answer is relatively straightforward: the initial preponderance of an 'official' parade was clear both from the distinctive clothing many of the marchers wore, and from the fact that a barrier – and sometimes physical barriers – separated those marching from dour looking police officers and the occasional bemused-looking elderly person; and by the time we had reached Piazza Verdi and the day's closing stages (for many activists the most important part of Pride) the crowd looked much the same as any other LGBTQ party in the square. But obviously not all in the crowd of onlookers were simply spectators, something that became more than clear when the boundary between roads and the pavement evaporated and the streets became an indiscriminate mass of colour and movement. Was it in any sense possible to delineate within this mass the boundaries of something like the queer activist 'community' of Bologna?

Obviously the answer is no; and yet whilst clear borders between 'queer' and 'not queer' may not have emerged, there are still senses in which it was possible to distinguish those who were more likely to identify as 'queer' than others. Take my friend Federica, for example: for as long as I have known her she has been involved in heterosexual relationships with men. Yet for the same political and personal reasons as many other young people with an interest in the politics of sexuality, she would rather self-identify as 'queer' than 'straight'. That day she was not due to take part in any of the sections of the parade, as she belonged to no group in particular. By the time the distinction between marchers and spectators had dissolved however, she and I were in the midst of the crowd. She wore no uniform, and in that respect looked no different to anybody else in the streets.

What she had done however was draw a thin moustache above her lips with an eyebrow pencil: a tiny gesture, but one replete with meaning. Not only did it serve to make her noticeable – and different – from anyone else in the crowd, it did so in an ideally 'queer' way, by destabilizing her gender identity and transforming her into a strikingly beautiful androgynous figure, as in Sontag's description of 'camp' as 'love of the unnatural: of artifice and exaggeration' (1990: 280 cited in van de Port 2012).

Laura is another case in point: though I have only known her to have relationships with other women, she self-identifies as 'queer', rather than 'lesbian', because, as she would often tell me, she believes that desire has priority over any attempt to fix the nature of the desired object. The night of Pride, in contrast to others with short spiky hair or leather clothing, Laura, as always, wore her hair long, had bright red lipstick on, and – again making her immediately noticeable and different from anyone else in the crowd – had put on a luxurious dressing gown, the symbolic meaning of which it is unnecessary to describe.

The fact that a woman should paint a moustache on, wear a dressing gown to a party, or have a fling with someone of the same sex despite being habitually heterosexual, will not sound surprising to anybody remotely familiar with queer activism (see van de Port 2012 for a non-activist comparison). These are simply minor examples of some of the many things that make those who identify with queer politics different from those who do not; this is clear also in

Angela's description from the beginning of this chapter of what makes 'queer' groups like SexyShock different from others – it is, as it were, their lack of uniformity that makes them uniform. This is nowhere more evident than on the day of Pride.

In other words, although it is impossible to distinguish in any clear sense a community of queer activists in Bologna, even on the day of the year that they are most visible, there are things that make them different from others, and one of those things is precisely the way in which they think about difference. Painting on a moustache and wearing a dressing gown to a nightclub are enactments of this way of thinking – they literally make a difference between oneself and others. Hence the tension I described earlier: difference is both what makes them different from one another – because it is understood to be a ubiquitous construction – but also different from others (and therefore the same) – because others do not think about difference this way.

Is it really the case that non-queer activists do not think of difference this way? That question is difficult for me to answer, as my fieldwork was largely spent with those who self-identified as queer. Needless to say, the last thing I want to do at this point is to contrast those with whom I worked with a spectral 'Euro-American' logic, and to discover that they are the point-for-point opposite.

Thankfully however, I do not have to do this work, because it has already been done for me. I noted earlier the similarities in the trajectories of queer thought and anthropology (see also e.g. Strong 2010). Just as they share perspectives on the constructed nature of difference, so they also share an object with which they contrast themselves. They do not call it 'Euro-American thought', they call it other things – 'heteronormativity', or 'cisnormativity', or 'cisgendered', the latter two having been specifically invented in order to mark this hitherto unmarked category, in exactly the way in which anthropologists have come to use 'Euro-America' as a catch-all term. Again, in the absence of fieldwork data I make no empirical claim as to whether those categories have meaning in Bologna – only that for queer activists in the city, as elsewhere, they stand for difference from themselves; this is also evident from merely a glance at the queer literature canon, a good portion of which is polemical and puts itself in opposition to precisely these categories of thought, many of them similar to those which anthropologists class as 'Euro-American'. But, of course, defining oneself in opposition to something is still a way of defining oneself.

Conclusion

Tensions between group and individual identities are of course not uncommon, and they are certainly not so within the sphere of LGBTQ activism, as both Green and Dave demonstrate. What I suggest is particular to the situation I describe here though is the fact that this tension itself revolves around the notion of difference. It is precisely the idea that difference is constructed together with an ethical commitment to produce such difference that makes queer activists in Bologna look more or less the same. As I will discuss in later chapters, this tension resembles – but also differs from – the tension in anthropology that emerges around the notion of 'strategic essentialism', first proposed by Gayatri Spivak as a way of accounting for the persistent power of identity in spite of its deconstruction (1988). The term has since come in for a range of criticism, and it is not my intention to engage with it in great depth here. What I wish to point out though is the presupposition of which it is by definition guilty: that the 'essentialism' it describes is only 'strategic'. When used in description it foregrounds, in other words, the concept of a fixed identity, but it does so only by tacitly assuming that such fixed identities are really only chimera, an assumption that usually reappears in analysis (cf. Sylvain 2014: 8).

I raise this issue not because I wish to suggest that a form of 'strategic essentialism' is at work in the tension I have described amongst queer activists; quite the reverse, in fact. What I wish to argue is that whilst the idea of strategic essentialism foregrounds a notion of identity in order to reassert an underlying politics of difference, what happens with regard to queer activism in Bologna is that a politics of difference is put in the foreground in order – at least occasionally – to fix a kind of identity. It is, as it were, a kind of 'strategic anti-essentialism'.

In proposing this idea my intention is not to suggest that there is a more 'authentic' identity politics at work beneath the ideas about difference which dominate queer activism in Bologna, for this would be to commit the equivalent sin of which the idea of 'strategic essentialism' is guilty, privileging one side of the tension over the other. Neither do I opt for another obvious anthropological solution, which would be to re-describe the whole situation within a meta-framework of performativity; essentialism and anti-essentialism both thus become two sides of the same (performative) coin, either to be deployed as and when is convenient. It should be unnecessary to point out that this coin is loaded. In characterizing essentialism as performative, it returns us to an idea of 'strategy' or choice which cannot but be antithetical to the very idea of essentialism, and simply stating otherwise, or adding the word 'radical' to the notion of performativity, will not resolve this problem.

My aim here instead is merely to describe a paradox which is to some extent constitutive of queer activism in Bologna, namely that of producing identity out of the production of difference;[4] and, in subsequent chapters, to connect that paradox to a similar one in contemporary anthropological thought about difference.

Notes

1. I use the term 'strategic' as it evokes Spivak's (1988) concept of 'strategic essentialism' (see below). 'Tactical' would be equally appropriate, if not more so, given that I am referring to the effect of the deployment of anti-essentialism in specific contexts, rather than more broadly.
2. To give it its full title, a *centro sociale occupato autogestito* (CSOA) is the Italian term for a global phenomenon in which a space is employed for use by a community, often, at least in Italy, of activists. They are commonly abandoned buildings, and may be occupied illegally or given over for use by the local authority.
3. It is notable that Marina assumed – safely, in all likelihood – that everyone in the room would more or less share the same perspective on these broader issues.
4. Or truth out of falsity, in van de Port's terms (2012).

Part III

5

Why Will Recursivity Run Out of Steam?

The title of this chapter deliberately echoes the now famous critique of critique by Bruno Latour in *Critical Inquiry* (2004). That piece was a polemical and highly influential intervention in the field of science studies (and beyond) in which Latour argued that the analytical weaponry with which his colleagues were equipping their students was out of date, and ill-suited to fighting 'new threats, new dangers, new tasks, new targets' (2004: 225). Critique, he argued, has run out of steam at least in part because it has rendered itself invulnerable to the operations it performs on its various objects. 'Better equipped than Zeus himself', Latour says of the critic, 'you rule alone, striking from above with the salvo of antifetishism in one hand and the solid causality of objectivity in the other' (2004: 239). But, he adds, 'The Zeus of Critique rules absolutely, to be sure, but over a desert' (2004: 239).

This third and final part of this book is written with similarly polemical, if also much more modest, intent. It is both polemical and modest because it is trapped, as it will suggest that much contemporary anthropology is, and in a manner similar to Latour's lonely Zeus of Critique, between two poles of argument: between making a particular, contingent and descriptive claim about some ethnography, and making a broader, more analytical and more general point about anthropology and anthropological theory.

'Trapped', the reader might imagine, is not the correct term for this condition. Indeed, some might argue (and have done, as I will set out below – see e.g. Holbraad 2017) that it is this peculiar combination of humility and grandiosity, of contingency and necessity, which provides anthropological claims with their distinctively anthropological character. Without it we run the risk of becoming 'butterfly-collectors' (Leach 1961: 2) or (bad) philosophers (Pedersen 2012). But what kind of a claim is that claim itself? If it is the distinctive claim of anthropology, then can it itself be contingent?

The purpose of these final two chapters will be to investigate precisely that question, by pushing that claim to its constitutive limit. Like some of the examples they will describe, the chapters themselves will be perched somewhat uncomfortably between a (polemical) analytical argument about the nature of the relationship between concepts and ethnographic data in anthropology, and a (modest) ethnographic argument about how my ethnographic data on the ethics of LGBTQ activism in Bologna may speak to this question in its own way. In order to make the distinction – the reason for which I hope will become clear – between the two poles as explicit as possible, the division between the two arguments will roughly correspond to the division between the two chapters.

The first chapter will attempt to articulate some of the frustration that contemporary answers to the question 'how should my analysis relate to my ethnography' may produce in anthropologists. Indeed, it will do so by experimenting with deliberately widening, rather than narrowing, the gap between ethnography and analysis precisely by posing this question independently of my ethnography of LGBTQ activism in Bologna. That is an unusual analytical move, I realize, but I hope the reasons I make it will be clear by the chapter's conclusion.

The second chapter, on the other hand, will make the reverse move by drawing out the connection between this question and my own ethnographic work (beyond the obvious fact that any anthropologist has to deal with it as a question in some manner or another). It will show how the ethnographic analysis I have laid out in previous chapters should enable me to challenge some of those contemporary answers provided to that question. Yet they do not. Trapped, as they are, within the same recursive logic of which they aim to be critical, they can only reinforce its basic contentions, and in doing so, fail. What I hope to reveal precisely in that failure though are the limits of recursivity, and an alternative language – or at least the point that there must be an alternative language – with which to answer the question posed.

The Problem

As I have mentioned, the concerns of this first chapter will be largely analytical. As such it will stand out somewhat from the rest of the book – the ethnographic basis of which I hope is clear – and may appear to some readers to be a curious if not outright unwarranted excursion away from the latter's central themes. For now, in its defence, let me reiterate that this is a deliberate and strategic decision; I hope it will be clear by the conclusion of Part Three of the book why I have gone to the trouble of making explicit the difference between its concerns and those of the others, but also why it is precisely in the explicit and strategically produced nature of that difference that an analogy may be drawn between the two. Whether or not that analogy should be drawn will be precisely the subject of that conclusion. In other words, to the question 'how does this relate to your ethnography', at least a part of my response is that the point of this chapter is to interrogate the conditions of possibility of asking that question, rather than presupposing its legitimacy.

This first chapter's major premise is that there seems to be a consensus, across a range of anthropological schools of thought, sometimes implicit but often – as in the primary example I treat in this chapter – explicit and well-theorized, about the fact that the best kind of anthropological analysis is that which is most difficult to distinguish from ethnography. That what we might once have thought of as 'anthropological theory' should not be considered different from ethnographic description, or perhaps from the theories of those whom we study. As Tim Ingold has recently noted, 'it has become commonplace – at least over the last quarter of a century – for writers in our subject to treat the two [anthropology and ethnography] as virtually equivalent' (2008: 69).

Indeed, the range of questions to which it is claimed that answers should be found not through abstract reasoning or 'model-theoretic apparatuses' (Faubion 2011) but in ethnography has expanded to include methodological and epistemological ones, such as how anthropology should understand translation (Viveiros de Castro 2004a), cultural change (Vilaça 2015), use examples (Krøjer 2015), generate politico-economic concepts (Jiménez and Willerslev 2007), and reinvigorate its notion of truth (Holbraad 2012), to name but a few. In fact, one of the few recent anthropological collections devoted specifically to epistemology is frequently concerned with claiming, as the argument of one of its contributors is described by the editors, that 'anthropology has no need of any epistemology other than ethnography' (Toren and Pina-Cabral 2011: 6).

This is roughly speaking what Candea and I elsewhere call 'ethnographic foundationalism' (forthcoming). That term is intended to denote the perception that what gives anthropological analysis its distinctive identity is its relationship to ethnographic material, rather than any particular epistemological bent or stance.

Ingold makes that remark about how easy it has become for us to equate ethnography with anthropology as part of an argument, subsequently repeated elsewhere (2014), for distinguishing between the two (2008; see also Cook 2016). Whilst that sounds rather similar on the surface to the purpose – widening, not narrowing, the gap between theory and ethnography – Ingold in fact identifies ethnography with 'descriptive or documentary aims ... which impose their own finalities on trajectories of learning, converting them into data-gathering exercises destined to yield "results," usually in the form of research papers or monographs' (2014: 390). Anthropology, on the other hand, is an 'ontological commitment ... to join in correspondence with those with whom we learn or among whom we study' (2014: 390). Arguing against theorizing from the armchair, Ingold claims that its 'paradox' 'is that in order to *know* one can no longer *be* in the world of which one seeks knowledge. But anthropology's solution, to ground knowing in being, in the world rather than the armchair, means that any study *of* human beings must also be a study *with* them' (2008: 83 italics in original).

Ingold, in other words, far from suggesting that there might be a difference between description and analysis, is arguing the reverse: any anthropological endeavour, he suggests, if 'it is to do justice to the implicate order of social life, can be neither descriptive nor theoretical in the specific senses constituted by their opposition. It must rather do away with the opposition itself' (2008: 81).

Ingold repeats this argument in a critique of Da Col and Graeber's proposal for something they call 'ethnographic theory', despite the fact that 'ethnographic theory' is also intended to stimulate 'ethnographically grounded, theoretically innovative engagements with the broadest possible geographic and thematic range' (2011: viii), as its name suggests. They come at the problem of theory in contemporary anthropology from the opposite direction to Ingold – disapproving of what they think of as the imposition of concepts from European philosophy onto ethnography, rather than of the cold, descriptive enterprise of data collection – but their solution is roughly the same: that 'theory' must be 'ethnographic'.

One suspects, in turn, that perhaps at least one example of the imputed imposition of European philosophical concepts onto ethnographic data that Da Col and Graeber have in mind is anthropology's recent interest in recursivity and ontology. This, as with Ingold's criticism of their own argument, is despite the fact that the notion of recursivity is explicitly premised on there existing a continuity between ethnographic data and anthropological concepts and on a critique of philosophical abstraction. So, for example, Henare et al. argue in the introduction to *Thinking Through Things* that 'instead of just adapting or elaborating theoretical perspectives ... to reconfigure the parameters of "our" knowledge to suit informants' representations of reality, [the ontological turn] opens the way for genuinely novel concepts to be produced out of the ethnographic encounter' (Henare et al. 2006: 8).

We have then a series of recent and influential reflections on the problem of how our observations and descriptions and our arguments and analyses should relate to one another, in which the response to that problem is not only identical, but is in fact identity, an identity between theory and ethnography. These arguments largely compete over who has best achieved this or whose method is most likely to do so, rather than about this principle itself.

Think, equally, of the analogy I suggested in my Introduction, between the idea that anthropology should be in the business of 'giving voice' to informants and Latour's far more empiricist injunction to 'just describe'. Whilst motivated by entirely different ideas, they share the certainty that there should be as little space as possible between the objects of our analysis and that analysis itself.

If in this chapter I will concern myself largely with recursivity rather than these versions of ethnographically foundationalist claims, or others such as Ingold's description of anthropology as 'philosophy with the people in it', or Da Col and Graeber's 'ethnographic theory', that is because the premises and conceptual architecture of the recursive turn are so clearly laid out; in this respect, far from misdirecting some more proper anthropological spirit, one might think of it as simply making explicit and seeking properly to justify what has long been implicit in our epistemological orientation.

So, in short: analysis should explain, represent, give voice to or just describe the ethnographic data with which it is paired. If it does not succeed in performing those or other related tasks, one is liable to find oneself a target of a fairly straightforward kind of anthropological critique which will highlight the fact that one has failed in relation to one's ethnography. Perhaps there is not enough of the latter to justify the conclusions drawn, or perhaps the conclusions drawn do not appear to reflect the evidence mustered in their favour. A classic example is ethnocentrism: applying categories or concepts to contexts in which they are not appropriate; the logic of the market does not explain the kula.

As a precept however, this only gets us so far. Granted that there ought to exist some kind of relationship between the concepts we employ and the ethnographic data with which we do so, this does not tell us what kind of relationship that ought to be.

One solution is to claim that the analytical concepts we employ are simply predicates of the things to which we apply them, and as long as this relationship holds there is no problem. Provided we can demonstrate that the kula is a type of gift economy, we have our answer to the question of what analytical concept to employ in describing it. This solution has the advantage of providing an unproblematic basis for comparisons: are notions of honour and shame, or the power of flutes, similar or different across the Mediterranean, or Melanesia (e.g. Blok 1981; Hays 1986)? The question is answerable insofar as we can determine the extent to which the ethnographic data in question shares or does not share the same attributes which describe our predicate.

A failure to provide the kind of analysis that will allow for comparison – or at least for discussion of some form at the level of abstract predicates like 'gift economy' or 'honour and shame' – can lead to a second kind of charge, of a different form to that described above, which, though less common, is just as cutting: to be parochial, to speak only to one's own ethnography, is to be, at best, boring, and at worst, not an anthropologist (Willerslev 2011; Ingold 2014). To label oneself or one's argument as 'Foucauldian', 'structuralist' or 'Strathernian', or even post-, anti-, or non- any -ism or -ian is to put oneself or one's argument in conversation with a wider body of work. That such conversation, about related – in some way or another – issues, is both possible and necessary in anthropology is as much of a truism as it is to state that such conversations must in some way be based upon empirical data.

But this returns us to our original problem, of how exactly that 'based upon empirical data' is supposed to function. Let us call the first solution provided above, of abstracting analytical concepts as predicates from objects, 'pluralist', in line with Holbraad and Pedersen's recent characterization of it, which draws heavily on the work of Marilyn Strathern (Holbraad and Pedersen 2009).

As Holbraad and Pedersen point out, the imaginary upon which this understanding of the relation between analysis and its objects is built is one of a world composed of things: many, many things, in fact, 'an inordinately large field of data', as they put it (2009: 373). The pluralist solution to the problem of how to get a handle on this vast array of anthropological objects is that already outlined – collecting and organizing them according to predicates they do or do not share. Probably the most obvious instance of this activity is the notion of culture, in which objects are organized into bounded units that can, broadly speaking, be mapped onto particular territories.

This imaginary has been subject to repeated and withering critique since the early 1980s, most famously through the insights of the 'writing culture' movement and its associates (e.g. Clifford and Marcus 1986). I will not dwell at great length on these criticisms here, firstly because they are now exceedingly well-known, but also because whilst as critical insights they have a taken for granted status in contemporary anthropology, their proposed solutions appear to have fallen by the wayside, at least on the British side of the Atlantic. They thus have only a limited place in this – again, partial – narrative.

The basic insight of the 'writing culture' movement with respect to anthropological categories seen as abstract predicates was that those categories themselves are not, in fact, abstract, but just as 'cultural' as the objects they are supposed to organize. The chimera of 'distance' they provide between the anthropologist's analysis and his ethnographic data is just that: a chimera. As Holbraad and Pedersen put it, in the post-structuralist imaginary 'all categories are by definition cultural because they always come from somewhere' (2009: 377). That includes, of course, even the category of 'culture' itself, at least in any particular instance, and hence the consequent impossibility of bounding anthropological objects within a particular territorial location (e.g. Marcus and Fischer 1986). As I have noted however, though these epistemological critiques were virtual truisms by the time I began my graduate studies thirty or so years later, the putative solutions these same authors provided were much less in vogue. Quite the contrary, in fact: as Holbraad notes of his own graduate training, 'reflexivity' – perceived at least as an obsessive insistence on deconstructing one's own ethnographic authority in favour of 'dialogue' – had already by then fallen out of fashion (Holbraad 2012: 30).

At this stage, it makes sense briefly to pause in relating this narrative as we have reached the point from which this account – and, perhaps, many others of its generation, implicitly at least – departs. To return to Latour's military analogy, by the time I and my cohort arrived for basic training, we already had some preconceived ideas about what we were about to be trained to face, and what form that training would take – or rather, what form it would not take. We knew, for example, that some weapons once available to our superiors were now banned from the field: 'positivism' in its various guises was deemed archaic and possibly unethical. But likewise, 'dialogue', 'text' and 'postmodernism' were all also unlikely to form part of our conceptual arsenal.

The reasons for the absence of the latter set of ideas are varied. Certainly, some excesses of auto-critique put off many. The one I wish to focus on here however relates to the conflicts for which we were being trained, because, I suggest, epistemologically speaking they remain largely unchanged, in contrast to the way in which different generations of students have been pre-pared to face them. We must still somehow account for our ethnographic data with our analysis, and we must still do so in a manner that allows us to speak to one another. 'Reflexivity', in its excesses, or their portrayal, retreated from the field of battle when it came to the first of those aims. As Holbraad puts it, 'the original remit of anthropology – the exciting prospect of making sense of sociocultural phenomena the world over – was lost' (2012: 30).

So, imagine yourself in our position: of knowing (vaguely, at least) what it is that we must do as anthropologists-to-be, namely to collect ethnographic data and then to do something with it that would interest our peers and supe-riors; but knowing also that most if not all extant meta-arguments for how exactly to 'do something with ethnography' that would both account for it in some way and also connect it to those of our colleagues were understood to be fundamentally flawed.

The Recursive Solution

That situation may have been the point of departure for many of my generation of (British) anthropologists as we began our training, but as that training has progressed a new set of conceptual resources has emerged that specifically sets out to address that problem. Needless to say, I do not mean to imply that in the intervening period there have been no other attempts to deal with the relation between ethnography and analysis, or that the absence of such attempts makes for bad anthropology. I suggest simply – again from a partial perspective – that for the most part this problem has been dealt with largely implicitly. Ethnographic data has still been accounted for; connections have still been made across the discipline. But what we have not possessed is a deliberate and explicit account of how that occurs, only the fragments of approaches that we no longer have complete faith in (positivism, reflexivity, etc.).

The approach that I will describe as 'recursive', in line with the clearest and most programmatic statements of its method and intent (e.g. Holbraad 2012, 2013; Pedersen 2012), explicitly seeks to fill that explanatory gap. It presup-poses some of the insights described above, which might be drawn either from the 'writing culture movement', or, as in this case, from the work of Strathern and others (e.g. Viveiros de Castro 2003; Wagner 1975). Here I want to high-light two such insights, which are not in and of themselves contentious, and in fact lead proponents of recursive approaches in anthropology to treat the question with which this chapter is principally concerned. The first is the basic Durkheimian presupposition that cultural categories are variable; the second is the recognition that anthropological categories are also contingent, and no more abstract than the ethnographic objects they describe. Hence the neces-sity of treating the problem of how to describe categorical variability.

As I have already noted, the 'writing culture' solution to this problem is – or at least is characterized as – the deconstruction of anthropological categories until (it is hoped) they somehow possess the same epistemological status as those to be investigated, thus allowing for a 'dialogue', of some form, but refusing the possibility of explanation or real description: 'making sense of', in Holbraad's terms.

The recursive turn in anthropology provides a different solution. Rather than assuming that – in spite of their acknowledged variability – cultural categories as ethnographic objects can be explained in terms of our own (the Durkheimian solution) or at least put in some form of dialogue with our own (the 'writing culture' solution), it proposes instead that when we encounter a situation of conceptual or categorical alterity we acknowledge it as such.[1] Such a situation, incidentally, can occur anywhere and everywhere. The claim is not that alterity is an object in the world; it is instead alleged to be a consequence of our conceptual poverty (Holbraad 2012, 2017). A classic and oft-cited example is the Nuer assertion that twins are birds (e.g. Carrithers et al. 2010). The pre-writing culture solution would be to render this as a belief or a metaphor (our category, not theirs), as indeed Evans-Pritchard did – or at least is alleged to have done (1956: 131–32; see also Evens 2012; Littlejohn 1970); the writing culture solution – in its caricatured form – would be to assert that our own assumption that twins are not in fact birds is merely an assumption, and cultural and contingent as such, without telling us much about what the Nuer mean when they claim the reverse. By contrast, proponents of the recursive turn argue that if we encounter something that we cannot explain with our own concepts without rendering it foolish or absurd, that is evidence for nothing other than the tautology that we simply lack the conceptual resources with which to explain it adequately. Hence a different solution is required.

For an example of that solution the obvious place to look is to its thus far clearest and most schematized example, namely the work of Martin Holbraad on Cuban divination, in which a cogent and coherent programme for recursive anthropology is set out (Holbraad 2009, 2012).

The problem Holbraad is faced with is the same in form as that of the 'twins are birds' issue: Cuban diviners claim that the verdicts they deliver to clients are indubitable. That is, divinatory statements of the kind 'you are bewitched' cannot be false and are not open to doubt. To the sceptic who points out that people in Cuba and elsewhere often do, in point of fact, doubt the truth of divinatory verdicts, Holbraad elegantly responds that what they doubt is not the truth of the verdict but its divinatory nature: accepting the claim of practitioners that their verdicts are indubitable means accepting it as an analytic statement true by its own virtue, because doing anything else is already a denial of the claim.

Clearly however, as Holbraad goes on to show, a statement such as 'you are bewitched' does not share the characteristics of other putatively indubitable truths with which we are familiar such as indeed analytical ones of the form 'a bachelor is an unmarried man', or Kripkean *a posteriori* necessities like 'water is H_2O' (Holbraad 2012: 71). In fact, 'you are bewitched' appears to share all the characteristics of a regular representational statement of fact. Yet regular statements of fact are, of course, by their nature open to doubt. Thus, the problem: divinatory truths are indubitable, and at the same time appear to represent a certain state of affairs in the world, thus laying themselves open to doubt.

The failure of analysis, therefore – presuming that this logical absurdity is indeed a failure – must rest with one or other of those facets of divinatory truth; and given the earlier point that not to accept fully the indubitable nature of verdicts logically entails reducing them to beliefs and being locked into what Holbraad calls a '"smarter-than-thou" stance vis-à-vis divinatory practice' (2012: 55), the facet to be doubted must be the possibility of doubt itself, and therefore the representational nature of divinatory verdicts.

Since any representational truth must by definition be open to the possibility of doubt, it follows that divinatory truth is non-representational. Since that ethnographic concept – a truth that has no representative relation to states of affairs in the world, and whose opposite is not falsehood – has no equivalent within our analytical repertoire, Holbraad must invent one, which he does in the form of 'inventive definition' or 'infinition', which is, therefore, both a description of divinatory verdicts and an instance of itself (Holbraad 2009), or 'metarecursive', in Holbraad's terms (2012: 237).

Infinitions are non-predicative truth statements. Like Wagner's 'inventions' (1975), they derive their truth not from their possession of an external relationship to things in the world to which they can be applied – like, incidentally, the pluralist solution to our dilemma outlined above – but from the intensively transformative effects they have on the concepts to which they relate. Thus, as in one of Holbraad's provocative examples, to say – or rather to infine – that 'Wagner is a genius' (2012: 44) is not to connect two pre-existing entities via an external relationship of meaning, but to transform both entities into something new ('Wagner-the-genius'). In the same way, divinatory verdicts are precisely not open to doubt because they do not represent a state of affairs in the world but modify the objects to which they apply: 'You are bewitched' 'transforms me from a person who stands in no particular relation to witchcraft into a person who is being bewitched' (Holbraad 2009: 88). Similarly, 'infinition' itself puts together concepts like '"speech act", "inauguration", "novelty" and "meaning"' (2009: 87) in order to produce a new concept, that of 'infinition'.[2]

Needless to say, this is a gloss that cannot possibly do justice to an extremely sophisticated argument that unfolds over the course of the monograph and several articles referenced here. It should be already enough, however, to provide some of the contours of how the recursive solution to our problem is supposed to function. Towards the close of the monograph, in fact, Holbraad lays out explicitly the schema involved, which I quote here in full:

Step 1: Describe your ethnography as well as you can, using all the concepts at your disposal in order to represent it as accurately as possible. Use ordinary representational criteria of truth to judge the accuracy of your descriptions: match them with the facts as you found them in the field.

For 'concepts at your disposal' in the case of the problem of divination, we can read 'representational truth'.

Step 2: Scan your descriptions for logical contradictions. Occasions in which your descriptions tempt you to say that your informants are being 'irrational' are good candidates for logical scrutiny. When you can show the contradictions involved, you have identified 'alterity'.

For logical contradictions, we might read 'truths that are both indubitable and representational, and therefore open to doubt'.

Step 3: Specify the conceptual conflicts that generate the contradictions. Which concepts are involved? What are the associated assumptions, corollaries, concomitants, consequences, and so on? How do they relate to the more transparent and logically unproblematic parts of your ethnographic description? Answering these questions provides you with the heuristic tools you will need for step 4.

Step 4: Experiment with redefining in different ways the concepts that generate contradictions. Ask questions of the form 'What if x were thought of as ...?' 'What does y need to be in order that ...?' Modify the meanings of your concepts by bringing them into different relationships with each other. Your criterion of truth is the logical cogency of your infinitions. This involves two minimum requirements: (a) that your infinitions remove the contradictions that motivate them; and (b) that they do not generate new ones in relation either to each other or to other parts of your ethnographic descriptions. Your aim is to straighten out the logical torsions of your ethnographic account, not merely to displace them. NB (*remember!*): While the concepts you are infining in these ways are derived from your (variously un/successful) descriptions of the ethnography, responsibility for your acts of reconceptualization is your own. Your ethnography won't give you the answers, only the terms with which to generate them. Feel free to draw on fellow anthropologists, philosophers and other thinkers for inspiration and comparison but again, remember the following:

Step 5: The litmus test for gauging the success of your recursive, motile, infinitive, and ontographic analytical experiment is its transparency with respect to *your ethnography*. This means that, while your infinitions' claim to truth resides in their logical cogency, the final test they have to pass is representational: If and only if your infinitions allow you to articulate true representations of the phenomena whose description initially mired you in contradiction, your work is done. (2012: 255)

Finally, infinition, as a modified concept of truth that does away with the contradictions outlined above, obviously draws on the work of philosophers (like Deleuze 1994) and anthropologists (like Wagner, Strathern and Viveiros de

Castro) and renders the concept of indubitable divinatory verdicts into something we can make sense of, rather than a logical absurdity.

In sum, then, what the recursive turn provides us with is a coherent language with which to discuss the dilemma I raised at the outset of this chapter. It answers the basic problems of both positivism and reflexivity. What is our analysis supposed to do with our ethnography? Represent it as transparently as possible. How do we do that given that our concepts are as contingent as those we investigate, and may therefore only be capable of rendering the latter absurd or simply false? We invent new ones (by transforming old ones) which are thus by definition contingent upon the data they are invented to represent, and not abstract, in the pluralist sense. In other words, it fulfils both of the requirements I identified at the outset of this chapter: it allows us both to account for our ethnography in a fairly straightforward sense, whilst also putting our analysis in conversation with that of others; and therein, I suggest, lies the problem.

Motion in Circles

Latour's critique of critique is based in part on the idea that critical analysis does two things: first it demolishes the fetishes of those it investigates (science, religion, etc.); then, having undermined the believer's faith in whichever particular phenomenon is at issue by suggesting that that phenomenon is merely a projection of his own fear or desires, it explains those fears or desires with reference to another phenomenon of the same order (power, discourse, etc.) but which is treated as a fact, instead of a fetish. The critic, in other words, cannot lose: anything that he does not happen to believe in can be treated in the first move, and anything that he does happen to believe in can appear with the second. Hence, as Latour puts it, the addiction of critique: 'You are always right!' (2004: 239).

Importantly for the point of view Latour himself seeks to advance, the two moves must always occur consecutively (2004: 240). One cannot simultaneously be Derrida and G.E. Moore, deconstructing with one hand whilst holding up the other as evidence of reality.

The argument I will outline below will resemble Latour's in the sense of highlighting some of the ways in which the recursive turn appears – perhaps surprisingly – to be an unsatisfactory solution to the problem with which this chapter is concerned, not because the armour it proposes we don has an Achilles heel, but precisely because it does not: like that of critique, it is impregnable. But the way I will advance this argument is not by suggesting that recursivity fulfils our needs with respect to ethnography and analysis in inappropriately distinct fashions; quite the reverse, in fact. What I will suggest instead is that the recursive turn tries to answer simultaneously two questions that in fact it might be helpful to consider as quite different.

Recursivity has been described by its proponents as 'a machine for thinking in perpetual motion' (Holbraad 2012: 265), a metaphor which elegantly captures its ambitions. My point here though, to mix metaphors paradoxically, will be that it is precisely insofar as it constitutes such a machine that it may be doomed to run out of steam: any analytical criticism, as I show in this chapter, is defused from the outset, and any ethnographic one will, as I show in the next chapter, automatically result in failure. Like critique, its strength is its weakness, and vice versa.[3]

I opened this concluding part of this book by describing in advance the way in which it would find itself trapped between analytical polemics and ethnographic modesty. For the remainder of this chapter and the next I will illustrate what that means. So far in this chapter I have raised and characterized a particular problem in anthropology – how to conceive of the relationship between ethnography and analysis – and outlined just a few of the answers to that problem, ending with the apparently faultless solution of the recursive turn.

At the beginning of the chapter I raised the question of its place in the book and its apparently abstract nature; one reason for that, as I noted, is that its purpose is precisely to ask about abstraction – or the recursive alternative I describe below, abstension – and their relation to ethnography, and framing that question in relation to ethnography would be to presuppose one kind of an answer. Another, and more important reason, is set out in the arguments below: that asking that question does indeed presuppose an answer to it, but of the opposite form. To ask about the relationship between ethnography and analysis – something that has not only occupied some of the finest anthropological minds of the last century, but is also something that we do on a regular basis – is already to presuppose a difference between the two, because the question itself is by its nature analytical. Whilst it has occupied some of the finest anthropological minds of the last century, it has not occupied those of their interlocutors. As I will seek to outline below, the recursive turn obfuscates this fact – a fact also evident from its own analyses – by conflating the two levels, which then precludes one from making that very critique.

This chapter, in other words, is deliberately purely analytical both because its point is that the question it addresses is also purely analytical, and to make the further point that such a purely analytical critique is inadmissible by the logic of the recursive turn, our most coherent available answer to that question. The next and final chapter will make some of the same points, but it will endeavour to make them ethnographically. In doing so it will demonstrate how arguing against recursivity ethnographically is doomed to fail: both because ethnography cannot be made to answer a question that is purely analytical, and also because no ethnography of any kind could be made to refute the logic of the recursive turn without inadvertently reinforcing it. Hence the somewhat unusual argumentative sequence – analysis and then ethnography: the central point of this part of the book is that some (necessary, to my view) analytical arguments cannot be made with ethnography, including that argument itself, one that thus also – by definition – not only cannot be recursive, but cannot even be admitted as an argument if the premise of recursivity is accepted.

The (Stolen) Anthropological Concept

This is not to say, of course, that this premise has been universally accepted. Recursivity has come in for some quite trenchant criticism of various kinds already (e.g. Bessire and Bond 2014; Course 2010; Heywood 2012; Laidlaw 2012, 2013; Laidlaw & Heywood 2013; Vigh and Sausdal 2014). Here though I want to focus on two kinds of problems that one might raise regarding it, which will take the same form as the two requirements I have mentioned above – to account for one's ethnography and to do so in a way that speaks to other ethnographic material – in order to show how neither of them quite hit the mark as critiques. But my point in doing so is to highlight the fact that they do not do so because the recursive turn is inherently impregnable to such arguments, not because it makes two moves when it should be making one, but because it makes one move when it should be making two.

Let us begin with the first kind of criticism that is often levelled against anthropological arguments: the charge of failing to account for one's ethnography. For despite the eminently clear fashion in which the schema laid out above is alleged to allow us to represent our ethnography as transparently as possible, this is in fact the most frequent form that criticism of the work of the turn's proponents takes. Some for example might wonder whether all Cuban diviners, or Mongolian or Amerindian shamans, think about truth or nature or spirits in exactly the same way, and thus whether accounts which focus on one particular – and fairly exotic – way of doing so are not somewhat unbalanced, a point Holbraad has attempted to refute explicitly (Holbraad 2012: 248). A more pressing and concerning – even to Holbraad (2017) – variant of this 'ethnographic' critique though is the observation made by a number of friendly sceptics (e.g. Candea 2017; Heywood 2012; Scott 2011) that in spite of the most fundamental claim of the recursive turn, namely that it is able to account for alterity, it does so in a manner that makes such alterity – from quite remarkably diverse parts of the world (Amazonia, Melanesia, Cuba, Siberia) – all look rather similar. This is the problem that Holbraad labels that of 'underwhelming originality' (2017) as he draws attention to the similarities between his own argument regarding 'infinition' in Cuban divination and Wagner's on 'invention' amongst the Daribi. His solution to – or dissolution of – this problem will also shed further light on the ways in which concepts and ethnography are alleged to be related by the recursive turn, and so is worth explaining.

The basic misapprehension that grounds this criticism, according to Holbraad, is precisely about the nature of anthropological concepts. Drawing on the earlier article, co-authored with Morten Pedersen and mentioned above, in which a post-pluralist agenda for anthropology is drawn out of the work of Marilyn Strathern (Holbraad and Pedersen 2009), Holbraad points out that to see 'infinition' and 'invention' as akin to one another one must first see them as purely abstract concepts in traditional pluralist fashion. They must appear as generic categories – like 'gift economy' – that are transposable or applicable to a variety of ethnographic contexts.

Whereas the point of the recursive turn is that this cannot be the case: anthropological concepts emerge in relation to specific ethnographic data because of the 'alter' nature of such data; because of their alterity – the impossibility of explaining them with concepts we already have – we are obliged to invent new ones (by transforming old ones). Thus 'infinition' is not a case of 'invention' being 'applied' to Cuban divination, but of a set of concepts – including, undoubtedly, 'invention' – being put into relation with Cuban divinatory truth to produce a new concept, 'infinition', or perhaps better yet, 'infinition-in-Cuban-divinatory-truth'.

In representing the 'anthropological concept' in this way, the point that Holbraad and Pedersen seek to make is that such concepts are indissolubly and intensively (Holbraad and Pedersen 2009: 379; and see Viveiros de Castro 2013: 486) linked to the contingent data from which they emerge. They are 'abstensions', rather than 'abstractions'. It is only by 'cutting off the ethnographic tail' (Holbraad 2017) of such concepts that one is able to see them as being alike in any abstract sense. Thus, in so far as this relationship can be demonstrated to obtain – as should be clear is the case in Holbraad's work, for example – the 'ethnographic critique' is defused from the outset.

The second kind of criticism that may be levelled against anthropological accounts – that of failing to allow for conversation across contexts – is, as I have mentioned, rarer, because the kind of pure description that would precipitate it, whilst occasionally invoked rhetorically (e.g. Latour 2005), is difficult to produce in practice; it is a truism to point out that ethnographic accounts do not emerge from an analytical vacuum and that the demands of the academy oblige us to be at least intra- if not often inter-disciplinary.

But in this case this critique emerges as a logical consequence of the recursive turn's response to the first problem. If anthropological concepts are so inextricably linked to the contexts from which they emerge, then how is it possible for one 'abstensive' concept ever to speak to another?

The answer is contained in the idea of 'abstension' itself; given that what motivates the argument for recursivity in this sense is precisely a recognition of the equally complex nature of 'abstractions' – like, say, truth – and the things they are supposed to abstract from – Cuban divinatory practice – then its products – 'infinition-in-Cuban-divinatory-truth' – cannot thus be thought of as somehow more or less complex than their component parts. Just as an abstension is a melding together of two equally complex things – something that looks like a concept and something that looks like an ethnographic datum

– so the abstension itself can be happily put into relation with other such – again, equally complex – things, like other abstensions: 'invention-in-Daribi-ritual', for example (Wagner 1975). In other words, whilst the first kind of critique cuts off the ethnographic tail of an anthropological concept, this kind of critique cuts off its analytical tail.

So, to sum up, the recursive turn has a coherent answer and impregnable armour when it comes to both of the most fundamental battles that an anthropologist is likely to fight, and furthermore that armour is one and the same in both cases. To the critic who wants to know how it could be that the most ethnographic variant of 'ethnographic theory' can make Cuban diviners look like Mongolian shamans or Daribi ritual practitioners, it answers that the question is misplaced because one end (the ethnographic end) of the 'anthropological concept' has been ignored in its asking. To the critic who wants to know how analysis that is so contingent on ethnographic variety is capable of speaking to any other kind of analysis, it points out that the critic has cut off the analytical end of the concept and missed the point that its creation is precisely about putting things of equal complexity into relation with one another, and therefore putting it into relation with other such concepts is simply an operation of the same order.

How is it then that the recursive solution to our problem – how should analysis and ethnography be related – could appear unsatisfactory? The issue, I suggest, is that what it does not allow us to do is to account for how we are able to ask this question itself.

Note that – unlike Latour's characterization of critique – the recursive turn's answer to both of those questions is essentially the same. Its success relies on collapsing the distinction between concepts and the things to which they are applied, a point with much-discussed ontological implications (e.g. Henare et al. 2006), and an extremely clear example of the idea of ethnographic foundationalism. The whole point of an 'anthropological concept' is precisely that it is not purely conceptual (Holbraad 2017; Holbraad and Pedersen 2009). It is a 'thing-cum-scale', like 'infinition-in-Cuban-divinatory-truth'. Its recursive nature is self-evident, and hence it is simultaneously the answer to both questions. But what about the concept of the 'anthropological concept' itself? Just as an 'anthropological concept' is self-evidently recursive, so that concept is self-evidently not. The stipulation that a recursive relationship must obtain between analysis and ethnography cannot itself be derived from ethnography.

This problem is akin to what Ayn Rand – admittedly an unlikely source of anthropological wisdom – has called the 'fallacy of the stolen concept' (Rand 1990: 59): a variation of the Epimenides paradox of Cretan liars, a 'stolen concept' fallacy is a type of self-refuting statement which depends for its truth on a premise the validity of which it denies. Proudhon's axiom that 'property is theft' is an example, the concept of theft lacking sense independent of the concept of property. In this case though, the stolen concept is that of the conceptual itself: the 'anthropological concept' asserts the mutual imbrication of concepts and objects, indeed denying the 'purity' of concepts in anthropology per se; except, that is, for the 'anthropological concept' itself, which emerges from a series of highly conceptual, abstract and analytical ruminations that have nothing to do with ethnography (e.g. Holbraad and Pedersen 2009), much like this chapter, and indeed a great many similar reflections on the same question.[4]

To a certain extent this point might be explicitly conceded by an advocate of recursivity, which nevertheless sees in such circularity a virtue, rather than a vice: hence, in part, its characterization as a machine for thought in perpetual motion. But a central point of this chapter is that this characterization only holds true if you think of movement as going around in circles (an idea perhaps best symbolized in the ouroboros emblem of *HAU*, intended to symbolize the notion of 'ethnographic theory'): a conceptual critique of recursivity, of which this chapter is an example, will always be ruled out of court because it relies on the same analysis/ethnography distinction that recursivity simultaneously upholds and denies. Like Latour's Zeus of Critique, the proponent of recursivity can only ever be right when confronted with either an ethnographic or an analytical critique, because their answer to the fundamental question with which this chapter is concerned produces in form (highly analytical discussions of abstract concepts like the 'anthropological concept') what it refutes in content (the distinction between concepts and objects, analysis and ethnography). The more rigorous and well-conceptualized these arguments are (as in the case of the recursive turn), the further they move from ethnography; the more systematized and comprehensive the claims, the more abstract the reasoning. But in pointing this out, I am already guilty of reproducing that distinction, and there ends any chance of the machine for thinking in perpetual motion thinking itself out of what looks increasingly like a rather small circle. This is akin to what I have elsewhere seen described as the problem of Dumbo's feather: Dumbo, the eponymous hero of a classic Disney film, is a baby elephant who can fly because of his very large ears. Dumbo, however, does not like having big ears, so he tells himself he can fly because he has a magic feather. Anthropological accounts often have big theoretical ears, but they would sometimes rather believe instead that they have a magical ethnographic feather.

Conclusion

Lest these arguments all appear rather negative, let me now attempt to put them in what I hope is a somewhat more productive fashion as an introduction of sorts to the next chapter. Because the argument set out above is not about why the recursive turn's answer – our most cogent answer as it stands – to the question of how analysis and ethnography should relate is the wrong one; it is about why that answer is frustrating precisely in so far as it cannot be wrong.

Speaking of the tension within feminist thought between a conscious and deliberate pluralism and an equally conscious and deliberate consensus and 'continuity of purpose' – in a manner not unlike my characterization of the tension between identity and difference in LGBTQ activism in Bologna, as the next chapter will make clear – Strathern writes:

> [I]f feminist scholarship is successful in this regard, then its success lies firmly in the relationship as it is represented between scholarship (genre) and the feminist movement (life). Play with context is creative because of the expressed continuity of purpose between feminists as scholars and feminists as activists. Purposes may be diversely achieved, yet the scholarship is in the end represented as framed off by a special set of social interests. Feminists argue with one another, in their many voices, because they also know themselves as an interest group. There is certainty about that context. (Strathern 1987a: 268; see also 1988)

A characteristic and enlightening comparison with anthropology follows:

> The anthropologist is in a rather different position. There appears no such anthropological interest group. For anthropology, play with internal contexts – with the conventions of scholarship (genre) – *looks like* free play with the social context of anthropology as such (life). In fact the resultant uncertainty is intrinsic to anthropological motivation and the drive to study. (Strathern 1987a: 268, author's italics)

What anthropology lacks, in other words, that feminism and in some ways, I will suggest in the next chapter, LGBTQ activism possess is an explicit and expressed representation of its own distinctive questions and interests, echoing the arguments of Jean-Klein and Riles noted in my Introduction (2005). That is why 'play with internal contexts' – such as blurring the boundaries between concepts and objects or analysis and ethnography – '*looks like* free play'. But 'internal contexts' are 'internal' to something; blurring those boundaries, as I argue above, actually reproduces them, because it is only anthropologists who do so, in order to answer peculiarly anthropological questions like 'how does my analysis relate to my ethnography'.

If seeking to bridge the gap between analysis and ethnography is what anthropologists do, it is also exactly what makes that gap unbridgeable in a sense, because it is precisely that activity that gives anthropological analysis its distinctive identity, making it thus irreducibly different from its ethnographic objects. Only, as Strathern notes, we do not represent it as such, and this has consequences. One, as I have sought to show here, is that arguments like that of the recursive turn appear irrefutable, because wholly conceptual critiques of them – such as this chapter, and such are by definition the only possible such critiques as the next chapter will show – appear beside the point because such critiques only relate to anthropological analysis.

Yet the parallels between that description of anthropology and the depictions of LGBTQ activism I have provided in previous chapters should be obvious. If what makes anthropological analysis distinct – its unexpressed continuity of purpose – is its paradoxical attempt to collapse itself into 'ethnographic theory' (Da Col and Graeber 2011; Pedersen 2012), then what gives LGBTQ activism its distinctive flavour is the anti-identitarian nature of its politics, but precisely insofar as this is what makes it distinctive, this is also what constitutes its identity. The next chapter will be an exploration of these parallels, together with an argument about their limits: for, appropriately, both ethnographic and analytical reasons, the argument I seek to make in this final part of the book cannot be derived purely from ethnography. As I show, to do so would be both to reproduce inadvertently the premise of the recursive turn, and to fail to do that which LGBTQ activists seek above all to accomplish: to 'make a difference'.

Notes

1. A corollary of this is the implicit assumption that anthropology only ever really comes into its own in such situations.
2. Though this may look to some like a description of an Austinian performative or illocutionary speech act, Holbraad is clear that in his eyes it is more complicated, as his concept of infinition is as much about truth as is a regular propositional statement, only it is a truth that is 'done' rather than 'said' (Holbraad 2012: 58).
3. A point that Delchambre and Marquis make about Latour's own work (2013: 566).
4. One could also compare this critique with the *peritropê* of the *Theaetetus* – if all concepts in anthropology are abstensive, then the concept of the abstensive concept should be as well, and is evidently not.

6

Making Difference

In the previous chapter I posed a question that I argued is central to any anthropological account, namely how its analysis is related to the ethnography it is supposed to account for, and laid out a very brief genealogy of answers to that question, concluding with the most recent attempt to tackle it, namely the recursive turn.[1] I sought to show how the recursive turn was able both to represent ethnography in as transparent a manner as possible and to account for how such representations can be put into relation with representations from other ethnographic contexts, essentially by collapsing the distinction between the two questions, and claiming that concepts and objects, analysis and ethnography, are mutually intertwined, as in the description of the 'anthropological concept' (see also Scott 2013: 864).

I ended that chapter, however, by arguing that such a claim is self-refuting to the extent that it rests on a premise that it denies: the claim that the 'anthropological concept' is a mixture of analysis and ethnography is itself purely analytical. Furthermore, it is the only such claim that the recursive turn admits, for once it is accepted any other such similar arguments – like indeed that of the previous chapter – that rely on the analysis/ethnography distinction are ruled out of court.

In the final sections of that chapter I suggested that what Strathern calls 'play with internal contexts' (1987a: 268) in anthropology – like blurring the boundaries between analysis and ethnography – only looks like free play because we lack a language with which to represent what those contexts are internal to. In fact, it is precisely the blurring of such boundaries that produces such a lack. If what makes anthropological analysis distinctive is its attempts to collapse the boundary between analysis and ethnography – to produce 'ethnographic theory' (Da Col and Graeber 2011; Pedersen 2012) – then of course this results in the paradoxical assertion that what makes anthropological analysis different from other things – like ethnographic data – is the extent to which it makes that difference disappear.

That description should, I hope, call to mind some of the arguments set out in previous chapters regarding the problem of difference in LGBQ activism. In particular, the central issue dealt with in Part Two of this book, namely the paradox of seeing the production of difference as necessary and virtuous, and that fact simultaneously constituting a common purpose and identity in LGBTQ activism.

This final chapter of this book will explore those parallels. In doing so it will to some extent follow a recursive logic, precisely by putting the analytical questions raised above into relation with the ethnographic ones I have already set out. Just as, for example, Holbraad finds in the ethnographic concept of truth in Cuban divination ('infinition') an analytical concept which helps to account for how truth might retain a status in anthropology (again, 'infinition') (2009: 82), so this chapter will explore how ethnographic understandings of identity and difference may relate to the analytical question of, precisely, the identity of anthropological analysis and its difference from ethnography.

So to some extent this chapter will make the obvious logical move – anticipated in the last – of using a contingent piece of ethnography to make a modest claim, namely that the belief in the necessity and virtue of producing difference on the part of LGBTQ activists in Bologna challenges the insistence of recursivity on the mutual imbrication of analysis and ethnography, because in order to make sense of that belief a difference between the two must be produced, as I will show.

But, as the above should make clear, that move cannot fully succeed. To assert the ethnographic basis of the difference between analysis and ethnography would seem to be just as paradoxical and self-refuting as to assert the analytical basis of their identity, as the recursive turn does.[2]

In its partial failure, however, I hope that this final chapter is able to open up the recursive circle somewhat, albeit in a distinctively post-recursive fashion. Part Three of the book has so far been an experiment in such post-recursive analysis: it has asked a question – how should analysis relate to ethnography – and in the very asking of it provided an instance of an answer. Because to some extent that question is wholly divorced from the ethnographic questions that have occupied the remainder of this book; thus in asking it we presuppose a certain kind of answer, as the last chapter argued, also thereby becoming an instance of its own argument.

But, as I have indicated, the question is only to some extent divorced from the ethnographic material with which this book is concerned. In putting that question and that material back into relation – returning to 'the point of bifurcation', as Strathern puts it (2011: 90) – this chapter will attempt to highlight some (differently) productive consequences of a paradox that both unites and divides anthropology and LGBTQ activism.

It will do so via an admittedly complex series of analogies, the value of which I hope will be clear by its conclusion, but whose complexity is unavoidable because a part of their purpose is to draw out likenesses and differences over, precisely, likeness and difference between their terms: in other words, to address the issues of analogy or comparison themselves. I will begin by again making use of the work of Marilyn Strathern on feminism in order to note some of the ways in which it is like LGBTQ activism, particularly with regard to their relationships with respectively, patriarchy and identity, and suggest an explanation for why what I have described as a paradox in LGBTQ activism may not be so paradoxical after all. I will then extend the analogy between feminism in the work of Strathern and LGBTQ activism to include their relationship with anthropology. As Jean-Klein and Riles note (2005), Strathern's point in her own comparative exercise is that the differences between anthropology and feminism are productive ones, to which they add that if such differences are not obvious they must themselves be produced (and that is exactly what Strathern does in her accounts). In the case of my own comparison however, producing difference as an analytical exercise from produced difference as an ethnographic object only yields further paradox.

My point in drawing this out will be to try to stabilize at least one kind of difference between LGBTQ activism and anthropology, one which I hope will shed some light on the previous chapter's discussion of recursivity: that such stabilization itself is neither possible nor desirable in anthropology, as it is in LGBTQ activism. What is political necessity to the latter is analytical choice (Strathern 2011) to the former.

Feminism and LGBTQ Activism

At this juncture, it will be useful to return briefly to the argument of Chapter 4, in which I set out what I described as a constitutive paradox of certain forms of radical LGBTQ activism in Bologna. This kind of activism is activism insofar as it seeks to 'make a difference' to the world around it; but what unites it in this endeavour is the belief that difference must and should be reproduced on a constant basis. In other words, what gives this kind of activism its distinctive flavour – its identity – is a fundamental denial of categories of gender and sexual identity, and indeed of identity as given per se.

Thus, the paradox is that an emphasis on the necessity and virtue of producing difference – as in, identity of any form is understood as a type of performance, and what defines this form of activism is the attempt to subvert such identities by performing difference from them – becomes an identity itself, a defining attribute of those who hold to it. What makes queer activists of this variety distinct from, say, the radical lesbian activists Sarah Green studied (Green 1997), or from rights-based activists who lobby for more recognition for identities like 'gay' and 'lesbian' (see e.g. Rahman and Jackson 1997), is the value they place on 'real difference', in Massimo's words. But precisely in making it distinct – and indeed in isolating a certain variety of difference as 'more real' than others – this activism itself is made 'real' and distinct.[3] As in my description of activists' antinomianism in Chapter 2, defining oneself in opposition to something is still a form of self-definition. That identity may be produced by self-definition in opposition to something is also evident in Chapter 3, where the problem of We Are Church is that its relationship to the actual Church looks too much like that of the activists with whom it wishes to dialogue, and thus – in this respect – it is too similar to those activists for the dialogue to be interesting; and all of this becomes doubly paradoxical when what one defines oneself against is self-definition itself.

This description, as I have mentioned, resembles Marilyn Strathern's characterization of feminism, and in the latter we may also find some answers to the question of why it may be less paradoxical than it might at first seem. In the case of feminism, for Strathern:

> Theoretical differences contribute, then, to a debate constituted and sustained by cross-reference. In our self-representations, feminists are in constant dialogue, an interlocution that maintains internal connections. It looks as though there is an impossible array of positions, but the positions are openly held in relation to one another. They comprise 'a self-referential body of thought' ... Much feminist writing is consequently concerned with making explicit one viewpoint with respect to others ... In the English-speaking world, for instance, to which my remarks largely refer, Marxist/Socialist feminism places itself in relation to both Radical and Liberal feminism. The strategy of separatism or the arguments of biological essentialism have to be countered. But these other viewpoints are never dispatched. No viewpoint alone is self-reproductive: all the positions in the debate comprise the theoretical base of any one. In other words, the vast number of internal debates (criticism; counter-criticism and commentary; writers talking about one another; a fragmentation at the level of the individual arguments) together create a field of sorts, a discourse. Feminism lies in the debate itself. (Strathern 1988: 24)

Feminism for Strathern, in other words, is intrinsically 'pluralist' in a manner akin to LGBTQ activism, a key aspect of its identity being an insistence on a multiplicity of perspectives; yet the theoretical premises of these perspectives – including, one presumes, that insistence itself – traverse their boundaries. Similarly, one of the central premises of queer activism as I witnessed it in Bologna was an insistence on promoting and retaining a diversity of different positions. Hence the assertion on the part of Marina and Massimo that their organization be defined as a network, not a group and not a singular entity but a proliferation of perspectives with no one dominant over others, in contrast to the hierarchical institution of Cassero.

Hence equally Laura and others' attack on Massimo for failing to sustain this principle and for assuming implicitly a leadership position and attempting to impose a single viewpoint on the network. More abstractly, Strathern's description also obviously resonates with my characterization of LGBTQ activism of this form as united precisely by the principle of the need for and virtue of producing difference. As she notes later in the same text:

> My account exploits perspectival devices, including the us/them dichotomy, as essential fictions to its argument. I even include 'the feminist voice' as one

perspective. But I hope I have not thereby homogenized it. For Owens (1985: 62) notes that the 'feminist voice is usually regarded as one among many, its insistence on difference as testimony to the pluralism of the times', thereby making it victim to assimilation as an undifferentiated category in itself. Its internal differences are suppressed in the adoption of 'the feminist view'. (1988: 38)

Strathern's characterization of the 'essential fictions' of her account in *The Gender of the Gift* as 'perspectival' suggests that the comparisons she goes on to evoke with regard to anthropology and feminism are matters of different viewpoints on the same objects. In fact, however, the comparison is more disjunctive (Lazar 2012), more perspectivist than perspectival, a distinction she invokes in later work (e.g. 2011: 93), drawing on the insights of Viveiros de Castro (1998) amongst others, as well as her own Melanesian material. By this I mean that the relationships she describes feminism and anthropology as possessing to their respective objects are not directly equivalent, a point she brings out with Donna Haraway's well-known trope of the hybrid:

Feminists and anthropologists comprise different communities of scholars; Haraway's image of half-animal, half-machine captures their incompatibility. It is not that they cannot come together or that they fail to communicate ... Feminist and anthropological scholarship endorse different approaches to the nature of the world open to investigation. These cannot be blended or matched. Their assumptions do not coexist in a part-whole relationship so that one could be absorbed by the other, nor do they have common objectives for mutual exchange between them: the one is no substitute for the other. (1988: 36)

Or similarly, in a separate article:

[T]he awkward relationship between feminism and anthropology is lived most dramatically in the tension experienced by those who practice feminist anthropology. They are caught between structures: the scholar is faced with two different ways of relating to her or his subject matter. The tension must be kept going; there can be no relief in substituting the one for the other. (1987b: 286)

What exactly is the nature of their different approaches? The answer, for Strathern, lies in the inherently conflictual approach that feminism takes to its object, the only perspective that it cannot by definition take into account, namely patriarchy:

Feminist scholarship, polyphonic out of political necessity, accommodates anthropology as 'another voice'. Within this epistemology, anthropological analysis of male-female relations in non-Western societies in the end cannot explain Western experience, which is also personal experience, although it may contribute to the further experiences about which feminists must think. At the same time, different viewpoints are sustained in coeval parallel; indeed, the multiplicity of experience is retained as a sign of authenticity. Each is a feminist voice, but the voices create no single viewpoint, no single perspective, and no part-whole relation between themselves. The only perspective lies in the common challenge of patriarchy. The contrast with modernist anthropology is obvious. That endeavour does not find itself in a dichotomous position with the world. Rather, anthropology seeks to pluralize its relationships with many cultures, many cosmologies. It creates its dichotomies within, as in its modelling of an us/them knowledge of its own conceptual constructs. (1988: 39)

The point I wish to bring out of this description of the differences between anthropology and feminism is that the latter is united by a specifically political purpose, as I noted at the conclusion of the previous chapter. What gives feminism, for Strathern, its distinctive identity – as opposed to anthropology – in spite of its insistence on plurality is its unity vis-à-vis the condition of women in the world. Hence the unproblematic nature of its plurality, for there remains a 'continuity of purpose' in its antagonistic relationship to patriarchy. Whether or not anthropology remains 'modernist' in the sense Strathern describes, it is still undoubtedly unlike feminism in this respect:

> Feminist inquiry suggests that it is possible to discover the self by becoming conscious of oppression from the Other. Thus one may seek to regain a common past which is also one's own. Anthropological inquiry suggests that the self can be consciously used as a vehicle for representing an Other. But this is only possible if the self breaks with its own past. These thus emerge as two very different radicalisms. (1987b: 289)

LGBTQ Activism and Anthropology

The point of this brief exegesis of Strathern's 'disjunctive comparison' (Lazar 2012) between anthropology and feminism is to make a further such comparison by examining what light it can shed on the paradox of LGBTQ activism as I have described it, and, in turn, to ask what this can tell us about the similarities and differences between the latter and anthropology. For I suggest that like feminism, the production of identity through the production of difference in the case of LGBTQ activism is not in fact paradoxical precisely because of its nature as activism.[4]

In order to be activism, as I have described it – in order to be of use as collective political action – it must maintain a certain relationship of difference from the world, a point I made in my Introduction. It must, in other words, possess an ambiguous connection to the target of its activism, made meaningful in relation to that object, but only in so far as it opposes it.

That could be a broadly accurate description of activism in general, but in the case of this form of LGBTQ activism there is an added layer of complexity because the objects it opposes are categories of identity. Identity is its equivalent of feminism's patriarchy, the perspective it cannot adopt and the difference it cannot produce. But without it – as, one imagines, in the case of feminism and patriarchy – this kind of activism makes no sense as activism. The relationship in question, in other words, is doubly equivocal, a perfect example of the kind of connection this book has been investigating more broadly: of course activism of this form looks like an 'undifferentiated category', in Strathern's terms, when put into relationship with what it opposes – 'undifferentiated categories' themselves; but it is precisely in relation to what it opposes that it has meaning as activism.

So, the ambiguous meanings of the phrase 'making difference' are in fact one: 'making difference' for LGBTQ activists in Bologna – the process by which they seek continually to subvert given categories of gender or sexual identity – is exactly what constitutes 'making a difference' – their political action in relation to the world of identity. The identity produced by the fact that they share a belief in the necessity and virtue of 'making difference' only finds its expression in the relationship of conflict or opposition that is 'making a difference' as an activist, i.e. against the category of identity itself. The transformation of the 'politics of difference' (Green 1997) into the politics of identity – defined precisely against identity politics – is in this case not a paradox but a necessity for the kind of political action LGBTQ activists in Bologna pursue.

Now, to return to the original question of this part of the book, how does this relate to the recursive turn and the problem in anthropology of how to conceive of the connection between ethnography and analysis? In the case of anthropology, I suggest, we are faced with an inverted version of the paradox above (in another example of disjunctive comparison, the implications of which I will draw out further below): as in Strathern's description of the difference between feminism and anthropology with respect to their particular 'others' quoted above, LGBTQ activism takes up a position of conflict and opposition with respect to its object, identity. Anthropology, on the other hand, at least in its contemporary recursive form, seeks to 'make sense of' and incorporate its object, ethnography: hence ethnographic foundationalism. In the former case, the paradox results from the fact that in uniting to oppose identity, LGBTQ activism gains its own identity and thus becomes akin to the object it opposes; the paradox in the latter case is that the endeavour of trying to make sense of ethnography, and to incorporate ethnographic data and analysis together, is precisely what makes this activity itself – anthropological analysis – distinct from ethnography. In producing identity – in being recursive, for example, in collapsing the distinction between the analytical and the ethnographic – anthropology produces itself precisely as different and distinct from the object with which it seeks to identify.

To get at how exactly this comparison helps us to deal with the latter paradox it is worth examining precisely how it is supposed to function: given that the paradoxes are inverted, it is not immediately clear how the two are being put into relation. Indeed, this is the broader point that Strathern makes in her argument about the relationship between feminism and anthropology. Superficially they look easily comparable, similar in many respects; one thing, appropriately, she notes explicitly that they have in common is a concern for difference, just as I have done in the case of LGBTQ activism and anthropology:

Feminist theory also has an interest in difference – in constantly bringing to mind the 'difference it makes' to consider things from a perspective that includes women's interests. Insofar as men's and women's interests are opposed, perpetual effort must bring this to attention. Again, homogenization makes no sense. Feminism's and anthropology's concerns in promoting difference would seem to be further grounds for mutual convergence. (1987b: 286)

In fact, however, her point in making the comparison is that in spite of the apparently numerous resemblances between feminism and anthropology, they are very different in some crucial respects, a number of which I have already described. Hence the distinctive nature of Strathern's comparison itself, which is based not on common ground but on difference (1987b; 1988). As Jean-Klein and Riles point out in making a similar argument with regard to anthropology and human rights, it is precisely Strathern's point that these differences are actually what makes anthropology and feminism of use to one another, and so ought to be maintained. Or better yet, as Jean-Klein and Riles put it: 'if at times it seems like there is no difference between anthropological practice and human rights practice, then perhaps difference, like relevance, must be produced, as an effect, not simply found in the world' (2005: 188). 'Producing' the difference between feminism and anthropology is exactly what Strathern's account accomplishes.

In analogous fashion, for activists like Laura, Marina, Massimo and others, alternative forms of activism like the rights-based activism of Cassero, or any kind of gay identity-based activism, all look far too much like the identities they seek to throw off – a 'repetition of differential sameness', in Zigon's terms (2013a: 719). They are imitative, or derivative, of the identities they critique. Queer activism, on the other hand, is the constant attempt to produce a difference – 'make difference' – from these identities, in order to 'make a difference' – be of 'use' – to the world at large.

A further analogy here suggests itself: Jean-Klein and Riles are writing of the – equivocal – relationship between anthropology and human rights. They explicitly situate their argument as mirroring Strathern's comparable points about anthropology and its – hybrid – relation to feminism; the analogy I add here is to the similarly 'partial' connection between anthropology and LGBTQ activism.

As in Strathern's argument, and as I noted in my Introduction, anthropology and LGBTQ activism share a constitutive concern for difference and a plurality of perspectives. A succession of literature reviews on the anthropology of gender and sexuality since the early 1990s makes clear just how deep the impact of queer theory has been on the discipline (e.g. Boellstorff 2007; Morris 1995), and the influence of thinkers such as Judith Butler hardly needs stating. Furthermore, ethnographic studies that demonstrated the variability of the ways in which cultures understand categories of gender and sexuality were among the factors that led to the move away from identity politics amongst many LGBT activists – a point Sarah Green brings out of her ethnography of lesbian activists in London in the 1980s (1997) – so the connection is far from being only one way.[5]

What makes this last analogy of use though in (finally) dealing with the question I originally raised in this part of the book is that for it to function correctly it has to break itself down. Unlike the other analogies with which I have compared it – human rights and anthropology, feminism and anthropology – this is not a consequence of a judgement about how the two may be of service to one another, but a logical necessity based on how the analogy works. Jean-Klein and Riles, and earlier Strathern, argue for why it is valuable – and indeed exemplify how it is possible – to produce a difference between anthropology and the respective objects to which they connect it (and from which they subsequently disconnect it); but if the relationship between anthropology and LGBTQ activism is like the relationship between LGBTQ activism and the world around it, it is necessarily already a relationship of produced difference. The problem thus is how to produce difference from a found object in the world when that found object is precisely produced difference.

I have already described the way in which the connection between LGBTQ activism and its object, the world of identities it opposes, is a paradigmatic exemplar of the kind of relationship this book has investigated. Not only is it equivocal in the sense that LGBTQ activism is related by difference and opposition to the target of its activism; that is true of activism in general. It is also true of antinomianism amongst activists and moral codes, of the interrelated but highly varied and conflicting understandings of being left-wing in Bologna, and of the troubled relationship to the Vatican that We Are Church possesses, as various chapters of this book have argued. The relationship between LGBTQ activism and identity is equivocal in a yet further sense however, because its relationship of difference is with identity itself.

I have also suggested that anthropological analysis possesses a similar, but at the same time very different, relationship to ethnography – or, as the recursive turn might have it, to alterity, or indeed difference. Recursive anthropology would have us collapse the difference between the concepts we employ and the ethnographic data – difference itself – with which we employ them (Jensen 2013: 312). But as the last chapter argued, doing this is exactly what gives that kind of analysis its distinctively analytical character. In attempting to close the gap between concepts and things, we rely on – or better yet produce (or even 'infine' perhaps) – a concept that is exclusively conceptual, namely the concept of the 'anthropological concept' itself.

What I am doing now though is asking how it is possible to make an analogy between those two – similar but different – relationships through such a comparison. To do so is to be recursive: to ask how the ethnography with which I have been dealing can be put into relation with my analytical concepts, to show that they share similarities; to do the opposite, in short, of what I sought to do in the previous chapter.

But just as the two relationships are – internally, so to speak – about producing identity through difference and producing difference through identity, so they are also externally, because they mirror one another: to make my analysis look very different from my ethnography – as I did in the last chapter – is to fail to produce identity, and thus to fail to be anthropologically recursive in an obvious sense. On the other hand, to produce an identity between my ethnographic data and these analytical questions would be equally nonrecursive, as those data concern precisely not producing identity but instead 'making a difference'. In other words, in making this last analogy I cannot help but reproduce its terms, and thus – like the relationships it both connects and disconnects – produce both identity and difference. Which is, of course, to muddy the waters further, precisely what I have been arguing that both LGBTQ activists and anthropologists do – albeit in different ways.

Making a (Final) Difference

What I mean by 'in different ways', as I hope is now clear, is that although both produce identity and difference together, the degree of emphasis placed on either one is reversed, just as the paradoxes I have highlighted are inverted. Whilst my activist interlocutors are very explicit about their views on difference and the importance of producing it, they leave largely implicit the degree to which this very fact makes them alike. I have argued that, as in Strathern's description of feminism, this is because this similarity is a question of a practical orientation, a necessary aspect of being an activist by definition, and thus can be more or less taken for granted. The 'continuity of purpose' can be accepted as a given.

In anthropology's case, at least as I have been characterizing it, what we tend to like to make explicit is the degree to which our analysis is closely related to our ethnography, as exemplified in the turn to recursivity. Though the pages of anthropological journals are packed with highly abstract and conceptual ruminations, for reasons beyond the scope of this book, reasons that one presumes are as much to do with disciplinary history and politics as they are intellectual, it is extremely rare to read contemporary work that explicitly and rhetorically privileges theory, analysis or generalization over ethnography and particularism (for two recent counter-examples see Willerslev 2011 and Ingold 2008, 2014). Though again the genealogy of this tendency lies outside of the scope of this book, some have traced it as far back as Malinowski's excoriation of Frazerian anthropology, and indeed Frazer is the inspiration for Willerslev's attempt to rejuvenate the idea of 'theory' (2011; see also Strathern 1987a).

Thus, in making the analogy or comparison I have attempted, I have in both cases sought to make explicit the aspect that remains implicit internally to the analogy's terms – to 'say something different', as Viveiros de Castro puts it (2003, 2013: 474), both from my ethnography and from the recursive trend in anthropological analysis, by both putting them together and holding them apart.

In respect of LGBTQ activism, I am under no illusions about the value, or lack thereof, to activism itself of pointing out the implicitly identitarian product of its explicitly anti-identitarian politics, though I have also sought to highlight why this is not in fact a paradox. In a passage that could again apply equally well to LGBTQ activism, Strathern writes of feminism: 'Feminists can only operationalize their perspectives if these are held to have some congruence with reality. Thus they do not need to know that "really" they cannot distinguish themselves from the oppressive Other; on the contrary, what they need to know are all the ways in which "really" they can and must' (1987b: 291).

Anthropology however, as Strathern and Jean-Klein and Riles have argued, has a different task; and on that side of the analogy, making explicit that very difference I hope serves a purpose, constituting what Jean-Klein and Riles call 'care for the discipline itself', through – if also against – ethnography, 'the only form of engagement that our profession is uniquely qualified to administer' (2005: 174).

Towards the conclusion of the last chapter I argued that recursivity, the most coherent paradigm for addressing the question this part of the book has posed, as a 'machine for thinking in perpetual motion', confines that motion to what it sees as a virtuous circularity. It is thus revolutionary in both senses of the word.[6] Its analytical arguments are often said to be instances of themselves – as they are recursive – and to perform themselves into being, the paradigmatic example being the ontological argument that concepts and things are one and the same (Henare et al. 2006; Holbraad 2009; Scott 2013). Thus, 'infinition' is an instance of itself. One effect of this, as I argued, is that once they are asserted their premises can be denied.

Are 'revolutions' – or indeed 'paradigms' – useful ways of thinking about transformations in anthropological knowledge though? In one final instance of a 'post-recursive' comparison, I suggest that the analogy between LGBTQ activism and anthropology may be helpful in answering this question. Writing still of the difference between anthropology and feminism, Strathern notes that the notion of a 'paradigm-shift' that some feminist anthropologists hoped that feminism would occasion in anthropology is based on a misplaced understanding of how anthropologists – and feminists – relate to one another. Paradigms, in Kuhn's usage of the term (Kuhn 1970), are by definition broadly shared understandings of how the world works. When they 'shift', that shift is revolutionary in the sense that one set of assumptions that inform a scholarly community's work are displaced by another. But, as she continues:

> These are the characteristics of a closed system. Revolution serves only to close the system again: successive paradigms replace or substitute for one another. Overt competition between paradigms is short-lived because the proponents of the new paradigm claim they have solved the problems that put the old one in crisis. Yet this hardly fits the present case of feminist scholarship, insofar as it has an interest in sustaining antagonism between 'paradigms'. Here it is the very championing of a new 'paradigm' that makes the old one problematic. Indeed, it is in feminists' overt

interests to take a conflict view of their social context. If so, its explicit conceptual frameworks cannot be regarded as paradigms. (1987b: 284)

As should be clear by now, this characterization could be extended to LGBTQ activism. Not only is it, as activism, based on a similarly 'conflicted' view of the world around it – both in the sense of being equivocally related to that world but also in the sense of being opposed to it – but its promotion of difference results in the same polyphony of perspectives that characterizes feminism. Hence the fact that so much of this book has described disagreement and debate over the proper methods and aims of LGBTQ activism, and indeed over the meaning of its primary objects, difference and identity. Indeed, as should also be clear it is doubly true of LGBTQ activism in some forms, as its emphasis on the constant need to produce difference precludes any paradigm-like identity beyond that emphasis itself.

Furthermore, as Strathern goes on to argue, this antipathy to the kind of consensus that Kuhn describes amongst natural scientists also holds true of anthropology: '[T]here is no one anthropology; its practitioners range from determinists to relativists, from those interested in power relations to those who give primacy to cultural models, from the political economists to the hermeneuticists' (1987b: 284; see also Nader 2011: 213).

So, to recall again the argument of the last chapter, my point throughout Part Three of the book has not been to demonstrate why the recursive turn's answer to the question of how our analysis should relate to our ethnography is wrong or incorrect. Quite the opposite in fact, as I have sought to show how once its basic premise is accepted, it is to all intents and purposes irrefutable. It is the closest thing to a genuinely coherent answer to the question posed.

But this is precisely why I have suggested it may occasion a degree of frustration. It is paradigmatic in Strathern's sense, in addition to being revolutionary, because it seeks to provide us with a shared understanding of a basic problem in anthropology, one that aims to replace previous attempts to do so. But as I noted in the introduction to the last chapter, genealogies of anthropological answers to this question are usually rather partial, as my own was: 'positivism' had its internal variations and its critics, just as did 'reflexivity' and 'writing culture'.[7] Anthropologists may in general share certain common purposes – like feminism and LGBTQ activism – such as seeking to relate their analysis to their ethnography, but this does not imply that they do not wish to be able to argue with one another over how best to do this, indeed just as feminists and LGBTQ activists do. The debates the recursive turn has produced are evidence of this.

Its circular logic, however, as I have sought to show, is inescapable whether one sees it as vicious or virtuous. Arguments that perform themselves – such as that for 'infinition' – are by their nature not very easy to disagree with.

By contrast, if there is an advantage to my attempt here to make explicit the implicit paradoxes of both LGBTQ activism and recursive anthropological analysis, and to make an analogy between them, it may lie in showing how such performances are so often accompanied by their own refutations. LGBTQ activism performs the difference it seeks to make to the world, but in doing so becomes akin to that which it opposes. Recursive anthropology performs the identity it seeks to create between analysis and ethnography, but in doing so distinguishes its analysis from that ethnography.

Finally, the analogy I have myself drawn between these two forms of relationship also both performs and refutes itself, depending upon which of its terms one chooses to emphasize. On the one hand, what I have sought to do is to experiment with deliberately widening, rather than narrowing, the gap between anthropological analysis and its object; to ask what questions we are better able to address by highlighting the ways in which the concepts and issues that concern anthropology as a discipline are quite different from those of our interlocutors. Doing so, indeed, has allowed me to address that question itself, one that I have argued is a distinctly anthropological one, and thus exactly to that extent my argument has been an instance of itself: I have sought to 'make a difference' between my analysis and my ethnography by addressing the issue of the relation between the two. On the other hand, precisely in so far as I have done this by analogizing that relation and the relationship that LGBTQ activism possesses to identity, the difference I have made collapses back again into identity. That this collapse of difference into identity and vice versa occurs within as well as between the terms of the analogy – within the relationship of analysis to ethnography and that of LGBTQ activism to identity – ensures there is no way the argument can ever rest securely on its own premises. There is no solace to be found in a 'final' analogy in which the justification of the argument is discovered either in the practices of LGBTQ activists or the nature of anthropological analysis, or indeed in the recursive relation between the two.

But if pointing out the potentially self-refuting aspects of some forms of LGBTQ activist thought serves no obvious purpose to LGBTQ activism as activism, that does not imply that highlighting the ways in which anthropological analysis can be self-refuting is of no use to anthropology.

In Chapter 4 I used the neologism of 'strategic anti-essentialism' to describe the emphasis LGBTQ activism places on difference from identity and the fact that it leaves the identity this emphasis itself produces implicit. I was however careful to qualify that term in order to be clear that I was not implying that difference can only ever be strategic, a matter of choice, whilst identity is always given – which would be the reverse of the implication of strategic essentialism (identities are always performed whilst difference is a given). Why I did so is I hope now clear: the identitarian product of the anti-identitarian politics of LGBTQ activism is not a matter of choice but a necessary aspect of activism itself. LGBTQ activism – like feminism, as Strathern describes – may be internally perspectivalist, in the sense that it allows and indeed promotes a multiplicity of viewpoints within it, but, I suggest, despite its obviously 'Euro-American' character, it is closer to perspectivism with respect to its relationship to its object, identity. What I mean by this is that this relationship is prior to the terms related (Strathern 2011: 100). As in the case of feminism and patriarchy, there is no choice of perspective when it comes to identity: to be a queer activist is to have a specific kind of (oppositional) relationship to the category of identity. That is precisely why it is unhelpful – in terms of activism – to point out that from another perspective this may appear self-refuting: that 'other perspective' is unavailable from an activist perspective.

Clearly, different perspectives are available to an anthropologist. As Strathern notes, we may be determinists or relativists, interpretivists or structuralists and as she points out in a more recent piece, choices of analytical vocabulary are very important to an anthropologist precisely because of our concern for the relation between that analytical vocabulary and the ethnographic data it is chosen to describe (2011: 97).

The nature of these analytical choices as choices is exemplified by this last part of this book. Throughout it I have been choosing, at various points, to emphasize difference at the expense of identity (as in the last chapter) or identity at the expense of difference (as in this chapter). As I have just argued, depending upon the perspective chosen, my account may be read as an argument against recursivity (demonstrating the difference between analysis and ethnography by asking the question of how they are related, a question distinct from my ethnographic material) or an extreme version of it (producing an anti-recursive argument from anti-recursive ethnographic material, and thus showing how no argument can be properly anti-recursive).

Conclusion

As I noted at the outset of the last chapter, that there ought to be a relationship of some form or another between anthropological analysis and ethnographic data is probably an assumption that most anthropologists would share. I have tried to make that assumption explicit here, and so at no point have I suggested that a kind of anthropological analysis that had no relationship of any form to ethnographic data would be a sensible goal, or even possible; like LGBTQ activism's relationship to its object, the relationship between anthropological analysis and ethnographic data is perhaps a necessary one.

But that does not mean that the 'conception of relationship' (Strathern 2011: 97) must be uniform. Unlike LGBTQ activism, I suggest, we do have a choice when it comes to how we relate our analysis to our ethnography, a fact that the recursive turn obscures in its paradigm-like response to the question Part Three of this book has raised. If at points and for certain purposes it may be productive to see that relationship in terms of resemblance or recursivity, so equally there may be occasions when it is beneficial to focus on how that relationship may be one of difference rather than identity. In other words – and this point will re-emerge in the conclusion to this book – what if there is something distinctive about anthropological analysis that is not ethnography?

So, to conclude this last chapter, what I have sought to do in the final part of this book is to raise a question that is to my view both fundamental to anthropology and fundamentally anthropological, namely how our concepts and analyses are related to the ethnographic data they are supposed to explain or represent. By 'fundamentally anthropological' what I mean is that the very asking of it provides us with a kind of answer: to the extent that as a question it has little to do with the practices of LGBTQ activism – or indeed I suggest any other similar ethnographic data – it is itself a conceptual, analytical question and responses to it will be of the same kind, a fact that is fairly self-evident upon examination of various attempts to address it. This holds true also of the most recent one of the most cogent of such attempts, namely the recursive turn, which I suggested was indeed so cogent in its response that it leaves us without a means of addressing the issue anew. Once the (purely conceptual) notion of the 'anthropological concept' as admixture of conceptual and empirical is accepted no further such (purely conceptual) discussions are possible.

But what I have also sought to do is to illustrate the manner in which my own ethnographic data may speak to this question in a properly recursive fashion. In this chapter I have illustrated some analogies that may be drawn between the way in which anthropology's constitutive concern for the relation between analysis and ethnography is, precisely, constitutive, and thus distinctly analytical, and the ways in which certain forms of LGBTQ activism, in their concern to produce and assert difference from identity, can come to appear to possess an identity themselves.

The analogy itself though is as paradoxical as its terms in the sense that to function properly it must break itself down: if anthropological analysis is 'like' LGBTQ activism then it cannot be unlike it at the same time. What I have sought to illustrate also though – and here I have definitely tried to hold the two things apart – is that these questions of resemblance and division (Strathern 2011), identity and difference, function themselves in different ways for LGBTQ activism and anthropology. It makes no sense to suggest that LGBTQ activists of this variety can 'choose' to adopt the perspective against which they are activists; they cannot identify with identity and remain activists of their form. Anthropologists though may make, as I have done here, (analytical) choices regarding when to emphasize identity over difference or vice versa in terms of their accounts and what they are accounts of. I do not think it incorrect or mistaken to 'choose' to focus on identities between our analysis and our data, and indeed I have done so here to a large extent. But insofar as this argument has sought to 'make a difference' to anthropology by 'making difference' between it and LGBTQ activism, it is in suggesting that it would be a mistake to lose sight of the fact that this is a choice, and that other choices are also available to us.

Notes

1. I have followed proponents of the recursive turn in treating this question as if it is a distinctively anthropological one. In fact, some of the best examples of anthropological writing on the subject have made productive comparison with other disciplines, particularly history and hermeneutics more generally (e.g. Evans-Pritchard 1950; Geertz 1973; Gellner 1970; Goody 1976; Lévi-Strauss 1985).
2. In the sense that the claim that 'there is a difference between analysis and ethnography' would be an analytical claim based on ethnography.
3. Similar to the idea van de Port describes as 'fake is the greater truth' (2012: 871).
4. Or at least cannot appear to itself as paradoxical, as I go on to argue.
5. As was the thought and life of Foucault (see e.g. Halperin 1995 and Bersani 1995).
6. Appropriately so as it has recently addressed the concept of 'revolution' itself (Holbraad 2014).
7. And many anthropologists would not have identified with either.

Conclusion

A central theme of this book has been a certain kind of relationship, one in which it is the differences, not the similarities, between the terms that is at issue.

In Chapter 1 I set out some of the political context of Bologna as a centre for LGBTQ activism, highlighting the apparent ideological uniformity of 'redness' in 'Red Bologna'. But my point in doing so was to emphasize that beneath this uniformity lay a genuine diversity of political orientation and value, as the concepts people referred to when they spoke about being left-wing were not in fact the same. Being left-wing was the idiom through which people connected radically different political beliefs. This led to a comparison with the way in which we conceptualize ethnographic and analytical concepts in anthropology and the suggestion that they may productively be viewed in the same light, as equivocal homonyms. There is thus no insuperable problem if being left-wing means something different (indeed many different things) in Bologna to that which it usually means in anthropology; indeed, it is precisely that difference that is interesting.

In Chapter 2 I described some of the ethical context of life as an LGBTQ activist, pointing to the ways in which people can not only differ from one another but also from themselves, so to speak. Through the concept of *doppia morale* I sought to show how it is possible to relate equivocally to an ethical injunction in such a way that the possibility of its betrayal is already inscribed in that manner of relating, thereby also suggesting that the choice sometimes framed as existing in the anthropology of ethics, between understanding morality as a set of rules or a process of reflection, is a false one; recognizing a moral code does not necessarily entail complete subjection to it.

Chapter 3 investigated the consequences of a failure to agree on differences. The police and the Church are different in some fairly obvious senses from the LGBTQ activist community, and so – for We Are Church in particular – they understood the problem of a dialogue to centre on the construction of common ground. But though We Are Church and its LGBTQ activist interlocutors may have found some affinities over love and authenticity, what they did not agree upon was exactly how they differed: We Are Church's attempts to emphasize resemblances made it appear a fringe group unable to represent Catholicism in general because it did not appear different enough to LGBTQ activists.

Chapter 4 dealt with a key moment in the debates I observed over difference amongst LGBTQ activists in Bologna, namely the 2012 Italian national Pride, using the latter as a prism through which to investigate the problem of how to build a community out of people who understand difference to be ubiquitous. I showed how Cassero's attempts to enrol queer activists in their vision of Pride failed because of differences over the notion of difference, and how Massimo's attempts to unite the more radical members of the city's LGBTQ activist community also fell foul of their resistance to a unified vision of difference, even one that claimed to be more 'real' than Cassero's. But it was also, in many ways, a unified community that came out on the day of Pride itself, if only because its belief in the virtue and necessity of performing difference clearly distinguished it from those watching on the side-lines.

Chapter 5 deliberately and explicitly switched registers from ethnography to analysis in order to raise the question of the relation between the two, one both connected and disconnected from the previous chapters. It argued that contemporary currents in anthropological theory that urge us to collapse the distinction between theory and ethnography in fact rely upon it.

Chapter 6 brought ethnography back to the question raised by the preceding chapter by drawing out some analogies between the relationship that some forms of queer activism have to their object, identity, and that of anthropological analysis to ethnography. It highlighted a similar, though inverted, paradox in both cases, but concluded by suggesting that the fundamental difference between queer activism and anthropology is that in the case of anthropological analysis and ethnography, the differences, or resemblances, between the two should not be understood as fundamental (an assertion this conclusion will complicate somewhat).

Different Differences

To the extent that this book has been about difference, it has mirrored a recent preoccupation in anthropological theory with difference, and different notions of difference.

As I have repeatedly noted, LGBTQ activism and anthropology share a constitutive concern for difference. But though I have sought throughout this book to describe the various ways in which difference enters into LGBTQ activism, I have yet to do so in any specific sense for anthropology. Indeed, doing so seems somewhat unnecessary: the manner in which anthropology is and always has been occupied with people and things that are or at least appear to be different from the things with which 'we' are familiar is obvious, even in an increasingly globalized world.

Yet – and perhaps this is related to anxieties over the place of anthropology in a world of similarities – there are some differences between the ways in which anthropologists of earlier generations wrote about difference and the way in which it emerges in contemporary writing (Jensen 2013: 309). In my Introduction, I recalled Herzfeld's pioneering critique of anthropology's focus on the exotic even amongst the near to hand (1987), and suggested that perhaps precisely because of its success it is less applicable today than it was at the time of its writing. But difference as a central theme remains, even if it is articulated differently, as it were.

As I hope is clear from Part Three of this book, my choice in emphasizing the way in which difference – not resemblance – is important in the relationships I have been describing – whether of activists to political ideologies, to their romantic partners, to moral codes, to fellow activists – has been for both ethnographic and analytical reasons. Ethnographic in the sense that putting the argumentative weight on difference is exactly what my LGBTQ activist interlocutors do; but also analytical because doing so has allowed me to make a comparison of a certain form with contemporary anthropological theory. I hope it is clear why I have chosen to make explicit the separation between the analytical and the ethnographic. In this conclusion, my aim is to expose some of the consequences of that focus on difference.

With regard to the analytical connection, I have so far confined the comparison to discussions of recursivity, but as I also noted in my introduction, the ethnographic relationships I have been describing resonate with broader contemporary writing on difference in anthropology, writing upon which much of the recursive turn is based. I have in mind an increasing body of work that goes beyond simple discussions of cultural difference or relativism; it is one that does not take the concept of difference itself for granted and instead asks questions about the difference, as it were, between differences (Viveiros de Castro 2004a, 2013: 482), an idea that is perhaps best encapsulated in Roy Wagner's now famous aphorism that, in his fieldwork with the Daribi, 'their misunderstanding of me was not the same as my misunderstanding of them' (1975: 20). At issue in the work of Wagner, Marilyn Strathern, Tim Ingold and Eduardo Viveiros de Castro, amongst others, through concepts such as 'equivocation', 'invention' or 'analogy' (e.g. Ingold 2000; Strathern 1988; Viveiros de Castro 2004a; Wagner 1975), is not just the question of how far people in the world differ from one another, but how they also differ over difference, much like the LGBTQ activists I have described here.

In other words, insofar as there exists a current of concern with difference in contemporary anthropology, it is itself different from the sort of which Herzfeld was so critical. As the title of a recent *Common Knowledge* symposium – 'comparative relativism' – playfully makes clear, it presumes neither commensurability nor absolute alterity, interrogating instead how such relationships between cultures (or ontologies) can be variously understood. Indeed, it goes further beyond Herzfeld's critique in the sense that some of the theories of difference it proposes are themselves derived from difference, by which I mean they are – or claim to be – based significantly upon insights derived from ethnographies of peoples in Amazonia, say, or Melanesia, thus undermining the idea that anthropological notions of difference must fundamentally draw their strength from its colonial heritage, or its Euro-American origins.

The work of Eduardo Viveiros de Castro is an exemplar of this kind of current in anthropology, clear and elegant in its language and incredibly thought-provoking in its argument. It is also probably the most extreme version of the 'different differences' problem – a bomb placed under Western philosophy, as Latour puts it (2009) – and for this reason I describe it here briefly as a foil against which to put the broader point of my conclusion. That broader point will concern exactly how different contemporary anthropological conceptions of difference really are (cf. Heywood 2012; Keane 2013: 187; Laidlaw 2012): in many respects they are radically so, to use a favourite adjective of this kind of writing; but in at least one respect I will suggest they are eminently conservative in their conception of difference. After establishing this resemblance between apparently different conceptions of difference, I conclude the book by making one final difference and sketching out an alternative anthropological conception of difference.

In his landmark 1998 article on Amerindian perspectivism (1998), Viveiros de Castro draws on the work of a range of Amazonianist ethnographers as well as his own fieldwork in order to advance an argument that both clarified a number of hitherto unsystematized resemblances amongst various Amerindian myths, practices and rituals, as well as challenging a foundational analytical perspective in anthropology, namely the idea that difference in the world is to be explained by cultural variation. Viveiros de Castro turns this assumption on its head by documenting the ways in which – for a range of Amerindian peoples – it is nature, not culture, which differentiates, bodies rather than souls which define perspectives, and a common humanity that unites not only people but people and other species. What is universal in this cosmology is not the universe itself but a single – human – perspective upon a multitude of universes.

In a wonderful example of this broader point Viveiros de Castro re-interprets Lévi-Strauss's anecdotal comparison of the Valladolid controversy and the drowning of captured Spanish soldiers by indigenous peoples of the Antilles (Lévi-Strauss 1952). Lévi-Strauss's point in making the comparison was that we are alike in our savagery, which indexes precisely the link that both the Spanish and their indigenous counterparts were seeking to discover between themselves (see also 1961: 81). Viveiros de Castro, by contrast, points out that though what both parties doubted was whether or not they had anything in common, their methods of investigating the presence or absence of difference were themselves notably different. What the Spanish at Valladolid doubted was whether or not Amerindians possessed souls like their own; their possession of bodies was not in question; natural resemblance was presupposed, the issue being whether or not the Amerindians were sufficiently culturally or spiritually akin to the Spanish to be recognizable to the latter as humans. For the inhabitants of the Antilles, by contrast what was taken for granted was the fact that their Spanish captives had souls; since even animals possess the same soul, this could not be in doubt. What was at issue instead was whether or not the bodies of the Spanish were the same as their own: ghosts have souls too, but they do not drown.

The ethnographic systematization Viveiros de Castro provides of already well-documented instances of what he describes is not – with some exceptions (e.g. Turner 2009) – much disputed, but as the author himself has turned increasingly to more broadly philosophical concerns (e.g. 2003; 2004a; 2011a), its analytical implications continue to be hotly debated, complex as they are. Anyone who has tried teaching the topic to undergraduates may not have to imagine the disheartening look on a student's face when, having got to grips with the facts of the argument, they declare 'so in their culture difference is natural', and realization of the paradoxical implications of that statement sets in.

Hence the status of Viveiros De Castro's argument in that paper as a paradigmatic exemplar of the kind of anthropology I have been discussing, for at issue is not merely difference, but a difference of differences, again, much as I have been describing in this book. Indeed, in his later work Viveiros de Castro elevates perspectivist translation – or 'equivocation' – to the status of a potential model for anthropological translation (2004a), an argument I have often referred to in this book.

Here though what I want to do is to reverse the prior focus of this book on difference and ask what implications emerge when we ask what resemblances exist between the model Viveiros de Castro describes and that with which he contrasts it, the implications precisely having to do with resemblance and difference. This I hope will both illustrate (and further complicate) the point of the preceding two chapters – that even in this extreme example anthropologists have a choice about what to emphasize – and, by way of conclusion to the book, offer up some final thoughts on what queer activism can tell us about anthropology.

The Natures of Difference and Different Natures

Anthropologists (along with a great many others) use the word 'nature' to refer to multiple different things. Amongst these things, two, in particular, are of interest for the argument here: firstly, an object, or perhaps even objects in general (world, matter, the environment, animals, volcanoes, jaguars and so on); secondly, a property of objects (the essential and constitutive aspect of something that makes it that thing and not another, and without which it becomes something else).

The argument I will make here is that at least some of the complexity and power of arguments concerning the multiplicity of nature is that as well as describing radical difference and equivocation (of a sort), often they themselves equivocate over these two possible referents of the word.

The purpose of the argument is not to challenge the ethnographic basis of such claims, which would be far beyond my expertise, and for the same reason this conclusion is likewise not in any sense intended to be ethnographically exhaustive in its depiction of perspectivism, or its cosmological opposite, perspectivalism. I sketch out the schematic features of both in order to illustrate the ways in which they appear in broader anthropological arguments over difference. My purpose in doing so is to clarify some of the implications of this work for anthropology: the meta-problems, if you will, involved in describing and accounting for its apparent radical difference from our own understandings of difference.

It is far beyond the scope and ambition of this conclusion to provide a comprehensive overview of the literature on perspectivism. As I have already suggested, my invocations of 'perspectivism' and 'naturalism' are not ethnographic, but anthropological, in that I am interested in how they have appeared in anthropological arguments, rather than their relationship to objects and behaviours in the world: in their status as indexing a 'relation of intelligibility between two cultures', not as 'veridical reflections' of those cultures (Viveiros de Castro 2014: 190), and in the broader arguments that have emerged from this relation. I will briefly sketch out some of perspectivism's relevant features below, largely as they emerge from the work of perhaps its most well-known exponent, Eduardo Viveiros de Castro (e.g. 1996, 1998, 2004a, 2004b, 2007, 2011a, 2012, 2014).

In the schema of perspectivist arguments, 'we' understand difference to be a matter of culture or worldview. For 'us', human beings are naturally identical and members of the same species, but spiritually and mentally diverse. Our bodies are the same, but our souls and our minds are different. We also live in the same world, but our ideas about it vary. There is 'a physical continuity and a metaphysical discontinuity between humans and animals' (Viveiros de Castro 1998: 479, 2004a: 475). 'Spirit or mind ... raises us above animals ... [and] makes each person unique before his or her fellow beings' (1998: 479, 2004a: 475). In that sense, we exist in natural unity and cultural diversity. This corresponds to the first sense in which I used the word 'nature' above: human bodies are the same sorts of object; the world is one thing. Cultures are multiple. Nature is not.

In the ethnographic literature on Amazonia, on the other hand, the situation is the mirror inverse of 'ours'. There, 'humanity' is 'the universal form of the subject' (Viveiros de Castro 1998: 470, 2004a: 468), and 'the common point of reference for all beings of nature is not humans as a species but rather humanity as a condition' (Descola 1986: 120; Viveiros de Castro 1998: 472). Hence, Amerindian words which designate 'human being' mark 'a social condition of personhood', not 'a natural species' (Viveiros de Castro 1998: 476). Hence, equally, the proliferation of origin myths in which the primordial condition is not a natural animality from which human beings must distinguish themselves through culture, but a humanity which animals proceed to lose (Viveiros de Castro 1998: 471, 2004a: 464, 2014: 68–69). All humans, which, as a designator of personhood not species includes some animals, share the same spirit, soul or perspective upon the world ('jaguars see blood as manioc beer, vultures see the maggots in rotting meat as grilled fish'; Viveiros de Castro 1998: 470). The body, in contrast, is an 'envelope' or 'clothing' which conceals an inner human essence (Viveiros de Castro 1998: 471), but is also responsible for the different objects seen (Viveiros de Castro 1998: 478, 2004a: 474). Here, in other words, we have a metaphysical continuity of subjecthood and a physical discontinuity of objects. Souls, which mark the person as human, are the same, whilst bodies, bundles of 'affects and capacities' which 'differentiate perspectives', are different (Viveiros de Castro 1998: 478, 2004a: 474, 2004b: 6). The worlds thus perceived also differ (hence, famously, 'multinaturalism') even as the form of the human perspective does not. Cultures are not multiple. Nature is.

The dilemma to which this gives rise is the status of that description itself: is that difference, between natures as different and cultures as different, a cultural one? Claiming that it is would diminish the radical nature of the difference in question (over nature itself) as well as leading inevitably to the conclusion that Amerindians are wrong, not only in the content of their worldview but in believing it not to be one. Culturalism when applied to perspectivism 'implies the negation or delegitimization of its object' (Viveiros de Castro 2004b: 5, 2014: 87). The option of describing it as a natural difference in seemingly recursive fashion is as hard to swallow as the culturalist option, as the practice of designating some peoples as 'naturally' different from others has a more than troubled political history (for discussion of which in relation to multinaturalism see e.g. Vigh and Sausdal 2014). This troubled political history is the source of some critiques of anthropology's 'ontological turn' that see it as exoticizing and othering of its subjects. As Vigh and Sausdal put it, 'Though ontology, as it glides from defining things, concepts and ideas to denoting people, groups and entire civilizations, is not necessarily articulated as rooted and territorialized, it is nonetheless theoretically constructed as naturalized and essentialized, internally coherent and bounded, as incommensurable worlds' (2014: 65).

These are what I mean by the 'meta-problems' to which the by now already classic plethora of ethnographic descriptions of perspectivism in Amazonia (and elsewhere – see e.g. Pedersen, Empson and Humphrey 2007; Willerslev 2007) have given rise. They are fundamental problems in anthropology, given the foundational status of notions surrounding 'cultural difference' in the discipline, and help to explain why these ethnographic descriptions have given rise to a whole corpus of methodological and epistemological reflections on the status of anthropological knowledge itself (e.g. Henare, Holbraad and Wastell 2006; Holbraad 2012; Viveiros de Castro 2004b, 2011a, 2014). They have been bombs placed under Western philosophy, as Latour describes them (Latour 2009).

Though Viveiros de Castro has elsewhere referred to his characterization of Amerindian cosmologies as 'tactical (procedural) quintessentialism' (Viveiros de Castro 2011b: 165), in perhaps his most sustained reflections on the methodological implications of Amerindian perspectivism for the basic anthropological projects of translation and comparison, he refers to the indigenous version of these as 'equivocation'. He goes on to elevate it to the 'condition of possibility' of the anthropological enterprise (Viveiros de Castro 2004b: 10, 2014: 89).

Equivocation, as I have noted elsewhere in this book, is neither direct culturalist translation of the traditional anthropological kind, nor essentialization or objectification, but 'the relational positivity of difference' (Viveiros de Castro 2004b: 12, 2014: 74). It is not about 'discovering the common referent ... to two different representations' (Viveiros de Castro 2004b: 6) but instead about not 'losing sight of the difference concealed within equivocal "homonyms"' (Viveiros de Castro 2004b: 7). The question I wish to pose here, however, is what kind of difference? Critiquing, in the same piece, work which imposes cultural constructionist frameworks onto indigenous perspectivist cosmologies, Viveiros de Castro notes, following Wagner, that 'there is all the difference in the world' between the two (2004b: 16; Wagner 1975: 51; see also Viveiros de Castro 2014: 62–63), and that reducing one to the frameworks of the other is 'to imagine an overly simple form of relation between them' (Viveiros de Castro 2004b: 16). But that, surely, is precisely the question, in many ways the most basic of anthropological questions: are they so different? Or, perhaps better, what is it in our descriptions of them that causes such differences to appear, and can these descriptions be differentiated yet further?

Clearly, even from the extremely minimal description I have provided of 'perspectivism' and what is often called 'naturalism', its Western counterpart, they are, in some respects extremely different. But given that the problem they raise for anthropological description is precisely about difference and its (potentially different) status in these cosmologies, it makes sense to be specific about what kind of difference this is.

To return to the distinction between referents of 'nature' I made above, it is evident that 'nature', in so far as it refers to a set of objects, is indeed distributed differently across these two schemas. Within naturalist cosmologies, as they are represented, there is one world, and a 'physical continuity' across bodies. 'Nature', in fact, in this sense, is what is responsible not for difference but for resemblance. It is the ground upon which comparative projects, cultural translation and indeed all forms of communication take place. As an object, in other words, it plays exactly the mirror image role that 'culture' occupies in perspectivist cosmologies. Take the following excerpt from Viveiros de Castro's landmark 1998 article on the subject, for example:

We must remember, above all, that if there is a virtually universal Amerindian notion, it is that of an original state of undifferentiation between humans and animals, described in mythology. Myths are filled with beings whose form, name and behaviour inextricably mix human and animal attributes in a common context of intercommunicability, identical to that which defines the present-day intra-human world. The differentiation between 'culture' and 'nature', which Lévi-Strauss showed to be the central theme of Amerindian mythology, is not a process of differentiating the human from the animal, as in our evolutionist mythology. The original common condition of both humans and animals is not animality but rather humanity. (1998: 471; see also 2012: 31–32; Vilaça 2014: 323)

In other words, Amerindian cosmologies also include the notion of 'an original state of undifferentiation between humans and animals'. Theirs is of humanity, ours of animality. Theirs of culture, ours of nature. That difference is of course enormously ethnographically significant. But it is worth noting that it is a perfect mirror-image inversion of what 'nature' does for 'us', as Viveiros de Castro himself points out (Viveiros de Castro 1998: 470): this is important not because it is a happy coincidence, but because, seen from the perspective of our anthropological meta-problem of what difference and resemblance mean, the only thing that has changed is the object. Both cosmologies possess notions of an originary, grounding resemblance between subjects. Both kinds of resemblance are given, essential features of life, not constructed or instituted by humans. In fact, if we were to reserve the word 'natural' to mean 'essential', rather than allowing it also to refer to animals or the environment, then there would be no difference between the two cosmologies in this respect at all. I repeat that I am not, in any sense, discounting the importance of the perspective from which they do appear different: I am merely pointing out that from another they appear remarkably alike. And since likeness and difference are at issue here, that other perspective is worth noting.

Something similar is visible if we examine the opposite pole of the two cosmologies. 'Culture' is what differentiates, in the schema of naturalism. It is what humans have, but we all have it differently. It is the object or medium of those projects of comparison, translation, communication or conversion that take place against the background of natural uniformity. It is variable, constructed and shifting. It is also, in those respects, the point for point opposite of 'nature' as it is described in Amerindian cosmologies, though of course the objects to which the word 'cultural' might attach remain the same. Take for example this description of the importance of bodily metamorphosis in perspectivism:

The performative rather than given character of the body, a conception that requires it to differentiate itself 'culturally' in order for it to be 'naturally' different, has an obvious connexion with interspecific metamorphosis, a possibility suggested by Amerindian cosmologies. We need not be surprised by a way of thinking that posits bodies as the great differentiators yet at the same time states their transformability. Our cosmology supposes a singular distinctiveness of minds, but not even for this reason does it declare communication (albeit solipsism is a constant problem) to be impossible, or deny the mental/spiritual transformations induced by processes such as education and religious conversion; in truth, it is precisely because the spiritual is the locus of difference that conversion becomes necessary (the Europeans wanted to know whether Indians had souls in order to modify them). Bodily metamorphosis is the Amerindian counterpart to the European theme of spiritual conversion. (Viveiros de Castro 1998: 481, 2014: 72; see also Vilaça 2005, 2011: 246–47)

Note again the equivalence established between the two schemas: (bodily) metamorphosis is (cultural) translation. That is, the objects transformed are entirely different in either case (souls and bodies), but the fact of transformation is not. Differences, in both schemas, are matters of contingent variability, not essential and stable properties. 'We need not be surprised' at the notion of bodies as differentiators because they function as differentiators in precisely the same way as souls do for us. The same point emerges from a summary of perspectivism in Viveiros de Castro's idea of equivocation:

> Such difference of perspective – not a plurality of views of a single world, but a single view of different worlds – cannot derive from the soul, since the latter is the common original ground of being. Rather, such difference is located in the bodily differences between species, for the body and its affections (in Spinoza's sense, the body's capacities to affect and be affected by other bodies) is the site and instrument of ontological differentiation and referential disjunction. (2004b: 6; see also Vilaça 2005: 450)

Here, again, we have the idea of 'culture' as a 'common original ground of being' – as a stable and essential resemblance between subjects, in other words – and the notion of the body as an instrument of 'differentiation'. The word 'ontological' here – as, perhaps, in other anthropological uses of it – is only denoting the object of difference, not the nature of it: what differentiates them (bodies) can change, just like what differentiates us (souls); what makes them the same (souls) cannot, just like what makes us the same (bodies). Or, reformulated: souls are the natural properties of humans in perspectivism ('*Culture is the Subject's nature*' (Viveiros de Castro 1998: 481, italics in original), and bodies are their natural properties in naturalism. Or, reformulated again, (cultural or natural) resemblance is 'given', and (natural or cultural) difference is 'performed', as we can observe in Viveiros de Castro's critique of Greg Urban's work on the Shokleng:

> At the end of reading *Metaphysical Community*, the reader cannot but feel a certain unease in noting that Urban's splitting of the world – into a given realm of jaguars and pine trees, and a constructed world of groups and emblems – is not the split made by the Shokleng. Actually, it is almost exactly the inverse... it is social organization that was 'out there', and the jaguars and tapirs that were created or performed by it. The institutional fact created the brute fact. Unless, of course, the brute fact is the clanic division of society, and the institutional fact is the jaguars of the forest. For the Shokleng, in fact, culture is the given and nature is the constructed. (Viveiros de Castro 2004b: 13)

The reading of this material I have proposed thus far is not an alternative to the traditional one of perspectivist literature, in the sense that it is all present in the original explanations, but it does take a different perspective, one created by the equivocation over referents of 'nature' and 'culture'. One might tabulate these perspectives in the following manner, making use of some of the categories Viveiros de Castro himself suggests need redistributing when dealing with perspectivist cosmologies (Viveiros de Castro 1998: 469–70, 2014: 56).

Here is a fairly uncontroversial rendering of naturalism:

Nature	Physical	Universal	Given	Necessary
Culture	Social	Particular	Instituted	Spontaneous

Here is the reading of the perspectivist scheme that gives rise to worries about essentialism and the 'ontologizing' of difference:

Nature	Physical	*Particular*	Given	Necessary
Culture	Social	*Universal*	Instituted	Spontaneous

In this first reading of the perspectivist schema, the attributes of 'instituted' and 'given', 'necessary' and 'spontaneous', have remained attached to their relationship with culture and nature, whilst the particular and the universal have shifted. This reading thus sees particular differences, because they are now labelled 'natural', as given and necessary: as essentialist, in other words.

Here, instead, is the one I have been outlining:

Nature	Physical	*Particular*	*Instituted*	*Spontaneous*
Culture	Social	*Universal*	*Given*	*Necessary*

This second reading leaves the universal and the particular in the same relationship to the given and the instituted as in the naturalism schema. But this is more than simply a question of whether or not multinaturalism or 'ontological' anthropology entails essentialism or not. It relates to the meta-problem of how the two schemas relate. Discard the middle table and we are left with the following:

Naturalism:

Nature	Physical	Universal	Given	Necessary
Culture	Social	Particular	Instituted	Spontaneous

Perspectivism:

Nature	Physical	Particular	Instituted	Spontaneous
Culture	Social	Universal	Given	Necessary

Recall that the question I suggested I would attempt to address here was that of how to articulate the relationship between cosmologies that are not merely different but differ over difference itself: contexts that are 'radically' or 'onto-logically' different from our own. The difference between perspectivism and naturalism has often been taken to exemplify this difference, and a glance at the tables above is enough to make clear why this is the case: the three boxes on the right-hand side have been switched around in moving from the first to the second.

That is one perspective. Another perspective is that it is only the two boxes on the left-hand side that have switched around. In other words, the objects which differ from one another in particular, instituted and spontaneous ways in naturalism (souls, for example, or ideas, or worldviews – 'social' things) are not the same objects which differ from one another in particular, instituted and spontaneous ways in perspectivism (bodies, for example, or worlds – 'physical' things), but the fact of their difference and particularity being a matter of variation and transformation (institution and spontaneity, not essence and necessity) does not itself differ across the schemas. It is the objects of difference that have changed, not the nature of difference itself. The differ-ence is over natural objects, not nature as essence. The difference between particular cases remains instituted, performed and variable.

In other words, from the point of view of what it means to be different, rather than what it is that is different, the two cosmologies do not, in fact, appear to be so different. Let us call the former the 'nature of difference'. If we proceed from the point of view laid out here – one that I again emphasize is only one such point of view; seen from another the two are as different as can be – then difference has the same nature in the two cosmologies: the particu-lar is instituted and spontaneous, not given and necessary, just as the universal is given and necessary, not instituted and spontaneous. The Other of the Other may not be the same as the Other of the Same (Viveiros de Castro 2004b: 12), but the relation between the Other of the Other and the Other of the Same is the same.

If we return to the table above, from the perspective I take here the boxes marked 'nature' and 'culture' actually tell us relatively little when detached from those to which they are analogized. The splendour and complexity of perspec-tivist universes for anthropology is not in the abstractive acrobatics of neolo-gisms like 'multinaturalism', but in their meaning: that nature can refer to certain kinds of objects and at the same time to essence and givenness (Viveiros de Castro 2014: 75). The reason why statements of the form *Culture is the Subject's nature* need italicizing is that the words 'culture' and 'nature' are doing both those different sorts of work at the same time: 'Culture', not meaning something that has been instituted or constructed but the possession of a view-point or a soul, is not the subject's body, but the subject's given essence.

If we thus detach the boxes containing the words 'nature' and 'culture' from the tables we are left with a shuffling around of objects, such as bodies and souls. Nothing else has moved. 'All the difference in the world', from one per-spective; not so different at all, from another.

Take, for example, the frequently cited anecdote from Lévi-Strauss, with which I began this discussion of perspectivism (1952: 12; see also 1961: 79–81). Lévi-Strauss's point in making the comparison was that we are alike in our savagery, which indexes precisely the link that both the Spanish and their indigenous counterparts were seeking to discover between themselves. Viveiros de Castro, by contrast, points out that though what both parties doubted was whether or not they had anything in common, their methods of investigating the presence or absence of difference were themselves notably different:

> Just as jaguars and humans apply the same name to two very different things, both Europeans and Indians 'were talking' about humanity, that is, they were questioning the applicability of this self-descriptive concept to the Other. However, what Europeans and Indians understood to be the concept's defining criterion (its intension and consequently its extension) was radically different. (Viveiros de Castro 2004b: 9; see also Viveiros de Castro 2014: 50–51)

The understandings in question are indeed radically different in terms of extension – body or soul; and intension, at least in so far as the meaning of 'humanity' for one is species and for the other a subject position. But, in fact, those are precisely the aspects of the other that neither party doubts. The Spanish assume a natural – in the sense of physical – continuity between themselves and the Indians. The latter assume a cultural – in the sense of metaphysical – continuity between themselves and the Spanish. Neither expects the universals they assume to vary with institutions or contexts. We can also infer from what we already know of perspectivism and naturalism that both will assume the discontinuities – the particularities of each – to be instituted and thus subject to change (in fact the *Tristes tropiques* rendering of this story has a colonist say that the Indians' 'grandchildren just *might* be up' to running their own society in the future, and in the *Race et Histoire* version he has Indians place those outside their group on a continuum related to bodies: 'monkeys', 'louse-eggs' and 'ghosts'; 1961: 79; 1952: 12). In both cases, what is shared is imagined as unchangeable and necessary, and what is different is imagined as transformable and spontaneous.

When Viveiros de Castro relates this story in his 1998 piece on *deixis*, the equivalence between the two forms of ethnocentrism is clearly on display: perspectivism and naturalism look alike, from this point of view. By the time it is retold in 2004 in his article on equivocation, from which the above quotation is drawn (Viveiros de Castro 2004a), the emphasis is on the 'radically different' location of humanity. But either perspective, one assumes, is legitimate, and if instead of focusing on the radical difference of location, we note the resemblance of form (continuities are assumed and necessary where discontinuities are not), then the meta-problem of the differences and resemblances between the two itself appears in a different light.

Necessary Resemblances

This perspective, from which these cosmologies do not appear so different, is that with which I am occupied here: the nature of difference. We can now frame a sort of meta-comparison, a comparison of comparisons, of the form Viveiros de Castro undertakes in outlining the notion of equivocation. Rather than focus on the object of such comparisons, however, in line with the argument so far, I will focus on their form.

In perspectivist cosmologies there are things which are universal and things which are particular. The relationship of likeness or resemblance implied by universality is given and necessary. It is not the case that things that are universal just happen to be so, nor that they happen to have been made to be so, but that they must be so, and are essentially so. The relationship of difference implied by particularity is instituted and spontaneous. It is not the case that things that are different must be different, nor that such differences are unchangeable, but that they are produced, and may be otherwise.

Exactly the same is true of perspectivalist cosmologies.

Both sides of our meta-comparison, therefore, take attributes that are universal and shared to be essential and necessary when comparing, and both sides take attributes that are particular and differ to be instituted and spontaneous when comparing.

For our meta-comparison to resemble its component parts, which it must do for there is nothing else to it, then that fact itself must be given and necessary because it is shared across them. It is, within the terms of the meta-comparison, universal, and what is universal within the parts of the meta-comparison is essential. Therefore, what is particular to the two sides of the comparison must equally be instituted and spontaneous, because it differs across them, just as what differs within them is instituted and spontaneous. In other words, just as discontinuities within the two cosmologies are matters of performance or construction (bodies or souls) so must be the discontinuities across the two cosmologies: the 'tactics' of 'tactical quintessentialism'. By this expression I take Viveiros de Castro to mean the strategy I noted above in regard to story of the Valladolid controversy: of emphasizing not likeness, but difference. What I add here is that such emphasized differences are necessarily strategic or tactical. Whereas the nature of difference, the essence of difference – as not, itself, essential or necessary – is, necessarily and essentially, the same across the schemas.

To state this more clearly: it is true ethnographically, as we have seen, that within the two schemas the difference between particular cases is instituted and spontaneous and what is universal is given and necessary. Therefore, that fact is itself universal across the two cases, and as such, logically, must also be given and necessary.

Meta-comparison:

Particular ('social' or 'natural' objects) = instituted, spontaneous

Universal (nature of universality and particularity) = given, necessary

Perpectivalist comparison:	**Perspectivist comparison:**
Particular = instituted, spontaneous ('social')	*Particular* = instituted, spontaneous ('natural')
Universal = given, necessary ('natural')	*Universal* = given, necessary ('social')

'All the difference in the world', seen from this perspective, is actually always only a certain kind of difference, one which is instituted and spontaneous; and because it is always that kind of difference, it is necessarily and essentially always that kind of difference. All the difference in the world is the same. From this perspective, then, this paradigmatic example of 'radical alterity' actually tells us that in a certain sense we are all the same, and we are necessarily and essentially so.

To draw out the connection between this rather abstract point and the ethnographic substance of this book, it is worth being a bit more specific about the meaning of a term I have so far been using as if it were relatively unambiguous: identity.

Identity and difference often sound as if they are opposed to one another, but as I hope Part Three of this book made clear, they usually also appear as two sides of the same coin. In fact, if we think of the meaning of identity as the essence of any particular thing that is not particularly surprising: in that sense, without identity there is no difference.

From this point of view there is no logical problem with asserting the instituted or constructed nature of both identity and difference. Indeed, if one is instituted, then so must the other be as well. If identity – as what makes one thing different from another – is constructed then of course so is the consequent difference.

Identity however can also mean something other than a thing's essence, an ambiguity I have occasionally exploited in this book: it can also mean a relationship of resemblance between two things, and in this respect obviously it must be the opposite of difference (cf. Sökefeld 1999). This is where the connection with the comparison made above between perspectivism and perspectivalism emerges: if we insist – as we do for example even when we talk about 'strategic essentialism', or 'tactical quintessentialism' – that identity in the first sense, and consequently difference, is constructed, then we cannot do the same for identity in the second sense. If there is nothing given that differentiates one thing from another then their identity or resemblance – in that respect – must itself be given. Precisely, in fact, as is true in the case of the given (cultural) resemblance between souls in perspectivism, the given (natural) resemblance between bodies in perspectivism, and – precisely because in both cases resemblance is given – the given resemblance between the two systems. What I am suggesting, in other words, is that if all we can assert is that all identity – in the first sense – is instituted and contingent, and that therefore no difference is given, then that assertion itself cannot be contingent. If all difference is constructed, then we are – in that respect at least – all the same, and we are so essentially.

The irony is not new. Michael Herzfeld makes this claim quite explicitly in his entry on 'Essentialism' in the *Encyclopaedia of Social and Cultural Anthropology*: 'Knowing this contested history [of eugenics in biology] enables us to focus on the *necessarily contingent* character of all forms of essentialism' (Herzfeld 1996: 189, my italics). It is also present as the implied opposite of ideas such as 'tactical quintessentialism': if essentialism is tactical, or strategic, what else can anti-essentialism be but given and necessary? But it is notable that it is visible in the kind of contemporary work in anthropology that is alleged to be most sensitive to difference, indeed, to have revolutionized our notion of difference itself.

This is where the final comparison with my ethnographic material emerges, and why I hope I can justify a degree of ambiguity in the way in which I have been using the term 'identity'. For in the case of queer activism I have been describing, the two senses of the word collapse into one, making the problem just outlined explicit: I have suggested that queer activism is about 'making a difference' by 'making difference' from essential identities. Paradoxically, that is its own identity. But the kind of identity produced by its production of difference is both identity as essence and identity as resemblance: it is identity as essence in so far as the activity of producing or constructing difference from essential identities is itself essential to queer activism; and precisely because it is identity as essence in this sense, it is also identity as a resemblance with other essential identities such as those they oppose.

In other words, queer activism as I have described it makes clearly visible the consequences of anthropology's uniform conception of difference: it asserts that all difference is constructed, and in so doing delineates for itself an essential identity, and moreover one which resembles other such essential identities, thus collapsing constructed and contingent difference into necessary resemblance. What it makes explicit is what I have just sought to show through the comparison of perspectivism and perspectivalism: that assertions of the constructed nature of difference are – and are necessarily – also assertions of the given nature of resemblance.

As I have noted, my aim in drawing this point out is not to criticize this kind of activism, just as the point of the earlier comparison of Amerindian and Euro-American comparisons was – obviously – not intended to be critical of either. It is legitimate to ask however – as a great many anthropologists have, and as this book has sought to do – whether the methodological assumptions of anthropological theory need to mirror – need necessarily to resemble, if you will – ones we find out there in the world. Indeed, there are several problems with doing so, as I outline below.

A Proposition

Having posed the question, I conclude with a deliberately controversial proposition, which inverts, in a rather hesitant fashion, the conclusion of Part Three of the book: throughout the latter, when referring to the difference between the concerns of anthropological theory and analysis and those of ethnography, I emphasized the produced and strategic nature of such difference. Indeed, a central plank of its argument was that for my language of analysis to be properly recursive in relation to my ethnography, I had to 'make a difference' between the two. In other words, whilst I experimented with switching perspectives from one that would emphasize resemblance to one that would emphasize difference, what I took for granted was that the nature of such differences meant that they would have to be made.

That assumption in LGBTQ activism, or Amerindian perspectivism, or Euro-American perspectivalism, has no problematic basis, and is obviously a matter for description and nothing else. But making that assumption about the relation between ethnography and anthropological analysis is not a matter of description, and entails some consequences: it suggests, for example, that without the production of such differences, analysis and ethnography will necessarily collapse into one another. It also entails the necessity of addressing questions of anthropological methodology – such as those the latter part of this book has addressed – through ethnographic material because the relation between the two is assumed. But since this itself is a methodological question, not one of description, there is no reason to assume it could not be subject to change.

Furthermore, there are problems that ensue from building theoretical edifices out of indigenous thought in terms of difference itself: one such problem relates to the highly schematic and homogenized status of cosmologies of difference as, for example, I have laid them out here and as they are often invoked in anthropological debates around the notion of 'difference'. The schemas themselves are as essentialist – as in, homogenizing – as the anthropological arguments (for difference as always and everywhere non-essential) that they support. It is hardly necessary to stretch the imagination to think of instances in which those we might habitually describe as 'perspectivalist' in their thinking treat difference as given and necessary, rather than spontaneous: this is not only true (some of the time) of some of the arguments concerning eugenics and its complicated political history that Vigh and Sausdal, and Herzfeld presumably have in mind, but also (some of the time) of animal scientists (some of the time), of geneticists, or (some of the time) of mathematicians (e.g. Brodwin 2002; Candea 2010c; 2013). An ethnographer of Amazonia, one assumes likewise, will not find it difficult to think of instances either in litera-ture or in their own experience in which the same is true of perspectivists – for example, it is often remarked that not all animals possess the attribute of personhood (e.g. Viveiros de Castro 1998: 471).

Another, related, problem is that of just how different the models of thought we discover in our ethnography end up being from our own preferred brand of Euro-American thinking: this is akin to the point Candea has made about the resemblance between the 'metaphysics of the other' described by much contemporary anthropological writing and our own 'other metaphysics' of Deleuze or Heidegger (2017), and indeed to the point of the preceding section, that the radical ontological difference of perspectivism is in some ways not so different from the cultural difference of perspectivalism after all.

To condense both problems into one: there are undoubtedly people in the world who think of difference (or at least some kinds of difference) as given and essential, and they also happen to be the people anthropologists are least interested in taking seriously.

I did not, as far as I am aware, meet such people during my fieldwork. Indeed, had I done so I would have been surprised, as – for reasons that should be clear by now – this conception of difference could not itself be more different from that of the queer activists with whom I spent most of my time. In other words, the proposition below is a final instance of 'making a differ-ence', in that if it resembles a conception of difference to be found in an ethno-graphic context, that context could not be further from my own; and for that reason there is also no way it can be mistaken for another recursive call to 'take seriously' a neglected ethnographic context – such a call might of course be made, but not by me.

My proposition is that we try to understand the difference between our analysis and our ethnography not as an object of production, or performance, or strategy, but as necessary and given and perhaps even essential. I am sug-gesting that whilst essentialism clearly makes for bad ethnographic descrip-tion when it comes to matters of fact in the cases of both perspectivism and perspectivalism, and indeed in my own ethnographic context, and bad politics when it comes to LGBTQ activism, it may not make for bad analytical strategy when it comes to thinking about anthropology itself.

This may sound rather radical but it is less so than it appears: think for example again of Herzfeld's comparison of exoticism in Greece and anthropol-ogy (1987); clearly to some extent that comparison was a descriptive one, grounded in an analysis of the history of anthropological concerns with differ-ence and of European margins. But it was also normative: it was a call for anthropology to exorcise its colonial demons through a focus on its own 'internal other'. The resemblance between a certain Euro-American mode of thought and a methodological issue in anthropology was clearly not imagined to be, therefore, a necessary one, and a part of the point of Herzfeld's argu-ment was that it ought to change.

Furthermore, it has changed: as I have sought to highlight, categories of anthropological analysis are now alleged to emerge from ethnographic contexts as varied as Melanesia, Amazonia or Cuba. Herzfeld's normative point has been taken so seriously that the methodological problems we now concern ourselves with are of a quite different sort – indeed about difference itself, as I have suggested – and the answers we propose are quite deliberately claimed to be rooted in contexts far from a colonial or Euro-American one.

But what if, instead of taking Herzfeld's point about anthropology and its resemblance to Euro-American thought and assuming that a better solution would be to discover a necessary resemblance elsewhere, a 'reverse ethnocentrism', as Vigh and Sausdal put it (2014: 53) – with, say, infinition in Cuban divination, or equivocation in Amerindian perspectivism – we stop assuming a resemblance of any kind at all? Why, indeed, should any ethnographic context reveal the answer to a question such as how to bound a field-site, or what a comparison is, or, indeed, what the relation between theory and ethnography ought to be? Whether or not identity, and consequently difference, to Amerindians, Euro-Americans or LGBTQ activists is a matter of performance is an ethnographic question; whether or not anthropology's own distinct identity in asking such questions is performed or essential is not; and precisely in so far as that distinction itself holds true it suggests an answer to the latter question. The difference between methodological questions in anthropology and our ethnographic descriptions is essential, not contingent.

I should be clear that this suggestion that we consider methodological questions in anthropology to be essentially distinct from any ethnographic ones does not exclude the truism that such methodological questions have a particular history, or that they come with certain kinds of (Euro-American) philosophical baggage; but the work of thinkers such as Viveiros de Castro, Wagner, Strathern and proponents of the recursive turn is collective testament to the fact that that history does not have to determine their future, and that baggage does not have to be left unexamined.

What alternative consequences does this proposition entail? For a start, it allows us to avoid what I have no doubt will be seen as the central problem of this book: it would no longer be necessary to address – even in the somewhat roundabout manner that I have done here – complex methodological questions through an engagement with ethnography of some form, and ethnography would no longer come combined with abstract ruminations about what it can tell us about anthropology as a discipline.

As should be obvious from the content of the latter part of this book, I consider such methodological issues to be deeply important, and I think simply ignoring or dismissing them is not a sustainable position. But my point is that we can only gain in our ability to answer them by recognizing the fairly self-evident truth that they are not of the same kind as ethnographic ones (cf. Ingold 2014). A large portion of Part Three of this book has been an attempt to show that this difference exists. But that this is in many ways self-evident should be clear to any reader whose reaction is to wonder why I have not discussed the connections between LGBTQ activism and political economy, say, or the broader place of the Catholic Church in Italian politics, or pursued some of the implications of the earlier chapters for the anthropology of ethics, or even just added some more description.

These latter sorts of questions are also, obviously, important, and the majority of this book has attempted to address examples of them despite the diversions of its final part. Would such questions be better addressed in the absence of diversions into methodological issues? Undoubtedly, and that is exactly the point I have just been making. But it is a point – a difference – that needs to be made, not taken for granted.

References

Agrama, H. 2010. 'Ethics, Tradition, Authority: Toward an Anthropology of the Fatwa', *American Ethnologist* 37, 2–18.

Albera, D. 2006. 'Anthropology of the Mediterranean: Between Crisis and Renewal', *History and Anthropology* 17, 109–33.

Anapol, D. 1997. *Polyamory: the New Love Without Limits; Secrets of Sustainable Intimate Relationships*. San Rafael, CA: IntiNet Resource Center.

_____. 2010. *Polyamory in the 21st Century: Love and Intimacy with Multiple Partners*. Plymouth, VA: Rowman and Littlefield.

ANSA. 2013. 'SEL Walks out over Northern League "Sodomite" Jibe in House. ANSA, 30 July 2013. Available online: http://www.ansa.it/web/notizie/rubriche/english/2013/07/30/SEL-walks-over-Northern-League-sodomite-jibe-House_9096764.html.

Arcigay. 2013. 'Onda Pride: Milano, Bologna, Napoli, Catania, Sardegna'. 10 June 2013. Available online: http://www.arcigay.it/41089/onda-pride-milano-bologna-napoli-catania-sardegna/.

Asad, T. 1986. *The Idea of an Anthropology of Islam*. Occasional Papers Series, Center for Contemporary Arab Studies. Washington DC: Georgetown University Press.

Banfield, E. 1958. *The Moral Basis of a Backward Society*. London: Free Press.

BBC. 2009. 'Berlusconi Demands Wife Apology'. BBC News, 4 May 2009. Available online: http://news.bbc.co.uk/1/hi/8032392.stm.

Beldo, L. 2014. 'The Unconditional 'Ought': a Theoretical Model for the Anthropology of Morality', *Anthropological Theory* 14: 263–79.

Belmonte, T. 1979. *The Broken Fountain*. New York: Columbia University Press.

Ben-Yehoyada, N. 2014. 'Transnational Political Cosmology: a Central Mediterranean Example', *Comparative Studies in Society and History* 56: 870–901.

Berlant, L. and M. Warner. 1995. 'What Does Queer Theory Teach us About X?', *PMLA* 110: 343–49.

_____. 1998. 'Sex in Public', *Critical Inquiry* 24: 547–66.

Berlinguer, E. 1977. 'Communists and Catholics: Clarity of Principles and Bases for an Understanding', *The Italian Communists* 4: 23–39.

Bersani, L. 1995. *Homos*. Cambridge, MA: Harvard University Press.

Bessire, L. and D. Bond. 2014. 'Ontological Anthropology and the Deferral of Critique', *American Ethnologist* 41: 440–56.

Bestor, T. 2001. 'Supply-side Sushi: Commodity, Market, and the Global City', *American Anthropologist* 103: 76–95.

Blaser, M. 2009. 'The Threat of the Yrmo: the Political Ontology of a Sustainable Hunting Program', *American Anthropologist* 111: 10–20.

———. 2013. 'Ontological Conflicts and the Stories of Peoples in Spite of Europe: Toward a Conversation on Political Ontology', *Current Anthropology* 54: 547–68.

Blok, A. 1975. *The Mafia of a Sicilian Village, 1860–1960: a Study of Violent Peasant Entrepreneurs.* New York: Harper & Row.

———. 1981. 'Rams and Billy-goats: a Key to the Mediterranean Code of Honour', *Journal of the Royal Anthropological Institute* 16: 427–40.

———. 'The Narcissism of Minor Differences', *The European Journal of Social Theory* 1: 33–56.

Boellstorff, T. 2007. 'Queer Studies in the House of Anthropology', *Annual Review of Anthropology* 36: 17–35.

Bonaccorso, M. 2009. *Conceiving Kinship: Assisted Conception, Procreation, and Family in Southern Europe.* New York and Oxford: Berghahn Books.

Bonelli, C. 2013. 'Ontological Disorders: Nightmares, Psychotropic Drugs and Evil Spirits in Southern Chile', *Anthropological Theory* 12: 407–26.

Du Boulay, J. 1974. *Portrait of a Greek Mountain Village.* Oxford: Clarendon Press.

Bourg, J. 2007. *From Revolution to Ethics: May 1968 and Contemporary French Thought.* Montreal: McGill-Queens University Press.

Brodwin, P. 2002. 'Genetics, Identity, and the Anthropology of Essentialism', *Anthropological Quarterly* 75(2): 323–30.

Brogger, J. 1971. *Montevarese: a Study of Peasant Society and Culture in Southern Italy.* Bergen: Universitetsforlaget.

Butler, J. 1990. *Gender Trouble: Feminism and the Subversion of Identity.* New York: Routledge.

———. 2010. 'I Must Distance Myself from this Complicity with Racism. "Civil Courage Prize" Refusal Speech. Christopher Street Day, 19 June 2010. Available online: http://www.egs.edu/faculty/judith-butler/articles/i-must-distance-myself/.

Candea, M. n.d. *In the Know: Being and Not Being Corsican in Corsica, France.* PhD Dissertation, University of Cambridge.

———. 2007. 'Arbitrary Locations: in Defence of the Bounded Field-site', *Journal of the Royal Anthropological Institute* 13: 167–84.

———. 2010a. *Corsican Fragments: Difference, Knowledge and Fieldwork.* Bloomington, IN: Indiana University Press.

———. 2010b. 'Anonymous Introductions: Identity and Belonging in Corsica', *Journal of the Royal Anthropological Institute* 16: 119–37.

———. 2010c. '"I Fell in Love with Carlos the Meerkat": Engagement and Detachment in Human-Animal Relations', *American Ethnologist* 37(2): 241–58.

———. 2011a. 'Endo-exo', *Common Knowledge* 17: 146–50.

———. 2011b. '"Our Division of the Universe": Making a Space for the Non-political in the Anthropology of Politics', *Current Anthropology* 52: 309–34.

———. 2013. 'Suspending Belief: Epoché in Animal Behavior Science: Suspending Belief', *American Anthropologist* 115(3): 423–36.

———. 2017. 'We Have Never Been Pluralist: on Lateral and Frontal Comparisons in the Ontological Turn', in P. Charbonnier, G. Salmon and P. Skafish (eds), *Comparative Metaphysics: Ontology after Anthropology.* London: Rowman Littlefield, pp. 85–107.

Carrithers, M. 2005. 'Anthropology as a Moral Science of Possibilities', *Current Anthropology* 46: 433–56.

Carrithers, M., M. Candea, K. Sykes, M. Holbraad and S. Venkatesan. 2010. 'Ontology is Just Another Word for Culture: Motion Tabled at the 2008 Meeting of the Group for Debates in Anthropological Theory', *Critique of Anthropology* 30: 152–200.

Cassero. 2010. 'Statuto'. 15 July 2010. Available online: http://www.cassero.it/il-circolo/statuto/.

Clarke, M. 2012. 'The Judge as Tragic Hero: Judicial Ethics in Lebanon's Shari'a Courts', *American Ethnologist* 39: 106–21.

_____. 2014. 'Cough Sweets and Angels: the Ordinary Ethics of the Extraordinary in Sufi Practice in Lebanon', *Journal of the Royal Anthropological Institute* 20: 407–25.

Clifford, J. and G. Marcus. 1986. *Writing Culture: the Poetics and Politics of Ethnography*. Berkeley, CA: University of California Press.

Cole, J. 1997. *The New Racism in Europe: a Sicilian Ethnography*. Cambridge: Cambridge University Press.

Cook, J. 2010a. 'Ascetic Practice and Participant Observation, or, the Gift of Doubt and Incompletion in Field Experience', in J. Davies and D. Mihavlova (eds), *Emotions in the Field: the Psychology and Anthropology of Fieldwork Experience*. Stanford, CA: Stanford University Press, pp. 239–66.

_____. 2010b. *Meditation in Modern Buddhism: Renunciation and Change in Thai Monastic Life*. Cambridge: Cambridge University Press.

_____. 2016. 'Ethnography: Translation'. Available online: https://culanth.org/fieldsights/874-ethnography-translation.

Cook, J., J. Laidlaw and J. Mair. 2009. 'What if There is no Elephant? Towards a Conception of an Un-sited Field', in M. Falzon (ed.), *Multi-sited Ethnography: Theory, Praxis and Locality in Contemporary Research*. London: Ashgate, pp. 47–72.

Course, M. 2010. 'Of Words and Fog: Linguistic Relativity and Amerindian Ontology', *Anthropological Theory* 10: 247–63.

Csordas, T. 2013. 'Morality as a Cultural System?', *Current Anthropology* 54: 523–46.

Da Col, G. and D. Graeber. 2011. 'The Return of Ethnographic Theory', *HAU: Journal of Ethnographic Theory* 1: vi–xxxv.

Dave, N. 2011. 'Activism as Ethical Practice: Queer Politics in Contemporary India', *Cultural Dynamics* 23: 3–20.

_____. 2012. *Queer Activism in India: a Story in the Anthropology of Ethics*. Durham, NC: Duke University Press.

Davidson, D. 1980. 'How is Weakness of the Will Possible?', in *Essays on Actions and Events*. Oxford: Clarendon Press, pp. 21–43.

Davis, J. 1973. *Land and Family in Pisticci*. London: Athlone Press.

_____. 1977. *The People of the Mediterranean: an Essay in Comparative Social Anthropology*. London: Routledge.

de la Cadena, M. 2010. 'Indigenous Cosmopolitics in the Andes: Conceptual Reflections Beyond Politics', *Current Anthropology* 25: 334–70.

de Lauretis, T. 1991. *Queer Theory: Lesbian and Gay Sexualities*. Bloomington, IN: Indiana University Press.

de Matos Viegas, S. 2012. 'Pleasures that Differentiate: Transformational Bodies among the Tupinambá of Olivença (Atlantic Coast, Brazil)', *Journal of the Royal Anthropological Institute* 18: 536–53.

de Rosa, G. 1966. *Cattolici e Comunisti oggi in Italia: via Italiana al socialismo e dialogo con I Cattolici*. Rome: Edizioni La Civilita Cattolica.

Delchambre, J.-P. and N. Marquis. 2013. 'Modes of Existence Explained to the Moderns, or Bruno Latour's Plural World', *Social Anthropology* 21: 564–75.

Deleuze, G. 1994. *Difference and Repetition*. London: Athlone Press.

Descola, P. 1986. *La nature domestique: Symbolisme et praxis dans l'écologie des Achuar*. Paris: Les Editions de la MSH.

di Giminiani, P. 2013. 'The Contested *Rewe*: Sacred Sites, Misunderstandings, and Ontological Pluralism in Mapuche Land Negotiations', *Journal of the Royal Anthropological Institute* 19: 527–44.

Dines, N. 2012. *Tuff City: Urban Change and Contested Space in Central Naples*. New York and Oxford: Berghahn Books.

di Nola, A. 1998. 'How Critical was De Martino's "Critical Ethnocentrism" in Southern Italy?', in J. Schneider (ed.), *Italy's 'Southern Question': Orientalism in One Country*. Oxford: Berg, pp. 157–77.

Douglass, W. 1975. 'Issues in the Study of South Italian Society', *Current Anthropology* 16: 620–25.

Easton, D. and J. Hardy. 1997. *The Ethical Slut: a Guide to Infinite Sexual Possibilities*. New York: Greenery Press.

Edel, A. and M. Edel. 2000 [1959]. *Anthropology and Ethics*. New York: Transaction Publishers.

Englund, H. 2008. 'Extreme Poverty and Existential Obligations: Beyond Morality in the Anthropology of Africa?', *Social Analysis* 52: 33–50.

Esposito, N. 1989. *Italian Family Structure*. New York: Peter Lang.

Evans-Pritchard, E. 1950. 'Social Anthropology: Past and Present', *Journal of the Royal Anthropological Institute* 50: 118–24.

———. 1956. *Nuer Religion*. Oxford: Clarendon Press.

Evens, T.M.S. 2012. 'Twins are Birds, and a Whale is a Fish, a Mammal, a Submarine', *Social Analysis* 56: 1–11.

Ewing, K. 1990. 'The Illusion of Wholeness: Culture, Self, and the Experience of Inconsistency', *Ethos* 18: 251–78.

Fabian, J. 1983. *Time and the Other: How Anthropology Makes its Object*. New York: Columbia University Press.

Faenza, L. 1959. *Comunismo e cattolicesimo in una parrochia di campagna*. Milan: Feltrinelli.

Falzon, M. (ed.). 2009. *Multi-sited Ethnography: Theory, Praxis and Locality in Contemporary Research*. London: Ashgate.

Faubion, J. 2001a. 'Toward an Anthropology of Ethics: Foucault and the Pedagogies of Autopoesis', *Representations* 74: 83–104.

———. 2001b. *The Shadows and Lights of Waco: Millennialism Today*. Princeton, NJ: Princeton University Press.

———. 2011. *An Anthropology of Ethics*. Cambridge: Cambridge University Press.

Ferrara, A. 2008. *The Force of the Example: Explorations in the Paradigm of Judgement*. New York: Columbia University Press.

Filipucci, P. 1996. 'Anthropological Perspectives on Culture in Italy', in D. Forgacs and R. Lumley (eds), *Italian Cultural Studies*. Oxford: Oxford University Press, pp. 52–71.

Fisher, I. 2007. 'Berlusconi Flirts. Wife's Fed Up. Read All About It'. *The New York Times*, 1 February. Available online: http://www.nytimes.com/2007/02/01/world/europe/01italy.html.

Follain, J. 2010. 'Silvio Cornered as Divorce Gets Nasty'. *The Times*, 6 June. Available online: http://www.timesonline.co.uk/tol/news/world/europe/article7144774.ece.

Fortes, M. 1959. *Oedipus and Job in West African Religion*. Cambridge: Cambridge University Press.

Fortun, K. 2001. *Advocacy after Bhopal: Environmentalism, Disaster, New Global Orders*. Chicago, IL: University of Chicago Press.

Foucault, M. 1985. *The Use of Pleasure: the History of Sexuality*, volume 2. New York: Random House.

_____. 1986. *The Care of the Self: the History of Sexuality*, volume 3. New York: Random House.

_____. 2000. 'On the Genealogy of Ethics: an Overview of a Work in Progress', in P. Rabinow (ed.), *Essential Works of Michel Foucault 1954-1984: Vol 1 Ethics*. London: Penguin, pp. 253–81.

Freud, S. 1957 [1917]. 'The Taboo of Virginity', in J. Strachey (ed.), *The Standard Edition of the Complete Psychological Works of Sigmund Freud, Vol. XI*. London: Hogarth Press, pp. 193–208.

Frohlick, S. 2007. 'Rendering and Gendering Mobile Subjects in a Globalised World of Mountaineering: Between Localising Ethnography and Global Spaces', in S. Coleman and P. Collins (eds), *Locating the Field*. Oxford: Berg, pp. 87–105.

Galt, A. 1980. 'Social Stratification on Pantelleria, Italy', *Ethnology* 19: 405–25.

_____. 1991. *Far From the Church Bells: Settlement and Society in an Apulian Town*. Cambridge: Cambridge University Press.

Gambetta, D. 1993. *The Sicilian Mafia: the Business of Private Protection*. Cambridge, MA. Harvard University Press.

Geertz, C. 1973. *The Interpretation of Cultures*. New York: Basic Books.

Gellner, D. 1990. 'What is the Anthropology of Buddhism About?', *Journal of the Anthropological Society of Oxford* 21: 95–112.

Gellner, E. 1970. 'Concepts and Society', in B. Wilson (ed.), *Rationality*. Oxford: Blackwell, pp. 18–49.

Gibson, M. 1998. 'Biology or Environment? Race and Southern "Deviancy" in the Writings of Italian Criminologists, 1880–1920', in J. Schneider (ed.), *Italy's 'Southern Question': Orientalism in One Country*. Oxford: Berg, pp. 99–117.

Gilmore, D. 1982. 'Anthropology of the Mediterranean Area', *Annual Review of Anthropology* 11: 175–205.

Giovannini, M. 1981. 'Woman: a Dominant Symbol Within the Cultural System of a Sicilian Town', *Journal of the Royal Anthropological Institute* 16: 408–26.

Goddard, V. 1996. *Gender, Family and Work in Naples*. London: Bloomsbury.

Goody, J. 1976. *Production and Reproduction: a Comparative Study of the Domestic Domain*. Cambridge: Cambridge University Press.

Green, S. 1997. *Urban Amazons: Lesbian Feminism and Beyond in the Gender, Sexuality, and Identity Battles of London*. London: Palgrave Macmillan.

Grillo, R. and J. Pratt. 2002. *The Politics of Recognising Difference: Multiculturalism Italian Style*. Aldershot: Ashgate.

Grottanelli, V. 1977. 'Ethnology and/or Cultural Anthropology in Italy: Traditions and Developments', *Current Anthropology* 18: 593–614.

Gupta, A. and J. Ferguson. 1997. 'Discipline and Practice: the "Field" as Site, Method and Location in Anthropology', in *Anthropological Locations: Boundaries and Grounds of a Field Science*. Berkeley, CA: University of California Press, pp. 1–47.

Hage, G. 2005. 'A Not so Multi-sited Ethnography of a Not so Imagined Community', *Anthropological Theory* 5: 463–75.

Hajek, A. 2011. 'Bologna and the Trauma of March 1977: the "intellettuali contro" and Their "Resistance" to the Local Communist Party', *Carte Italiane* 2: 81–100.

Halperin, D. 1995. *Saint Foucault: Towards a Gay Hagiography*. Oxford: Oxford University Press.

Harrison, S. 2003. 'Cultural Difference as Denied Resemblance: Reconsidering Nationalism and Ethnicity', *Comparative Studies in Society and History* 45: 343–61.

_____. 2006. *Fracturing Resemblances: Identity and Mimetic Conflict in Melanesia and the West*. New York and Oxford: Berghahn Books.

Hays, T. 1986. 'Sacred Flutes, Fertility and Growth in the Papua New Guinea Highlands', *Anthropos* 81: 435–53.

Henare, A., M. Holbraad and S. Wastell (eds). 2006. *Thinking Through Things: Theorising Artefacts Ethnographically*. London: Routledge.

Herzfeld, M. 1980. 'Honour and Shame: Problems in the Comparative Analysis of Moral Systems', *Journal of the Royal Anthropological Institute* 15: 339–51.

_____. 1984. 'The Horns of the Mediterranean Dilemma', *American Ethnologist* 11: 439–54.

_____. 1985 *The Poetics of Manhood: Contest and Identity in a Cretan Mountain Village*. Princeton, NJ: Princeton University Press.

_____. 1987. *Anthropology Through the Looking-glass: Critical Ethnography in the Margins of Europe*. Cambridge: Cambridge University Press.

_____. 1996. 'Essentialism', in *Encyclopedia of Social and Cultural Anthropology*. London and New York: Routledge, pp. 288–90.

_____. 2009. *Evicted from Eternity: the Restructuring of Modern Rome*. Chicago, IL: University of Chicago Press.

Heywood, P. 2009. 'The Two Burials of Aldo Moro: Sovereignty and Governmentality in the anni di piombo', *Cambridge Anthropology* 29: 1–29.

_____. 2012. 'Anthropology and What There Is: Reflections on "Ontology"', *Cambridge Anthropology* 30: 143–51.

_____. 2014. 'Neoliberal Nation? Mobbing and Morality in Italy', *Journal of the Royal Anthropological Institute* 20: 151–53.

_____. 2015. 'Freedom in the Code: the Anthropology of (Double) Morality', *Anthropological Theory* 15: 200–217.

_____. Forthcoming. 'Making Difference: Queer Activism and Anthropological Theory', *Current Anthropology*.

Holbraad, M. 2009. 'Ontography and Alterity: Defining Anthropological Truth', *Social Analysis* 53: 80–93.

_____. 2012. *Truth in Motion: the Recursive Anthropology of Cuban Divination*. Chicago, IL: University of Chicago Press.

_____. 2013. 'Scoping Recursivity: a Comment on Franklin and Napier', *Cambridge Anthropology* 31: 123–27.

_____. 2014. '*Revolución o muerte*: Self-sacrifice and the Ontology of Cuban Revolution', *Ethnos* 79: 365–87.

_____. 2017. 'The Contingency of Concepts: Transcendental Deduction and Ethnographic Expression in Anthropological Thinking', in P. Charbonnier, G. Salmon and P. Skafish (eds), *Comparative Metaphysics: Ontology After Anthropology*. London: Rowman & Littlefield, pp. 133–59.

Holbraad, M. and M. Pedersen. 2009. 'Planet M: the Intense Abstraction of Marilyn Strathern', *Anthropological Theory* 9: 371–94.

Holbraad, M., M. Pedersen and E. Viveiros de Castro. 2014. 'The Politics of Ontology: Anthropological Positions', *Cultural Anthropology*, 13 January. Available online: http://www.culanth.org/fieldsights/462-the-politics-of-ontology-anthropological-positions.

Holmes, D. 1989. *Cultural Disenchantments: Worker Peasantries in Northeast Italy*. Princeton, NJ: Princeton University Press.

Howell, S. (ed.). 1997. *The Ethnography of Moralities*. London: Routledge.

Humphrey, C. 1997. 'Exemplars and Rules: Aspects of the Discourse of Moralities in Mongolia', in S. Howell (ed.), *The Ethnography of Moralities*. London: Routledge, pp. 25–49.

Ingold, T. 2000. *The Perception of the Environment: Essays on Livelihood, Dwelling and Skill*. London: Routledge.

———. 2008. 'Anthropology is *Not* Ethnography', *Proceedings of the British Academy* 154: 69–92.

———. 2014. 'That's Enough About Ethnography!', *HAU: Journal of Ethnographic Theory* 4: 383–95.

Jameson, F. 1984. 'Postmodernism, or, the Cultural Logic of Late Capitalism', *New Left Review* 146: 53–92.

Jean-Klein, I. and A. Riles. 2005. 'Anthropology and Human Rights Administrations: Expert Observation and Representation After the Fact', *PoLAR: Political and Legal Anthropology Review* 28: 173–202.

Jensen, C. 2013. 'Two Forms of the Outside: Castaneda, Blanchot, Ontology', *HAU: Journal of Ethnographic Theory* 3: 809–35.

Jiménez, A.C. and R. Willerslev. 2007. 'An Anthropological Concept of the Concept: Reversibility Among the Siberian Yukaghirs', *Journal of the Royal Anthropological Institute* 13: 527–44.

John Paul II. 1994. 'Apostolic Letter *ordinatio sacerdotalis*, on Reserving Priestly Ordination to Men Alone'. Available online: http://www.vatican.va/holy_father/john_paul_ii/apost_letters/1994/documents/hf_jp-ii_apl_19940522_ordinatio-sacerdotalis_en.html.

Keane, W. 2013. 'Ontologies, Anthropologists, and Ethical Life', *HAU: Journal of Ethnographic Theory* 3: 186–91.

Kertzer, D. 1974. 'Politics and Ritual: the Communist Festa in Italy', *Anthropological Quarterly* 47: 374–89.

———. 1980. *Comrades and Christians: Religion and Political Struggle in Communist Italy*. Cambridge: Cambridge University Press.

———. 1996. *Politics and Symbols: The Italian Communist Party and the Fall of Communism*. Yale, CT: Yale University Press.

Krause, E. 2009. *Unraveled: a Weaver's Tale of Life Gone Modern*. Berkeley, CA: University of California Press.

Krøjer, S. 2015. 'Revolution is the Way You Eat: Exemplification Among Left Radical Activists in Denmark and in Anthropology', *Journal of the Royal Anthropological Institute* 21: 78–95.

Kuhn, T. 1970. *The Structure of Scientific Revolutions*. Chicago, IL: University of Chicago Press.

Laidlaw, J. 1995. *Riches and Renunciation: Religion, Economy, and Society Amongst the Jains*. Oxford: Clarendon Press.

———. 2002. 'For an Anthropology of Ethics and Freedom', *Journal of the Royal Anthropological Institute* 8: 311–32.

———. 2010. 'Agency and Responsibility: Perhaps You Can Have Too Much of a Good Thing', in M. Lambek (ed.), *Ordinary Ethics: Anthropology, Language, and Action*. New York: Fordham University Press, pp. 143–65.

———. 2012. 'Ontologically Challenged', *Anthropology of this Century* 4. Available online: http://aotcpress.com/articles/ontologically-challenged/.

———. 2013. 'A Generous Pluralism', *HAU: Journal of Ethnographic Theory* 3: 197–200.

———. 2014a. *The Subject of Virtue: an Anthropology of Ethics and Freedom*. Cambridge: Cambridge University Press.

———. 2014b. 'Significant Differences', *HAU: Journal of Ethnographic Theory* 4: 497–506.

Laidlaw, J. and P. Heywood. 2013. 'One More Turn and You're There', *Anthropology of this Century* 7. Available online: http://aotcpress.com/articles/turn/.

Lambek, M. 2000. 'The Anthropology of Religion and the Quarrel Between Poetry and Philosophy', *Current Anthropology* 41: 309–20.

———. (ed.). 2010. *Ordinary Ethics: Anthropology, Language and Action.* New York: Fordham University Press.

———. 2013. 'The Continuous and Discontinuous Person: Two Dimensions of Ethical Life', *Journal of the Royal Anthropological Institute* 19: 837–58.

Latella, M. 2009. *Tendenza Veronica.* Rome: Rizzoli.

Latour, B. 2004. 'Why Has Critique Run Out of Steam? From Matters of Fact to Matters of Concern', *Critical Enquiry* 30: 225–48.

———. 2005. *Reassembling the Social.* Oxford: Oxford University Press.

———. 2009. 'Perspectivism: "type" or "bomb"?', *Anthropology Today* 25: 1–3.

Lazar, S. 2012. 'Disjunctive Comparison: Citizenship and Trade Unionism in Bolivia and Argentina', *Journal of the Royal Anthropological Institute* 18: 349–68.

Leach. E. 1961. *Rethinking Anthropology.* London School of Economics, Monographs on Social Anthropology 22. New York: The Humanities Press.

Lempert, M. 2013. 'No Ordinary Ethics', *Anthropological Theory* 13: 370–93.

Lévi-Strauss, C. 1952. *Race et histoire,* in *Anthropologie structural deux.* Paris: Plon, pp. 377–422.

———. 1961. *Tristes Tropiques.* London: Hutchinson & Co.

———. 1985. *The View From Afar.* Chicago, IL: University of Chicago Press.

Littlejohn, J. 1970. 'Twins, birds, etc.', *Bijdragen tot de Taal-, Land- en Volkenkunde* 126: 91–114.

Lloyd, G. 2011. 'Humanity Between Gods and Beasts? Ontologies in Question', *Journal of the Royal Anthropological Institute* 17: 829–45.

Low, S.M. and S.E. Merry. 2010. 'Engaged Anthropology: Diversity and Dilemmas', *Current Anthropology* 51: 203–26.

MacIntyre, A. 1981. *After Virtue: a Study in Moral Theory.* London: Duckworth.

———. 1998. *Moral Pluralism Without Moral Relativism.* Paper presented at the 20th World Congress of Philosophy, Boston.

Mahmud, L. 2014. *The Brotherhood of Freemason Sisters: Gender, Secrecy, and Fraternity in Italian Masonic Lodges.* Chicago, IL: University of Chicago Press.

Mahony, H. 2013. 'Bulgaria and Italy Train in EU on Gay Rights Legislation', *EU Observer,* 16 May. Available online: http://euobserver.com/lgbti/120097.

Mair, J. 2014. 'Fo Guang Shan Buddhism and Ethical Conversations Across Borders: "Sowing Seeds of Affinity"', *Collegium* 15: 66–89.

Malkki, L. 1997. 'News and Culture: Transitory Phenomena and the Fieldwork Tradition', in A. Gupta and J. Ferguson (eds), *Anthropological Locations: Boundaries and Grounds of a Field Science.* Berkeley, CA: University of California Press, pp. 86–102.

Marcus, G. (ed.). 1999. *Ethnography Through Thick and Thin.* Princeton, NJ: University Press.

——— and M. Fischer. 1986. *Anthropology as Cultural Critique: an Experimental Moment in the Human Sciences.* Chicago, IL: University of Chicago Press.

Marx, K. 1845. *Theses on Feuerbach.* Available online: http://www.marxists.org/archive/marx/works/1845/theses/index.htm.

Mattingly, C. 2012. 'Two Virtue Ethics and the Anthropology of Morality', *Anthropological Theory* 12: 161–84.

Matysik, T. 2008. *Reforming the Moral Subject: Ethics and Sexuality in Central Europe, 1890-1930.* Ithaca, NY: Cornell University Press.

McCallum, C. 2014. 'Cashinahua Perspectives on Functional Anatomy: Ontology, Ontogenesis, and Biomedical Education in Amazonia', *American Ethnologist* 41: 504–17.

Merry, S.E. 2008. 'Anthropology and Activism', *PoLAR: Political and Legal Anthropology Review* 28: 240–57.

'Mio marito mi deve pubbliche scuse'. 2007. *La Repubblica*, 31 January. Available online: http://www.repubblica.it/2007/01/sezioni/politica/lettera-veronica/lettera-veronica/lettera-veronica.html.

Mol, A. 2002. *The Body Multiple: Ontology in Medical Practice*. Durham, NC: Duke University Press.

Molé, N. 2008. 'Living it on the Skin: Italian States, Working Illness', *American Ethnologist* 35: 189–210.

———. 2010. 'Precarious Subjects: Anticipating Neoliberalism in Northern Italy's Workplace', *American Anthropologist* 112: 38–53.

———. 2012a. *Labor Disorders in Neoliberal Italy: Mobbing, Well-being, and the Workplace*. Bloomington, IN: Indiana University Press.

———. 2012b. 'Hauntings of Solidarity in Post-fordist Italy', *Anthropological Quarterly* 85: 371–96.

———. 2013a. 'Existential Damages: the Injury of Precarity Goes to Court', *Cultural Anthropology* 28: 22–43.

———. 2013b. 'Trusted Puppets, Tarnished Politicians: Humor and Cynicism in Berlusconi's Italy', *American Ethnologist* 40: 288–99.

Morris, R. 1995. 'All Made Up: Performance Theory and the New Anthropology of Sex and Gender', *Annual Review of Anthropology* 24: 567–92.

Muehlehbach, A. 2009. '*Complexio oppositorum*: Notes on the Left in Neoliberal Italy', *Public Culture* 21: 495–515.

———. 2011. 'On Affective Labor in Post-fordist Italy', *Cultural Anthropology* 26: 59–82.

———. 2012. *The Moral Neoliberal: Welfare and Citizenship in Italy*. Chicago, IL: University of Chicago Press.

———. 2013. 'The Catholicization of Neoliberalism: on Love and Welfare in Lombardy, Italy', *American Anthropologist* 115: 452–65.

Nadel, F. *The Foundations of Social Anthropology*. Glencoe, IL: The Free Press.

Nader, L. 2011. 'Ethnography as Theory', *HAU: Journal of Ethnographic Theory* 1: 211–19.

Owens, C. 1985. 'The Discourse of Others: Feminists and Postmodernism', in H. Foster (ed.), *Postmodern Culture*. London: Pluto Press, pp. 57–82.

Parkin, D. (ed.). 1985. *The Anthropology of Evil*. Oxford: Blackwell.

Parry, J. 2000. '"The Crisis of Corruption" and the "Idea of India": a Worm's Eye View', in I. Pardo (ed.), *The Morals of Legitimacy: Between Agency and System*. New York and Oxford: Berghahn Books, pp. 27–55.

Paxson, H. 2004. *Making Modern Mothers: Ethics and Family Planning in Urban Greece*. Berkeley, CA: University of California Press.

Pedersen, M. 2011. *Not Quite Shamans: Spirit Worlds and Political Lives in Northern Mongolia*. Ithaca, NY: Cornell University Press.

———. 2012. 'Common Nonsense: a Review of Certain Recent Reviews of the "Ontological Turn"', *Anthropology of this Century* 5. Available online: http://aotcpress.com/articles/common_nonsense/.

Pedersen, M., R. Empson and C. Humphrey. 2007. 'Editorial Introduction: Inner Asian Perspectivisms', *Inner Asia* 9(2): 141–52.

Pels, P. 2002. 'The Trickster's Dilemma: Ethics and the Technologies of an Anthropological Self', in M. Strathern (ed.), *Audit Cultures: Anthropological Studies in Accountability, Ethics and the Academy*. London: Routledge, pp. 135–72.

Peristiany, J. (ed.). 1965. *Honour and Shame: the Values of the Mediterranean*. London: Weidenfeld & Nicolson.

Però, D. 1999. 'Next to the Dog-pound: Institutional Discourses and Practices about Rom Refugees in Left-wing Bologna', *Modern Italy* 4: 207–24.

———. 2005a. 'Left-wing Politics, Civil Society, and Immigration in Italy: the Case of Bologna', *Ethnic and Racial Studies* 28: 832–58.

———. 2005b. 'Inclusion Without Recognition: the Socialist Left and Immigrants in 1970s Italy', *Focaal: European Journal of Anthropology* 45: 112–26.

———. 2007. *Inclusionary Rhetoric, Exclusionary Practices: Left-wing Politics and Migrants in Italy*. New York and Oxford: Berghahn Books.

Piana, G. 2010. *Omosessualitá: una proposta etica*. Assisi: Cittadella.

Pina-Cabral, J. 1989. 'The Mediterranean as a Category of Regional Comparison: A Critical View', *Current Anthropology* 30: 399–406.

Pipyrou, S. 2014. 'Cutting *bella figura*: Irony, Crisis, and Secondhand Clothes in South Italy', *American Ethnologist* 41: 532–46.

Pitt-Rivers, J. 1977. *The Fate of Shechem, or the Politics of Sex: Essays in the Anthropology of the Mediterranean*. Cambridge: Cambridge University Press.

Pocock, D. 1986. 'The Ethnography of Morals', *International Journal of Moral and Social Studies* 1: 3–20.

Quinn, N. 2006. 'The Self', *Anthropological Theory* 6: 362–84.

Pratt, J. 1986. *The Walled City*. Göttingen: Herdot.

Rahman, M. and S. Jackson. 1997. 'Liberty, Equality Sexuality: Essentialism and the Discourse of Rights', *Journal of Gender Studies* 6: 117–29.

Rand, A. 1990 [1979]. *Introduction to Objectivist Epistemology*. New York: Plume Books.

Retzloff, T. 2007. 'Eliding Trans Latino/a Queer Experience in U.S. LGBT History: José Sarria and Sylvia Rivera Reexamined', *CENTRO: Journal of the Center for Puerto Rican Studies* 19: 140–61.

Riccamboni, G. 1976. 'The Italian Communist Party and the Catholic World', *Social Compass* 23: 141–69.

Robbins, J. 2007. 'Between Reproduction and Freedom: Morality, Value, and Radical Cultural Change', *Ethnos* 72: 293–314.

———. 2009. 'Value, Structure, and the Range of Possibilities: a Response to Zigon', *Ethnos* 74: 277–85.

———. 2013. 'Beyond the Suffering Subject: Towards an Anthropology of the Good', *Journal of the Royal Anthropological Institute* 19: 447–62.

———. Forthcoming. 'Where in the World are Values? Exemplarity, Morality, and Social Process', in C. Mattingly, R. Dyring, M. Louw, and T.S. Wentzer (eds.), *Moral Engines: Exploring the Ethical Drives in Human Life*. New York and Oxford: Berghahn Books.

Robertson, A.F. 2011. 'How Can Lukoho be his Own Grandfather? Being and Becoming in the Cartesian Gap', *Journal of the Royal Anthropological Institute* 17: 585–603.

Rubin, G. 1984. 'Thinking Sex: Notes For a Radical Theory of the Politics of Sexuality', in C. Vance (ed.), *Pleasure and Danger: Exploring Female Sexuality*. Boston: Routledge, pp. 267–319.

Russell, B. 1970 [1929]. *Marriage and Morals*. New York: Liveright Press.

Salmond, Amiria. 2014. 'Transforming Translations (part 2): Addressing Ontological Alterity', *HAU: Journal of Ethnographic Theory* 4: 155–87.

Salmond, Anne. 2012. 'Ontological Quarrels: Indigeneity, Exclusion and Citizenship in a Relational World', *Anthropological Theory* 12: 115–41.

Sanford, V. and A. Angel-Ajani. 2006. *Engaged Observer: Anthropology, Advocacy, and Activism*. New Brunswick: Rutgers University Press.

Saunders, G. 1979. 'Social Change and Psychocultural Continuity in Alpine Italian Family Life', *Ethos* 7: 206–31.

_____. 1984. 'Contemporary Italian Cultural Anthropology', *Annual Review of Anthropology* 13: 447–66.

_____. 1985. 'The Crisis of Presence in Italian Pentecostal Conversion', *American Ethnologist* 22: 324–40.

_____. 1998. 'The Magic of the South: Popular Religion and Elite Catholicism in Italian Ethnology', in J. Schneider (ed.), *Italy's 'Southern Question': Orientalism in One Country*. Oxford: Berg, pp. 177–205.

Scheggia, S. 2009. 'Don Nildo si defende: "Cantare é un dono di Dio"'. *La Repubblica*, 30 July. Available online: http://bologna.repubblica.it/dettaglio/don-nildo-si-difende:-cantare-e-un-dono-di-dio/1685035.

Schielke, S. 2009a. 'Being Good in Ramadan: Ambivalence, Fragmentation, and the Moral Self in the Lives of Young Egyptians', *Journal of the Royal Anthropological Institute* 15: 24–40.

_____. 2009b. 'Ambivalent Commitments: Troubles of Morality, Religiosity and Aspiration Among Young Egyptians', *Journal of Religion in Africa* 39: 158–85.

Schneider, J. (ed.). 1998. *Italy's 'Southern Question': Orientalism in One Country*. Oxford: Berg.

Schneider, J. and P. Schneider. 1976. *Culture and Political Economy in Western Sicily*. New York: Academic Press.

_____. 1996. *Festival of the Poor: Fertility Decline and the Ideology of Class in Sicily, 1860-1980*. Tucson, AZ: University of Arizona Press.

_____. 2003. *Reversible Destiny: Mafia, Antimafia, and the Struggle in Palermo*. Berkeley, CA: University of California Press.

Schwab, W. 2005. 'Noch einmal politisch korrekt feiern'. *Die Tageszeitung*, 23 June. Available online: http://www.taz.de/1/archiv/?id=archivseite&dig=2005/06/23/a0344.

Scott, J. 1977. *The Moral Economy of the Peasant: Rebellion and Subsistence in South-East Asia*. New Haven, CT: Yale University Press.

Scott, M. 2011. 'To Be a Wonder: Anthropology, Cosmology, and Alterity'. Paper presented at the 'Contemporary cosmologies and the cultural imagination' workshop at University College London on 11 May 2011.

_____. 2013. 'The Anthropology of Ontology (Religious Science?)', *Journal of the Royal Anthropological Institute* 19: 859–72.

Sedgwick, E. 1990. *Epistemology of the Closet*. Berkeley, CA: University of California Press.

SERG. 1981. 'The Anthropology of Southern Europe: Towards an Integrated Explanatory Framework', *Critique of Anthropology* 4: 55–62.

Shively, K. 2014. 'Entangled Ethics: Piety and Agency in Turkey', *Anthropological Theory* 14: 462–80.

Shore, C. 1990. *Italian Communism: the Escape from Leninism*. London: Pluto.

Silverman, S. 1968. 'Agricultural Organisation, Social Structures, and Values in Italy: Amoral Familism Reconsidered', *American Anthropologist* 70: 1–20.

Simon, G. 2009. 'The Soul Freed of Cares? Islamic Prayer, Subjectivity, and the Contradictions of Moral Selfhood in Minangkabau, Indonesia', *American Ethnologist* 36: 258–75.

Smith, A. 2010 [1759]. *The Theory of Moral Sentiments*. London: Penguin.

Sökefeld, M. 1999. 'Debating Self, Identity, and Culture in Anthropology', *Current Anthropology* 40: 417–48.

'"Sometimes I'm a Sinner": Silvio Berlusconi Admits He's Not Perfect as He Attacks Opponents for "Soviet-style Show Trial"'. 2011. *Daily Mail*, 11 February. Available online: http://www.dailymail.co.uk/news/article-1356046/Sometimes-Im-sinner-Silvio-Berlusconi-admits-hes-perfect-attacks-opponents-Soviet-style-trial.html.

Sontag, S. 1990. *Against Interpretation and Other Essays*. New York: Picador.

'A Special Report on Italy'. 2011. *The Economist*, 11 June.

Spivak, G. 1988. 'Can the Subaltern Speak?', in C. Nelson and L. Grossberg (eds), *Marxism and the Interpretation of Culture*. Urbana, IL: University of Illinois Press, pp. 271–315.

Stacul, J. 2004. *The Bounded Field: Localism and Local Identity in an Italian Alpine Valley*. New York and Oxford: Berghahn Books.

Stasch, R. 2009. *Society of Others: Kinship and Mourning in a West Papuan Place*. Berkeley, CA: University of California Press.

Strathern, M. 1987a. 'Out of Context: the Persuasive Fictions of Anthropology', *Current Anthropology* 28: 251–81.

_____. 1987b. 'An Awkward Relationship: the Case of Feminism and Anthropology', *Signs* 12: 276–92.

_____. 1988. *The Gender of the Gift*. Cambridge: Cambridge University Press.

_____. 1992. *After Nature: English Kinship in the Late Twentieth Century*. Cambridge: Cambridge University Press.

_____. 1995. *The Relation: Issues in Complexity and Scale*. Cambridge: Prickly Pear Press.

_____. 2004 [1991]. *Partial Connections: Updated Edition*. Lanham, MA: Rowman and Littlefield.

_____. 2011 'Binary License', *Common Knowledge* 17: 87–103.

Strauss, C. 1997. 'Partly Fragmented, Partly Integrated: an Anthropological Examination of "Postmodern Fragmented Subjects"', *Cultural Anthropology* 12: 362–404.

Strong, T. 2010. 'Kinship Between Judith Butler and Anthropology? A Review Essay', *Ethnos* 67: 401–18.

Sullivan-Blum, C. 2006. '"The Natural Order of Creation": Naturalising Discourses in the Christian Same-sex Marriage Debate', *Anthropologica* 48: 203–15.

Sylvain, R. 2014. 'Essentialism and the Indigenous Politics of Recognition in Southern Africa', *American Anthropologist* 116: 1–14.

Tarrow, S. 1967. *Peasant Communism in Southern Italy*. New Haven, CT: Yale University Press.

Thornton, R. 1988. 'The Rhetoric of Ethnographic Holism', *Cultural Anthropology* 3: 285–303.

Tiles, J.E. 2000. *Moral Measures: an Introduction to Ethics West and East*. London: Routledge.

Tönnies, F. 1887. *Gemeinschaft und Gesellschaft*. Leipzig: Fues's Verlag.

Toren, C. and J. de Pina-Cabral. 2011. *The Challenge of Epistemology: Anthropological Perspectives*. New York and Oxford: Berghahn Books.

Turner, T. 2006. 'Anthropology as Reality Show and as Co-production: Internal Relations Between Theory and Activism', *Critique of Anthropology* 26: 15–25.

_____. 2009. 'The Crisis of Late Structuralism. Perspectivism and Animism: Rethinking Culture, Nature, Spirit, and Bodiliness', *Tipiti* 7: 3–40.

Tsing, A. 2000. 'The Global Situation', *Cultural Anthropology* 15: 327–60.

van de Port, M. 2012. 'Genuinely Made Up: Camp, Baroque, and Other Denaturalising Aesthetics in the Cultural Production of the Real', *Journal of the Royal Anthropological Institute* 18: 864–83.

Vigh, H. and D. Sausdal. 2014. 'From Essence Back to Existence: Anthropology Beyond the Ontological Turn', *Anthropological Theory* 14: 49–73.

Vilaça, A. 2002. 'Making Kin Out of Others in Amazonia', *Journal of the Royal Anthropological Institute* 8: 347–65.

_____. 2005. 'Chronically Unstable Bodies: Reflections on Amazonian Corporealities', *Journal of the Royal Anthropological Institute* 11: 445–64.

_____. 2011. 'Dividuality in Amazonia: God, the Devil, and the Constitution of Personhood in Wari' Christianity', *Journal of the Royal Anthropological Institute* 17: 243–62.

_____. 2013. 'Communicating Through Difference', *HAU: Journal of Ethnographic Theory* 3: 174–78.

_____. 2014. 'Culture and Self: the Different "gifts" Amerindians Receive From Catholics and Evangelicals', *Current Anthropology* 55: 322–32.

_____. 2015. 'Dividualism and Individualism in Indigenous Christianity: a Debate Seen From Amazonia', *HAU: Journal of Ethnographic Theory* 5: 197–225.

Viveiros de Castro, E. 1996. 'Images of Nature and Society in Amazonian Ethnology', *Annual Review of Anthropology* 25(1): 179–200.

_____. 1998. 'Cosmological Deixis and Amerindian Perspectivism', *Journal of the Royal Anthropological Institute* 4: 469–88.

_____. 2003. *And*. Manchester: Manchester University Press.

_____. 2004a. 'Perspectival Anthropology and the Method of Controlled Equivocation', *Tipiti* 2: 3–22.

_____. 2004b. 'Perspectives: The Transformation of Objects into Subjects in Amerindian Ontologies', *Common Knowledge* 10(3): 463–84.

_____. 2007. 'The Crystal Forest: Notes on the Ontology of Amazonian Spirits', *Inner Asia* 9(2): 153–72.

_____. 2011a. 'Zeno and the Art of Anthropology: of Lies, Beliefs, Paradoxes, and Other Truths', *Common Knowledge* 17: 128–45.

_____. 2011b. 'Zeno's Wake', *Common Knowledge* 17: 163–65.

_____. 2012. 'Immanence and Fear: Stranger-events and Subjects in Amazonia', *HAU: Journal of Ethnographic Theory* 2: 27–43.

_____. 2013. 'The Relative Native', *HAU: Journal of Ethnographic Theory* 3: 473–502.

_____. 2014. *Cannibal Metaphysics: For a Post-Structural Anthropology*. Minneapolis, MN: University of Minnesota Press.

Wagner, R. 1975. *The Invention of Culture*. Englewood Cliffs, NJ: Prentice-Hall.

We Are Church. 2006. Press Release, 4 July. Available online: http://www.we-are-church.org/int/statements/b16-spain-july2006/Valencia_en.pdf.

Weber, M. 2001 [1930]. *The Protestant Ethic and the Spirit of Capitalism*. London: Routledge.

Weston, K. 1993. 'Lesbian/Gay Studies in the House of Anthropology', *Annual Review of Anthropology* 22: 339–69.

Willerslev, R. 2007. *Soul Hunters: Animism and Personhood among the Siberian Yukaghirs*. Berkeley, CA: University of California Press.

_____. 2011. 'Frazer Strikes Back From the Armchair: a New Search For the Animist Soul', *Journal of the Royal Anthropological Institute* 17: 504–26.

Williams, B. 1981. *Moral Luck*. Cambridge: Cambridge University Press.
Wilson, R.A. 2003. 'Preface to Special Issue on Political Violence and Language', *Anthropological Theory* 3: 267–69.
Wolfram, S. 1982. 'Anthropology and Morality', *Journal of the Anthropological Society of Oxford* 13: 262–74.
Yan, Y. 2011. 'How Far Can We Move Away From Durkheim? Reflections on the New Anthropology of Morality', *Anthropology of this Century* 2. Available online: http://aotcpress.com/articles/move-durkheim-reflections-anthropology-morality/.
Yanagisako, S. 2002. *Producing Culture and Capital: Family Firms in Italy*. Princeton, NJ: Princeton University Press.
Zigon, J. 2007. 'Moral Breakdown and the Ethical Demand: a Theoretical Framework for the Anthropology of Moralities', *Anthropological Theory* 7: 131–50.
———. 2008. *Morality: an Anthropological Perspective*. Oxford: Berg.
———. 2009a. 'Within a Range of Possibilities: Morality and Ethics in Social Life', *Ethnos* 74: 251–76.
———. 2009b. 'Phenomenological Anthropology and Morality: a Reply to Robbins', *Ethnos* 74: 286–88.
———. 2013a. 'Human Rights as Moral Progress? A Critique', *Cultural Anthropology* 28: 716–36.
———. 2013b. 'On Love: Remaking Moral Subjectivity in Postrehabilitation Russia', *American Ethnologist* 40: 201–15.
Zur, J. 1996. 'Reconstructing the Self Through Memories of Violence Among Mayan Indian War Widows', in R. Lentin (ed.), *Gender and Catastrophe*. London: Zed Books, pp. 64–76.

Index